Geordies — Wa Mental

To Richards
friend & comrade
Dave
Douglass
London Anarchist
Bookfare
Oct 2011

Geordies — Wa Mental

Wa Off Wa Fuckin Heeds!

by

David John Douglass

First limited edition published in Great Britain in 2002
by Trade Union Publication Service Books
This revised edition published in 2008 by
Read 'n' Noir
an imprint of ChristieBooks
PO Box 35, Hastings, East Sussex, TN34 1ZS

Distributed in the UK by Central Books Ltd
99 Wallis Road, London E9 5LN
orders@centralbooks.com

ISBN 1-873976-34-8
ISBN-13 - 978-1-873976-34-0

British Library Cataloguing in Publication Data.
A catalogue record for this book is available from the British Library

Part I
Geordies Wa Mental

Author's Introduction

I am a bloke who loves the crack, loves telling the tale and in my life I have experienced and accumulated a host of wonderous encounters and stories many of which are retold in this work. I am not however an egotistical person, I find talking about myself, rather than the situations I have been in and the peoples whose lives I have crossed very difficult.

In writing an autobiography and if not setting oneself centre stage of the production, at least making sure the spotlight is on your part, to some extent talking about oneself becomes inevitable. I have tried to tell my story in the historic and social backdrop in which it takes place, with certainly my colouration of events, and my impressions of the things around me, but do so without hopefully coming over too boastfully, where I fail in that I apologies.

Because much of my story sails close to the wind of illegality and I suppose some events might still be on file, I have blurred where necessary events, I have also changed some of the names of central characters. All of the events and characters are however real. I am also forced to leave out altogether some events and some people which have indelibly touched my soul and memory but which current domestic and international repressions will not allow me to describe.

I began this story in pure Northumbria dialect, or Northumbria la'lands, but it soon became clear this is a spoken twang, and whilst it is easy enough to write and listen to, it is a bugger to read. I have instead used slices and tracts of dialect and where no good reason appears to use standard English rather than 'Geordie' I have used the latter.

This story was written almost contemporaneously from detailed diaries and mutterings just into my teens to early articles on pit life at the age of seventeen to an early draft 'C'

Stream at Wardley when I was twenty-three and my childhood and teenage years were still vivid. I am a horder of notes, papers, diaries speeches and minutes and have exhaustively gone back through them to check my stories and dates and chronologies.

It might surprise some to find that I footnote much of this work; footnotes in autobiographies are not common. In this case it is necessary to stamp for posterity and particularly an accurate understanding of the history of the miners and their union the NUM, that this is not just anecdotal, or the figment of temper or bias. I know that when writing up histories of the labour movement dry dates and events lack colour and depth of living participants, but then anecdotal evidence is dismissed as unsubstantiated conjecture. To rectify this for future historians and future researchers I have footnoted those sources which verify my story and you will find useful as cross-references and evidence. To those who hate footnotes, just ignore them.

Dedicated to-

The ancient echo of a Celtic Northumbria, from the Solway Firth and Cumberland to the North Sea, from The Lowlands to South Durham. A distinct land, like Ireland, like Scotland, like Wales, like Brittany, like Cornwall.

Edwin the Angle, who left the last defenders of that vision yelling in defiance, floating thicker than seaweed between the Farnes as his blockade of Lindisfarne starved to deeth the host of 'Northumbria' Celts, and leaving the beaches and fields of Bamburgh to Beadnell stained reed for a generation with their blood. Edwin whose sons and army massacred the ancient British on mountain sides of the Cheviots and fell sides of Cumbria. Ida who for all that sowed the seeds of a new Northumbria, for a time an independent Northumbria, over which Edwin would preside from his capital Edwin's Burgh. But the ancient northern 'Welsh' hadn't lang to wait or the pointer to torn full circle "in immense sheets of light rushing across the firmament" the Vikings swept ashore and did unto Angle as they had done unto Celt.

To 'the harrying, heathen,' Vikings who Bede tells us In 793 "miserably destroyed God's church" at Jarrow.

To Halfden entering the Tyne with an armada of lang ships, finding willing allies on the banks and men as wild as thasells and willing to join with the new invaders in a vengeful quest for Angle blood. Thereafter and for two hundred years it would be Viking kings who ruled Northumbria, as aud Celt, Angle and Viking fused as one Northumbrian.

To a Northumbria as a distinct people, including the bulk of the lalands now Scottish and Northumbrian, a hybrid British Celt and Angle and Viking. Allied with Scot and Pict and later the Irish settlers, and aye for times langsyne by Arab traders, sailors and settlers. But for centuries and mer

Northumberland was a Viking land, a Norse land lang before any 'England' was invented.

To Edwin who constructed a northern kingdom and an independence of character and culture, the birth pangs of 'the Geordies' though that a misnomer for no George ever captured wor allegiance in truth.

To Harold Saxon king of the sooth, having the worst year of his life in 1066 as he marches north to meet the army of Northumberland under Tostig and King Harold of Norway. Amid the clash of axe-blows and broadswords just outside York, the mists of time clear and we see the messenger with bated breath, catch the beleaguered Saxon king with first the good news. The Viking king is slain, the army of Northumbrians fall back- and now the bad news, William The Conqueror has just landed on the south coast!

With the Normans came rule of a different sort, they would rule while those of every other race would toil. But not yet awhile as the north refused to accept the new world order. First William had to subdue the Northumbrian-Viking alliance led now by Malcolm, king of Scotland. Northumbria then being a sort of autonomous allie, Malcolm would fight hard to retain it for the realm of Scotland. He died fighting for that cause at Alnwick lured into an ambush and it was at Tynemouth's Priory he was buried, along side St Oswin and Osred the ancient kings of Northumbria. The Northumbria rebellion continued against William Rufus secure in Tynemouth's defences. For three hundred years, no Norman peace would rule this land.[1]

By 1069 The King abandons Northumbria and gives it to Robert Comines, who tries to suppress the natives by Invading Durham and massacres the locals. The day after the region rises and wipe out the Normans and Bob.

The Folk Moot (a peoples assembly) of Gateshead in

1080 who discuss the murder of a native Angle by the Norman Bishop Walcher, they avenge the Angle Tynesider with the cry

Gude Reed , Short Reed, (rede)
Slay we the bishop!

...which they did.

To William Wallace's right arm, hacked from his body in London and stuck on the aud Tyne Bridge as a warning to all who resist, the rest of his body similarly hacked to pieces and spread throughout the cities and towns of the island.

But now the blood of Africa, the Indies and Indochina enrich the broad base of Viking and Brit, Angle and Scot and Arab. A distinct people yet, a nation perhaps not now, but the history and relationship with and of Scotland is worth recording if only because southernocentric histories of 'England' have sought to exclude it and bury it.

To Percy, the ancient border scrapper, whe tuek the Northumbrian army to the battle that defeated the Douglas and the Scots, then turned that army into an alliance against England in 1403 when Henry IV forgot that 'Geordie' folk and Scot are blood brothers, and the question of Northumbrian nationality was far from settled at that time.

Percy with his aud adversary in the dungeon of his keep had not lang to make up his mind as to where politically and militarily the army of Northumberland would stand.

'Aye, whey nivor mind Douglas here's what wa gaana dey, ye'r gaanin free, yee and yer army, wa joining with the army of Wales and wa Ah'll gaan te London, at the heed on three greet armies Scotland, Northumberland and Wales and bollicks ti Henry IV.

And so it was that brave Percy the Hotspur dies in the field of battle against Henrys pretensions of 'England'.

To the Scottish republicans who cross the Tyne to Stella Haugh and take the city from the Royalists in 1640 forcing the clergy to flight. Charles bribes the Scots to leave and it is claimed the resulting recriminations spark the civil war.

To the bold pitmen of Benwell who marched at the heed of a twenty-thousand strong Scottish republican army to blast the Newcastle city walls with gunpooda during the civil war, both Royalist and Cromwellian armies fighting across Northumbria were Scottish. Newcastle chose the side of the king and Sunderland that of the Parliamentarians.

To John Lilburne of Bishop Auckland founder of the Levellers 1649, jailed by Cromwell. Had been flogged and pilloried eleven years earlier sparking anti-government demonstrations.

To General Foster and his heroic sister Dorothy who led the Northumbrian Rising of 1715 and nailed the flag of Northumberland to the Jacobite cause.

To Earl Derwentwater, the twenty-seven year old leader of the Northumbrian people's allegiance with the Jacobite cause of 1716 Bamburgh holding out till the end. James Radclyffe the third Earl captured stripped of his lands and taken to London and tortured in public to a bloody death (Sat 23rd Feb). His final words were that if he was to die here in London then carry him to Northumberland to lie in the Northumbrian earth of his fathers or as Joe Hill would later say before his execution in Salt Lake City, "I wouldn't be found dead here."

To the armed cavalry of Northumbrian Jacobites who rode through Northumberland with flaming torches to honour his death. To the Earls' nephew who died similarly in the later rebellion of '45 and the Northumbria Jacobites of the 1720s whose stories and battles are unrecorded save for their scratched messages on the walls of the dungeons of Bamburgh castle, taken like the men by those hostile to their cause.

To the Tyneside keelmen, miners and sailors who rose to

declare Tyneside for Charles Stuart and Scotland, marching in armed formation, small pipes chanting four years after the defeat at Culloden. Not wor fault that the French-Italian bonny lad, fearful of this armed proletarian column in his ranks, gave the waiting Tyneside insurgent rebels a body swerve and went doon the other side of the country, only to get cold feet at the open doors of London, fleeing back north to massacre, exile for himself and genocide for Scotland, supporter and non supporter alike.

To the revolutionary miners of Northumberland and Durham from the back end of the 1700s and the early decades of the 1800s who took up arms and fought back against the tyranny of the coal owners, shipmasters and political system. To the sixty Tynesiders captured by the Press Gang at North Shields, but in turn capture the ship and sail it to Scarborough for day out before escaping back up north in 1760.

To the Hexham rioters of 1761 who led by the miners of Allendale joined the general regional resistance to conscription and service for the crown, and suffered a massacre of 40 of their number, shot down by the Yorkshire Militia.

To the mass trespassers of 1771 who smashed down the fences and hedges, and stopped the enclosure of the Toon Moor.

To Robbie Burns speaking at Morpeth, Newcastle and Hexham in 1787 a great inspiration to the political and dialect movement of the region.

To the northern regiments stationed in Newcastle who mutinied and marched through the streets with arms shouting their discontent in 1795.

To the Free City of 1826 Carlisle, throwing off the controls and politics of the state, Tories and Constables sent packing or ducked in the Caldew. The commune is put down with extensive military violence and the use of artillery.

To Johnathan Martin of Hexham who loped over 'the border' and sets fire to York Minister in 1829.

To the revolutionary working class propagandists of the 1830s who produced penny instructions titled *Street Warfare* in the style of *The Anarchist Cookbook*, or the *Mini Manual of the Urban Guerilla* one hundred and thirty years later, for sale on The Side. The Side Saturday morning markets would see the sale of inflammatory publications and weapons including muskets, pikes and craes feet.

To the sixty-five armed working class detachments, which Devyr reported, were ready to rise.[2] To the demonstrators and rioters on the streets of Carlisle and Middleton-in-Teesdale who take the streets under the French Jacobin Tricolour demanding Liberty Fraternity Equality.

To the Rev J.R. Stevens who in a monster Chartist demonstration on the Moor 1838 declares himself "A revolutionist by fire, a revolutionist by blood, to the knife, to the death" and calls upon the people to arm to defeat the reform bill and light Newcastle with a blaze of fire which could only be quenched by the blood of those who supported "this abominable measure".[3]

To the lads of Crowley's Forge Winlaton, who produced Weapons for the French Communards, supplied the Northern chartists with every form of weapon from Crae's feet to small cannon, and formed an armed detachment, which ensured a Peterloo on the Toon Moor would result in a different outcome.

To Joseph Cowen, Radical Tyneside Republican and revolutionary Internationalist Libertarian, who raised guns and fighters for The Polish Democratic Society and Garibaldi's Sicilian campaign as well as directly in efforts to blow up Napoleon 111.[4] To Thomas Spense revolutionary democrat publicist and propagandist.

To the *Northern Liberator*, and *Newcastle Chronicle* mass revolutionary republican newspapers in support of the armed struggle wing of Chartism, Irish independence, Garibaldi, Hungarian and Polish Republicans and the native northern working class. To Blakey and Thomas Doubleday, Liberators local editors who sailed into the teeth of sedition and treason laws to continue their message of truth and class justice. The *Chronicle* was banned from all the Irish jails by the British state along with the Irish Nationalist papers.[5]

To George Julian Harney Northern Chartism's most dynamic and uncompromising spokesperson fearing no Gods, Masters, Priests, or preachers, demanded 'not just the Charter', and not just the ballot box either.

To the miners of 1839 who hijack a whole train to get to a Chartist meeting at Sunderland Town Moor, to the mass Chartist meeting at Darlington which vows "to repel force by force", to the people of Stockton facing down the influx of the 77th foot battalion in the face of a chartist uprising.

To the Chartists 'Sacred Month' the first attempt at a nationwide general strike for political change. Troops sent to Cramlington, Seghill and Winlaton to crush the movement. Thornley Colliery joins the strike. To the rioters of The Side. To the soldier rioters of 1841 who with five thousand locals attack the police to unarrest a solitary drunken mate.

To Garibaldi, who for a time stayed in Tynemouth, spoke around Tyneside to enthusiastic crowds inspired by his vision of a united socialist Italy, and the men of the Tyne who sailed off and joined his libertarian uprising in 1860.

To the Clousden Hill Free Communist and Co-operative Colony, of Forest Hall, established in 1895 On the

Communist social theories of Kropotkin and Morris. To *Freedom* the Anarchist newspaper founded by Kropotkin which in 1894 is reported circulating the pit villages of Sunderland and Silksworth.

To the International Anarchist Communist Group who in 1909 bought premises on Blackett Street Newcastle to open the famous Communist Club, a venue and bar much frequented by Tyneside workers and philosophers during its lifetime.

To the incendarist suffragists of 1913 who burned down the pavilion at Heaton Park, had a go at Heaton Rail station, and a house in Jesmond to the slogan "No peace until we get the vote." Then Esh railway station, Kenton Railway station and Shipcote School then Bombing Barras Bridge Post Office, and Gosforth Golf course the same year. To Emily Davison of Morpeth dying under the hooves of the Kings horse at Epson derby. And in 1914 'committed an outrage' at St Nicholas's cathedral.

To the revolutionary miners of Chopwell (Little Moscow) who in the 1926 General Strike derailed the scab Flying Scotsman and marched on Newcastle to hoist the red flag from the City Hall.

To the Shields Arab seamen who fought, guns and knives in hand to defend militant trade unionism in 1930's Tyneside and to Ali Said their leader, jailed and deported for giving voice to that tradition.

To the Jarrow marchers setting off in October 1936 for London having debated whether they should proceed to the capital as an armed detachment. Deciding instead to give petition and moral outrage a chance.

To the twenty-four Geordies who laid down their lives fighting with the Tyneside contingent doing internationalist duty in Spain against Franco's fascists.

To the anti-fascist fighters of Northumberland,

Cumberland, and Durham who spent their young lives in the four corners of the earth and oceans fighting the Nazis but hating Churchill.

To wor young internationalist 'sand dancer' Ian Davison jailed for life for armed struggle against the Zionist state of Israel.

To Davie O'Connel, Geordie class fighter, who died in jail serving life imprisonment for carrying out armed struggle in the cause of Ireland.

To the hundreds of jailed, beaten, sacked and blacklisted insurgent men,women and children of the coalfields of Northumberland and Durham who fought back with everything flesh and blood could muster in the great coal battle of 1984/5…

And to every mad bastard 'Geordie'/Northumbrian who ever lifted a claymore, pistol, moli, broon-ale bottle or brick in the cause of the lang-doontrodden toilers of the world!

I

Waggonway Street

Clouds of dull dirty steam hang over the street, an aura of a permanently impending thunderstorm, given credence by the periodic thumping of the colliery compressor forcing air down the shaft. Tirelessly, the dillyway rollers spin as the waggonway rope draws the 'teum' waggons back up the waggonway to outlaying pits.

Dave and dad (1948)

Waggonway Street, a continuous line of cramped, damp pit cottages, rammed one next door to the other, two steps downwards to gain entry by the half-door. Parallel to the street, the Waggonway, dissecting the back garden between the tattie rows and the rhubarb encased in galvie buckets with the bottoms knocked through.

Clap ya hands for Daddy comin doon the Waggonway
Wiv his pockets full O money and his poke full O hay
Aal the money for Mammy, Aal the money for Da
To buy a little motiecar for owa little la

The aud wifies dandling sang, adapted and freely nicked from the ancient pit waggoners

'Sair frowzy freckled and he's blind of an ee' version. Through the steam and fog of childhood, memory recalls the last time mothering care would sit me on a knee and bounce me to the tune.

Life gets hard after that…

Waggonway Street started at the border of the village, where the fields spanned off to distant sweet smelling or shit-

Wardley Colliery

smelling agriculture to the south-east, whilst the Waggonway itself inclined sharply uphill toward loading stations from Kibblesworth, Springwell, places only known to exist as their banners entered Durham on the Big Meeting Day.

Waggonway Street. It ended fifty yards from the pit tip. The full sets lowering down at regular revolutions of great iron wheels, braked by black faced waggoners hanging onto the backs of the wagons, white teeth visible like the Cheshire Cat lang before the outline of the black face took shape on the shoulders, or the white of the eyes peering out smiles making crack marks in the black. Wheels crossing the way-joints in measured rhythm, clank...clank...clank..never missing..clank. Little lads, runny noses, legs chapped from piss soaked short trouser leg bottoms, held up with braces. Flat caps, big khaki shirts, holey armless Fairisle cardies, ney socks, but mud splattered legs and red raw knees. Girls in langish muckraked-coloured cotton dresses, with matted lovely hair, cheeky faces and wellies, sing in monotonous mantra to the passing iron giants of coal: “Wo-on...two-o...thr-ee...fo-wer...five”

Scaren times, heart-thumping times, darin'times, when the waggoners eased on the brakes, jumped off the back wagons and ran alang, lowering the levers one after another, squeaking, creaking, coupling hooks snapping tight, the line of Iron and Coal thuds, thuds, thuds doon the line to a halt. For how lang, that was the contest, as wee bodies dived under the wheels of the wagons at one side and out the other. Who was to be last before the brakes eased off and wheels started to roll again ?

'Gaanon, gaanon thou next.

Ah's through, and heart pounding head thumping heart beat gives way to the sun still there in the sky at the other side of the waggonway.

At other times, as the wagons clanked more quickly on their way to the river, they are ambushed by 'Indians' ,boy-horses, rider on top, horse at the bottom, hand slapping the backside to make the legs run faster, firing bows and arrows at the iron invaders from those distant places ,only seen on Gala Day. Leaping ower the sleepers, shooting at the cursing waggoners: "Geroot O that! Hadaway, does tha wanta get kilt?"

The cottages bathed in the glow of the gas-mantles and an all pervading smell of burning lamp-oil together with a blazing inferno of hot coals in the range that cast a dancing aura of warmth and shadows across the ceiling and walls. Yet the damp remained and made a happy humidity for cockroaches scuttling in their undertakers garb from every dark recess and cupboard, clicking their death-watch through the night. Leaving their empty shells to be squashed by bare feet on urgent quest for the netty in the darkness of the neet. Frying on the fire, having successfully disguised themselves as coal. Womenfolk parading their battered remains on coal shuls to boast 'Noo then, whey's foond a bigger begger than that?' and wives would peer ower the wall. 'Ee, A'h bet that's the syme in was in Ned's bed the ither neet, and didaway before I could skelp it'

Not all creatures were as unwelcome as the cockroach, and most prized a regular spider. Wors a giant, of the thin langedlegged variety which she-because Da had christened her Mary-spread oot around her body just above the big mirror over the range. Da swore it was the same one that lived with us in Hebburn and had come on the removal cart with the rest of the stuff. I had been born in Jarrow (Jarra) a month or so after the stocks were laid on the new ship at the end of the street. Daily it had grown, till its bows loomed over the row and shadowed the sun off my pram like a benevolent oak tree by the time I could stagger to the end of the cobbled street it was sliding away into the river to a cacophony of welcoming foghorns and crane sirens.

Still the Geordie womenfolk hung out their Monday signals in huge billowing sheets hung in regular communal ranks across the road from hoose ti hoose, claes-props straining like masts before the stiff breeze.

Shipyards and mines, that was Jarra and Hebburn. Workers went from one to the other, the pit hooses yards from the shipyards, the early morn turn, shipyard workers and miners clumping the cobbles together, passing beneath the greet bows. Wor hoose was one of a street almost entirely occupied by the miners, as were the adjoining raws: Quality Raw, High Lane, Cross Raw, Chapel Raw. We lived in Arthur Street, three minutes from the pit, between Frederick Street and Railway Street. The story of the river, its lure and lore, flowed in wor young channels like tides. 'The *Kelly*, there y'are, lad', me Da taking out a black-and-white postcard of the famous Tyneside ship. A destroyer born and bred on the river, on its most famous of engagements, shell-shocked and blasted, it listed hyme, the bodies on deck, the water lapin' the gunnels, back tithe river where the Geordies stood and gyped with pride.

Years in Gateshead sea cadets and three-times-weekly attendance at training-ship *Flamingo*, with tarry ropes and flashing Morse tappers, reinforced the Da's instruction on the *Nelson* and the *King George IV*, built at the Armstrong

Road end of Vicars. Giant girthed monsters of steel and guns slipping between the swing bridge's narrow confines with only one inch to spare on either side. Canoeing the great depths, rising and falling with the swell, fighting the whirlpools, soaring with the currents, and feeling the swimmy, heady feeling of being at a great height, suspended over a thousand fathoms of dark grey water. Boating the awkward depths from the great swell at Bill Quay to Dunston, rowing or, in a fashion never fully mastered, trying to Cox under sail the cumbersome twenty-seven foot naval whaler, as passing merchant ships and small river-craft blew their indignation, sending tidal waves of wash to further test the boy matelotes, faces red, raw hands blue with cold, soaked to the skin.

Less challenging, more liberating, less controlled, were bikes. In terms of cutting loose, a bike and the freedom it gave was somewhere just under the first pair of skin-tight jeans. It was a means outwith parental control, a route to freedom, to the lower stretches of the river and the endless shimmering rocky coast. The bikes stand lined up, erect, their lowered pedal wedged on the pavement, saddlebags filled with bait and bottle. To wor minds, they chug over, awaiting only a powerful rev of the handlebar cover, then away to pedal the miles and catch first the smell then, in the distance, the sight of the sea, then the close-up roll and crash of the sea, wor sea, the North Sea. Screaming doon the sand, fleein' up pebbles and washed-up gunge, Tyneside faker ken, barefooted passage ower pebbles and rocks must be rapid and careless. We mock the fuel, stepping and picking with tender feet, arms flung oot rocking and slipping and stumbling, stubbin' is toes, fallen' back and forth, walking sidieways like a woonded crab.

Jarra or Wardley, the struggle against dust and dirt and sand and soil which swept the villages from colliery slag, from beach and quarry and wide fields, which found its way

Dave and sisters on the Waggonway, 1951

through every crack and gap and open door and bent the back of the womenfolk generation on generation. Carpets were virtually unheard-of but oilcloth did its best against the cold of the floor. To this the ingenuity of the womenfolk had added the progie mat: tattie sacks washed and darned, a bag full of wool rags cut into short lengths, and a side of peg with which the wool was 'proged' into the sack. The finished article was a little woolly mat to lie on the floor.

The fire could never die: it was the soul of the cottage with its stream of hot water down the arteries to fuel the passage of black and bloody colliers passing each other in shifts at the door, one leaving, one entering. Big black men sit down to dinner while clouds of coal dust fly from the back yards as 'lang 'uns' and jacket get a daddin' against the waal. Big mugs of tea and bowls of rice puddin' restrain the drooping eyes long enough for the tin bath to be placed before the fire and filled with steaming water. The bare black pitman sitting in his bath before the room fire, the womenfolk clearing away dishes and chatting to neighbours who walk to and fro through each others' kitchens and front rooms as a right of way barred to any other, a helpin' hand to wash the man's back and a bored look of indifference as he steps from it. Hers is a comradeship with another pitwoman, a fellow fighter in the war against dirt; he is—just something else to wash.

But the damp, rising and regrouping along the floors and rolling down peeling, ill-coloured wallpaper, invaded the raw and my lungs, and slowly TB and pleurisy stabbed at the small body and buckled me legs.

'Gerroot in the air, man.... Dinnet lie aboot here aal day.... Get thasell oot.' And oot into the sick of the street, trying to force small pedals round on a wee trike, and weeping, and little girls in ankle-socks and polka-dot dresses skipped from the neighbouring prefabs to sing: 'Cry-baby David, cry-baby David.' A thundering voice of manhood and darkness: 'Dinnet be soft, man, dinnet be soft, thou's a pipestaple, a wee-bit pipestaple". The damp clasped at me lungs and the trike was never seen again.

Months of the local doctor's alien gaze had found nowt but 'malingering caused by mollycoddling', but I was worse and, carried in me Ma's arms, a half-recalled bus journey to Gateshead children's hospital 'followed, by nine months of internment and life-saving treatment.

When I was had moved to a new estate named after Ellen Wilkinson. The estate was the socialism of many of the old miners, and the streets were named after the early pioneers of the labour movement. To my folks this council house was a dream. Its size, dry straight walls, three big bedrooms, living room, dining room, kitchen, inside toilet, bathroom and ootahoose: this was quite some step up from Waggonway Street and Pit Raw. In later years, my sister Veronica was to tell me we were middle-class now. The peggy mats were replaced by wall-to-wall fitted carpets throughout, although me Mam's Irish inventiveness continued to make good use of everything she found, like the two bedside bookcases she made from orange boxes

Dave and chum (1953)

lined and covered in wallpaper.

Starting school at a little over five, already designated a thicky, since I'd missed some. St Albans at Pelaw on the banks of the river. As yet, the river was unknown to me; in later years, it would be as blood in my veins. St Albans, adjoining a big wooden hut, which was St Albans Church, in years to come a source of drunken midnight mass amusement with its doddering old English priest, for hitherto all priests, would be Irish. St Albans: a redbrick and white-tiled Victorian working man's shithouse, with the benefit of girls. St Albans: with kids without proper shoes, but with running and snot-congealed kids, with black gabardine coats like my own, with wellies as daily footwear, but those who wore them needs must take them off at the door and walk barefoot 'or else bring your slippers', as if kids who wore wellies to mass on a Sunday had slippers. Mind, through me Da's strict Methodist abstinence I had boots, nor not the buets with the hobnails in that the lads wore, nor me Mammy had determined mine would be bloody booties, fur-flamin'-lined. I oft-times envied the wellies from the less temperate parents— booties highly suspect. The first canvas sandshoes, generally without socks, were allowed at the school, bad because in winter they got wet through and then froze and kept ya feet cold, and because of ney socks you weren't allowed to tek them off, unlike wellies, which were worn with big pit stockings.

St Albans: the big lads locked is in the putrid netty, and I scrabbled belly-flopper under the wooden bays through pools of piss to escape. St Albans: I arrive too late for the Coronation Mug complete with toothbrush and toothpaste. The brown bag delivered to everyone in the class but me, I hadn't been on the register when they were ordered, big tears rolling doon me cheeks, the poxy white mug with the queen on it. 'Ye didn't get one! Ye didn't get one!' my tormentors in their black gabardine Burberrys and bare red knees mocked, and I, picking up the nearest overheard domestic nationalist-versus-imperialist arguments of me folks, spat back: 'Ah divind want one, it's not MY queen!', not really knowing what the hell the queen was anyway, but I'd have loved a bonny mug and toothbrush for aal that.

St Albans: the chancer to the rescue, bonny lass in clean socks having her plastic tea-set demolished by a lad with a iron stick, dived from me imagined horse to wrestle him to the ground with me arm round his neck before he ran off. Games with the tea-set gave way to displays of her knickers and unbuttoning her dress in the new game of Doctors and Nurses. At playtime on the adjoining field which separated the wooden church to the Jewish man-God from the school's red brick and tiles, we made beelines to the wee 'hoose' we had built of abandoned stones and rubbish and obliging elderberry bushes, squatting in play, to hug mostly and feel the warmth of her grey cardigan, to hug and to smell her Parma violets and feel the smoothness of the skin on her face. 'A love', we called it, giving each other 'a love', and the cheeky displays of knickers as she drew up her dress and wiggled her bum to some tune she hummed which we associated with sexual naughtiness—'da da da da da, da da, da, da, da da da, da'—but never knew why. Lying flat on the grass, hidden from the sight of the school, I was allowed to pull her knickers down to her knees and examine her 'tupence', I think we called it, always as the Doctor. And I, falling spectacularly from fatal bullet wounds, would fall onto the operating theatre, where she as the Nurse got to work on my 'thingy', releasing it through my short trouser-leg and applying a dock leaf or a hanky as a bandage wrapped round its faceless swollenness. But the bell and hurried ranks of boys and girls brought separation.

Most boys played together, football and chasey, and fighting. I never made friends with the boys or really wanted to join their games. They didn't have that certain 'A'h divina what' or the smell of Parma violets.

Coronation day we were marched to Heworth and stood in ranks so deep yi couldn't see the road. I seen a greet black car, and heard the teachers cheer, then we got to go home. I got a clout on Coronation Day. Me Da says, 'Did ye see the queen then?' Ah says 'Ah seen nowt, Fa-ther.' The clout was for talking Geordie to me Da, and more particularly for calling him 'Fa-ther'; he thought both were acts of disrespect. At the time I thought the clout was for seeing nowt; in later years I always got to the front of crowds and usually got clouted and nicked; but at five such confusing dilemmas were rationalised by the belief that gettin' clouted was normal and I was intrinsically bad and full of bodily dysfunctions, something like fallin' doon.

It seems as though it's something ye can dey nowt aboot and happens for the same reason, just at any time of the day or neet, oot o' the blue, for nowt, it can't be for something, it just happens all the time: gettin' a clout, fallin' doon, cuttin' your knee and gettin' a clout for cuttin' your knee, bustin' ya nose, bleedin' on ya shirt and drippin' it in the kitchen and gettin' a clout, gettin' a clout and hurtin' ya knee, gettin' a clout and fallin' down and breakin' something and gettin' a clout for breakin' something and cryin' and gettin' a clout for cryin'. It was part of being a small person in a big persons' world full of things that knocked you over and tripped you up and fell on you, or broke when you looked at them, or bumped into you, or got you so you got in the way even when you were standing still. Every bus-stop in Britain is full of kids getting a clout, every beauty spot or church, every holy shrine, every fun-fair, every chip shop, every garden and graveyard, every ceremony, from burying the dead with feelings of reverence to enjoying themselves at the seaside or wedding, is not complete without giving them a clout, more regular than the clock, the clouting of the kids, like the clicking of the Waggonway Street cockroaches, goes on—in public, but nobody sees it, and kids learn it's just like falling doon.

It wasn't long before me Mammy give is a free transfer from St Albans to St John's in the Felling, to be part of St Patrick's parish, St John's was always called the St Patrick's school anyway, and it sounded better when writing home to Ireland. St John's nestled near the river, an occupied ruin just over the wall from an unoccupied ruin of some prehistoric riverside industry or long-forgotten castle, opposite the big Nobel and Lung heavy engineering factory. St John's was rumoured by the kiddhas to have been an ancient castle itself because of the tower with the battlements on the top, which was full of skulls and at the top armour and swords and lances. Everyone said they knew someone who had sneaked up the secret steps in the headmistress's (Mrs Kelly's) room. The secret steps were exposed to me once when I and several others went to her room for the stick. The lower steps were being used as

Mam: Margaret Nelson (1930)

bookcases but higher up they tailed out of sight and into the dark and dank, and quite took your mind off the impending doom until the stick fell like a bacon-slicer across the ends of me fingers; then the pain shocked the concentration back in time to watch me poor hand tremble as the second stroke fell across me palm and thumb. Only two on each hand this time, for fighting. They were added to the deep scratch on me face—bliddy Quinns always had long dirty nails like an aud rabbit.

Behind the school's walls, down the narrow lanes to the river, the men staggered from the pubs on a Sunday to pitch coins standing in small groups, or else two would strip to the waist and fight in a circle of watching boozers in their good suits, fight and punch with thuds like rocks against a sandbag, dull thuds, dark reluctant blood, nowt like this on the flicks.

The school yard was broken, cracked and filled with craters big enough to take cover in from enemy fire, keek ower the top, let gaan wi' ya rifle, dook, then raid oot the holes with bayonets fixed, screaming across the yard, the rattle of the Thompsons and Bren's all roond, knocked to the hard tarmac an' bleed real blood courtesy of the wall of footballers coming fernant and quite unaware of the war. To fight on, with real blood on ya face, firing from the hip, watching the enemy fall magnificently on every side.

The crumbling stone wall which stood in a square round the boys' playground with cracks and hollows was another world for the side creepers, kids who hung silently on its edge, on their knees every morning, playtime, and dinner-time, creeping roond its edges boulin' cars or tin tanks over the boulders, ploughing through the thick sand of its atomising wall, where tin soldiers peered oot of the hidden caves made by the hollows and shared with the lang-legged spiders.

In the classroom iron-legged ink-mottled wood-top desks stood in line, ranks upon ranks, a stone slate and chalk recording scratchy big efforts at lettering. Later, little boodie inkpots will stand: an endless source of smudging, or blue floods across the desk, or ink wars which persisted through the infants, juniors and seniors. The ink-war technology changed little over the years, a lump of blotting paper soaked in ink flicked from a pen or ruler re-christens the white shirt or clean dress with devastating effect, or a clean page written off in a bomb-burst of ink terror. Ink monitors, trusted clean kids, let loose on a galvie jug full of the stuff, trusted to its safe distribution. Little hands hold forth the pot as line by line the galvie jug lad walks doon the isle, like a priest at communion. Tipping each in turn, until—until that evil temptation takes grip and the jug is tipped, the pot filled, overfilled, and ink flows down the arms over the bare leg down the shoe and into a pool on the wooden floor.

In the cupboard, sit golden tins of Plasticine, wooden toys, brightly coloured little building bricks, and cardboard things, and boxes with trains and sunshine and seaside on, and woolen things and coloured strings, and bright pieces of plastic. 'Go to the toy cupboard, children, and choose one toy', was a rare and magical instruction, more often withdrawn than granted.

More usually the tones were the dull monotony of the times tables, like the clanking of the dillyway wagons. In mass chorus trance-like zombie children chant two twos are four, three twos are six, four twos are eight, five twos are ten, seven twos are fourteen, eight twos are sixteen, nine twos are eighteen, in a rhythm which nobody taught us but is reinforced by the teacher swiping the desk with the cane, crack, crack crack crack, something like the time-beater on a slave galley. And the catechism from infancy to teenage, the catechism:

'Who made you?'

'God made me.'

'Why did God make you?'

'God made me to know Him, love Him, and serve Him in this world and be happy with Him for ever in the next.'

In the juniors, each would sit carrying out the gestures which accompanied the words.

'What will God say to the souls of the just?'

'God will say to the souls of the just, "Come ye [ranks of small arms beckon and draw into self-embrace], blessed of my Father, possess ye the kingdom prepared for ye."'

'What will God say to the souls of the damned?'

'God will say to the souls of the damned, "Depart from me, ye cursed [arms fly out to the right, planned slapstick accidents occur throughout the room, the boy backhands the boy to his right, who has swiped at the girl to his right, who in turn has garroted a taller lad to her right] into everlasting flames [fingers jab toward the floor, the nearest thigh gets poked, fingers stub on desks, books in ready piles for distribution tumble to the floor], which were prepared for the devil and his angels."'

Hysteria grips the scene; small faces contort with suppressed laughter; here and there, hands grip sides or genitals to suppress the pain of mirth or a sudden urge to piss. The outrage of the catechism-waving teacher only adds to the glory of the mayhem.

'Get out, you clown!' A boy dragged from his seat by the ear.

'Silence! Clowns!' the baritone depth of the hippo female in full flight accompanied by smacks round offending ears—or any ears.

It was the same every time that passage was read. The turning of the first page lifted the curtain on a long-expected pantomime.

'Mary, Holy Mary, Mother of God.'

The vision had descended the instruction from out of a sunbeam, a request from the Holy Virgin herself, 'Say the family rosary', in a novena for peace. There would be no slacking in the campaign of rosaries. Knees would crack and ache on the hard floors, or wooden boards, the blur of words 'HolyMaryMotherofGodprayforoursinnersnowandat thehourofourdeathamen', the gold bit, the Glorybetithefather, the little round ones, the endless Hail Mary's full of grace. Faster and faster in a circle of beseeching HAIL MaryfullofgracetheLordiswiththeeblessedartthouamong womenandblessedisthebloodoftheywombJesus. One circle of beads finishes, another prayer starts up: OurFatherwhoartinheavenhahlowedbethyname ... round an' round till your heed swims in dizziness and knees rock back and forth in aimless motion. From living-rooms darkened and lit by candles where mother and sisters would kneel and pray in earnest endeavour to the mass classroom scenes of the rosary, Mary had so requested. Mary of the blue lang-heed scarf, Mary of the china foot and red nail-varnished toes, invariably with a chip off the big toe, whose tiny feet belie the fact that they are crushing a snake the size of a sea-serpent. Mary, whose hands outstretched, made her seem more a victim than the son who looked three times her age, even as he lay thin and pierced with barb and spear and china-white from loss of blood (as well as being china) draped across her knee in a white shroud like an oversized bairn needing a nappy change.

'Why do we pray to Mary and not straight to Jesus?' an inspired infant had asked. Because, he was told, like you, if you want something special and dare not ask your father, you will often go and ask your mother, knowing that she will pass on the request with more chance of success. It was a logical answer, though God always watching, being all-knowing, must have seen what you were after, perhaps he didn't listen all the time, only when he saw something interesting or SINFUL!

So the game of 'Dare to Heaven' came about. The later game of chicken was nowt in comparison. In that game you chickened out a car or a train, in wor game you played chicken with blasphemy and your immortal soul. In the ootahoose, two small bodies cuddled, a hand up each other's short trouser-leg, holding onto each other's pulsating juvenile cock, mouths dry in a mix of fear and heart thumping excitement.

'Would ye stop deyin this if the priest said so?'

'Na.' The grip would tighten the danger up a notch.

'Would ye stop deying this if an angel appeared?'

'Na, Ah'd say knackoff!' The grip remains in mutual cock-strangulation.

'Huw this is all gaanin on wa souls ye knaa', and we'd envisage ink spreading through a blotting paper as wa souls absorbed more sinfulness.

'Ah knaa, should we stop?'

'Nor.'

'Wad ye stop if the Angel Gabriel appeared?' And so the dare progressed, sometimes to Jesus himself, although the sound of the dustbin moving outside or a hard rap on the oottahoose door— 'Whatyees deeyin in theor?'—usually struck enough fear into wa hearts to stop the game for a week or so.

The confessional box, dark, smelling of incense and leather in the Felling, in St Albans: the dorty get always had his light on, I supposed so that he could see who had did what.

'Bless me, Father, for I have sinned, it is three weeks since my last confession.' Then you were into it, a percussion of sins, many made up to fill out the confession and pad the 'Ah have been immodest' in among the 'Ah hey back-answered my mother and father, Ah hey been disobedient', in the hope the priest wouldn't come back to it.

'Say five Hail Mary's and three Our Fathers.' The penance, though it got to be like counting up to a hundred when playing hidie, you always lost count and just waited what seemed like a fair enough time before getting up, walking out the door, brand new shiny soul again, and poor old Gabriel having to sharpen up the pencil and tear the old page out of the book again.

A gradual la'r slowly began clearing the mist and let shimmering shafts of perception through. Living things began to occupy my awareness, living things and once living things. I would find poor dead things lying here and there: the bird whose eyes would see no more blue skies; the lifeless beetle which would never again turn stone or seek the shade of a wall; a vole face down in the grass, alone and still, that would sense no more the surge of warm blood or sit on contented haunches, small paws gripping the great seed, savouring the pure tastes, looking here and there in the bright rays of the sun. Such abandoned and lonely creatures were to find posthumous solace as I bore them home, in matchboxes and tablet boxes, and laid all to rest in cardboard coffins, each with a small headstone: 'A poor bird'; 'Black beetle. RIP'. Next door's cat, a moldering dog: all tearfully laid to rest, but the father drew the line at the big horse which had died at the bottom of the Felling after being hit by a bus. His noble head had come to rest on the tarmac; his eyes rolled aboot in desperation; a leg kicked and flexed; his back was broken. I had tried to get to his side, to stroke his ears and give him comfort, but the polis had held is back and big tears rolled mercilessly down me face. He should have been buried. His great legs were strapped together and he was dragged off by a fire engine, his head trailing a long line of rich red blood along the Sunderland road, and a little lad sobbing helplessly.

By the time I was seven, this empathy had led to the earth-shattering discovery that meat was dead animals—like most kids I thought it simply food—worse, that animals were deliberately slain so folk could eat them. My vegetarianism started the moment of the revelation, although me Mam's Irishness codded me that such things, as sausages weren't meat. 'Sure, what sort of animal would a sausage come from?' she would ask. Likewise, such perfections as non-meat gravy escaped me for a few years. The principle was to become a battlefield with teachers and dinner ladies, who seemed to take my not eating meat as a personal slight—until I got to the seniors and was able to exchange the school dinner-plates of dry spuds with black bits in them for the self-selection freedom of the local cafés on the Felling High Street.

A red brick wall with a single opening separated the girls and boys' playgrounds. At times bunches of lasses would lead sorties into the boys' ground to capture a lad and drag him back through the gap in the wall, where he was forced to kiss a girl who had chosen him. At other times surreptitious knots of boys stand peering through the gap at girls hand standing against the wall, white legs akimbo and naked to their knickers, their shirts riding up to reveal bare waists and thin bodies in their skin, skirts falling nearly over their inverted faces. Undeterred on seeing the lads, and egged on by their friends, they continue, giggling upside down in an orgy of knickerism, the lads peering, hearts pounding, rooted to the spot.[6]

The Geordie-Irish predominate here, which in part is why I was sent. I carried a mild admixture of Tyneside twang and bits of me Mammy's Irishisms. The Geordie-Irish had Mammies years after the Geordies had Ma's. An IRA cell rapidly established, with black gabardine raincoats buttoned ower the shoulders like a Zorro cloak, riding wild imagined horses, the Geordie-Irish galloped the playground slashing with sabers or quickly changing to machine-guns or bows and arrows. British and Irish soon made British and German war games redundant, opposing sides diving for the holes in the playground. At dinner-time the cell escaped over the wall and attacked a crane standing empty on its tracks on 'the tank', a strange ashy mound running down to the river. Windows were smashed and the controls in the cab covered in paint, recovered from an abandoned paint drum, 'UP THE IRA' painted along the school walls, the tin flung away, the cell returned over the wall.

A group of lads, drifting through the field of horse plats, over unearthed lumps of wall and mysterious humps and bumps in the ground, head cautiously toward the ruins, where tinkers and their gallowas lived, among the ancient walls, under oilcloth tents.

Suddenly a shout, and in the distance from the ruin lowp four greet Alsatians like a pack of timber-wolves closing for the kill. Off like rockets, leaping the lumps, ploughing through the plats, up and over the school wall, to breathlessly join the end of the crocodile of children stamping off back into the corridor, and off into classrooms, adventure nigh forgotten. But no, bounding through the doors from outside, the four hoonds, tongues lolling, teeth flashing, defy the rules. Panicking teachers push the kids into classrooms and slam shut the doors, as the dogs bark and wheel up and down the corridor and leap up at windows, pushing at the doors with giant paws. From the other end the caretaker, armed with a broom and supported, nearly, by two male teachers, advances slowly on the dogs, shouting 'Geritche, gerr' in deep aggressive voices, until the dogs regroup and turn determinedly toward them, doing that big bounding motion, with stiff front legs and flat stamping paws, which means: 'Now I'm really mad.' Caretaker posse,

Dave, Mam and Dad (1954)

protected by the wildly waving broom, back off. Meantime every kid is up at a window, jumping on the desks, teachers running between kids and doors and dogs and classrooms. Doors open, dogs split up and hare off in different directions, one nearly getting his head through the door, pushing with his nose and tearing with his front feet while the teacher wedges arse, legs and arms to keep it shut and kids scream in mock and real horror. Kids follow teachers out of doors in rescue attempts and run screaming and shouting up and down the corridor, books scatter, displays fall from walls, the building nigh pulsates with tension, fear, excitement and joy, wild overpowering all-consuming whirlwind pushing aside puny attempts at control. We were the masters! For a while, us and the dogs were the masters!

It ended as the tinkers, blackened faces, holey, smoke-covered woolen cardies, leather caps and wellies, sauntered up the corridor of this alien place, hands in pockets, and whistled for the dogs, who turned barking in defiance, tossing their great heads and skipping gallisley, well pleased with themselves, towards their men. Wor liberators for nearly an hour. Calm descends like drizzle, and as heartbeats subside the screeching voice of a teacher could at last be heard again: 'Get back in your seats and face the front, anyone still talking in two minutes will get the strap', and any head which was turned so it might be talking, any owner of a mouth which could not be seen and prove itself shut, was dragged and bundled back out of the desk, his hand pulled up flat and whacked hard with the thick strap of leather cut into strips for greater impact at the ends.

Dave and Granda (1954): Kells, Eire

Some evenings me and me two sisters would travel on the bus from Wardley to the toon, to the Tara Club, of which me Ma was a founder member. Situated just over the Tyne Bridge, a great stone building with a massive central hall called The Arcade off which were smaller rooms, in one of which a fiddler stood and dragged out once wild tunes while little legs rocked and wavered in the ancient custom of teaching the kids Irish dancing. Me too, though there were few boys in the class. 'One two three four, five six seven, and one, two three, four, five, six, seven, and one, two the easy reel, but it wasn't, the double kick at the end of the crossovers usually knocked the skin off me ankle or found me on me arse amid giggling gaishers. Still, you could sit on the high dusty window-sills and eat your bag of Tudors, suppin' glasses of limeade, and watch the sisters deying complicated heel-rolls and ankle-clicks and, as the legs kick higher and bodies bounce, the fiddler catches his stride and, foot fair stamping, fires the tune along, something more like its taproom custom.

Or the haunting flute, the first instrument I ever heard, played low and mellow in wor Wardley kitchen, as me sisters and fellow dancers rehearsed for the big Feis, bobbing and jigging, sweating and wheeling, kicking and whooping,

Tara Club Dancers: sister Veronica in middle

while waiting dancers rehearsed the kicks and turns with their two fingers, dancing them on the arms of chairs. We were the Tyneside-Irish, the Felling was St Patrick's parish, and his day was special, with buckets of shamrock being distributed, and armies of folk wearing it around their daily business. At the ceilidhs, I would take the stage and give renditions of *The Wild Colonial Boy*, in the fields with the gang I would sing it, with another few verses I had added in making more of the heroic shoot-out scene. The green, white and gold of the Irish tricolour was oft-times seen flying round the estate on the end of a bamboo pole which we imagined as a pike or a lance.

The Arcade is gone now, killed by the city's murderers, who had been steadily pulling the city doon since the middle of last century. Mind, they had promised to put it together again brick by brick, stone by stone and, true to the pledge, it was dismantled with loving care, each piece painted with a number for easy reassembly, transported to a field in Heaton, where it sat, year by year, the numbers fading till at last all that could be reassembled was the central hall. The rest, just a pile of meaningless masonry, was quietly dumped.

The silence of Ireland. Stillness. Quiet. Crackling sticks burning in the fire of the blackened range, a little pile of turf used sparingly, and me Granny, minute on ancient worn-down shoes, moving as if on wheels about the cracked stone floor. We would sit, exhausted from the journey: Newcastle via Holyhead, or worse, via Liverpool to Dun Laoghaire, what seemed like a stagecoach hike on the bus from Dublin through deep lush green silence to Kells, County Meath, the

John Doonan playing at Birtley Fête (1964). Pit tip in background

Royal County, the county of the Irish Tara kings. Sitting exhausted, still feeling the rocking sensation of the boat hours after disembarkation. Me Granda by his crackling wireless, sucking on his pipe and raising his ancient bones every now and again to spit tobacco juice on the burning sticks in the range. A man of pure Irish brogue, he was a Protestant though not a strong one. Some said he had come from England though just how was never clear. To me he was as Irish as the bog.

Visits to the country cousins, uncles and aunties, were an endurance of alienness for the first few days, three times a year, always the same until our 'English grandness' wore away. We'd arrive at the road to the cottage, open fields and grazing beasts, the roads frequently chock-a-block with cattle on their way to market, driven along by a wee garson with a twig, the mud-caked giants of flesh and muscle bellowing or else trying to make a stand. 'Be up the fucking road now, will ye!' the garson, half my size, would shout without fear or inhibition and whack the bull with the twig. The bull would do a half-hearted double back-flick with his great hooves before nudging his way through the herd to the front, and a gentle stroll toward Kells.

The cottage smelling of turf, wood smoke, Irish homemade soda bread and spuds. 'Will ye no' have a spud?' It was the equivalent of 'Would you like a cup of tea?' All visitors along the road calling at the door were asked 'Will ye no' have a spud?' The spuds were always either ready in a pan, slowly simmer-ing in their thin flaking skins, or else keeping warm next to it, still in their black cauldron. Often as the bus made its way along the narrow road we'd pass a little old woman with a black shawl pulled over her head and shoulders like a figure from the Theatre Royal pantomime, back in a slow stoop, in her arms a huge bundle of sticks for the fire. It was wor Granny, and her stick collection happened every time she chanced out here or there. My attempts to help were abject failures, as I could never seem to get them to stay in a bundle; they were always twisting away from each other and falling from my grasp.

Likewise, carrying water from the pump a mile up the road was an agony, which she 'popped out' to do, a bucket in each hand. I made a pilgrimage with the one. The water from the pump was for drinking. The rain-barrels, one at the front and one at the back, held our bath water: skim off the stranded flies and leaves and take out a basinful, as caald as the North Sea, but smooth and soothing somehow. The errand to the pump was ney problem gaanin', empty bucket slung ower the shoulder, and pumping it full was a joy. The problems began the minute I tried to lift its brimming body off the neck of the pump. I'd have to get close to lift it, and inevitably it would tip in a great flood and soak me feet. Dripping wet, the bucket just scarcely off the ground, I'd limp the damn thing back, chipping at me ankles, one arm nigh pulled out of its socket, the handle digging deep into my red raw palm, deeper than the cane could strike, and changing hands every other step. No matter how full it was when I set off, only half, a bucketful ever got back.

But then I was free, free again to mount the great farm-gate that crossed the leafy driveway to the cottage, and travel with it in its great arc in a mindlessly happy game, catching speed and crashing into the gatepost, back and forth, a noisy creak of irritated metal and rusty hinges, with me standing tall on the top crossbar crashing back once more, again and again.

On a later visit me and another pitman's son, walking along behind the packed herd of twisting and complaining cattle the wee garson trail-hand turns to the big lads from ower the water: 'Shtay wid me beasts will ya, mister, while I see me ould un a minute.' The request was simple enough; we were walking that way, just keep ahint the kie while he had a minute with his Ma or his Granny. 'Whey aye,' they probably wouldn't even knaa he'd gone, would they? Ye bugger ney shuner had the garson disappeared ahint the hedgerow up the path when the herd decided to trot, the animals at the front starting into a gallop. 'Ger up in front,' I shouted 'Slow them doon', and that effort to get past them caused four or five to stop, turn and start heading back. In no time, the four or five mavericks at the front were in full bellowing charge doon the road, another group had lowped the ditch at the side of the road, pushing through a thick hedge into a beautifully set flower garden, where they played plough up the flowers and trample the women's vegetables. Others, leading the retreat, were charging back toward me! 'Stop, ye buggers! Whoa! Had up!' But to no avail. I wondered if 'Geritchi' might work. One of the few cars coming doon the road found a cow anxious to mount it as it did its damnedest to climb over the bonnet. Utter chaos spread oot on hooves in every direction as the wee garson, accompanied by a bloke on a bike, came harin' doon the road behind we. 'Stupid English omithorn.' The omithorns stood hapless while the man on the bike charged up after the leaders and, finding them quietly grazing the golf course, herded them back onto the road, where they stood like sheep. The wee garson leapt the ditch and followed through the hole in the hedge, where a greet bull wheeled to challenge him. The garson's bare foot lashed out at the beast's ribs with a shout of 'Be off, yi fucking bousy', and the bull cantered to the side, snorting, running back through the hedge, followed by the other renegades. Soon the herd was assembled and, leaving the hole in the hedge, the trampled garden, the car with the hoof-marks in the bonnet, the chewed-up golf-course and two red-faced English omithorns, the wee chap resumed his leisurely stroll ahint his herd.

It was to be on this fateful visit 'home' that the mate, in learned discourse to me and a couple of other open-mouthed garson's, explained where babies came from, about everyone, everyone, having to have sex before you could have a bairn. In answer to my shocked exclamation of total disbelief, he had replied, as if I was two years old: 'Course ya Ma and Da shagged, where the fuck de'ye think ye come from, like?' The idea was as repulsive as it was impossible. *My* Ma? *My* Da? Give ower, anyway what was shaggin', it had to be more than Doctors and Nurses, didn't it? Best not seem totally stupid, I'll pick it up as we gaan alang. Mind, he was really talking shite when he further divulged that babies came oot ya Ma's blit!

Months later, me and John, one of the lads, sat with wa chairs turned round the opposite way, with wa legs dangling over the sides and wa heads rested on the back of the chair, hands rested on knees, staring in unbroken gaze at his naked baby sister sitting legs outstretched on the floor, and trying to relate her delightful dimple of flesh with the idea of a baby steaming out of it like a train through a tunnel. John hit on it. It doesn't stay like that, little and that, it splits right roond to their arses and up to their belly-buttons, so the bairn can get oot. Aye nuw, that made mer sense. 'Ney wonder they're always skelpin wi', I ventured. 'Must hurt like buddy hell!'

But here in infancy a wee garson mesell, awe and strangeness locked a fixed smile for fear of making an expression more honest. Thousands of barefoot cousins charged down the road to greet is and, catching sight of is, mobbed me in shock and surprise. 'Look! Look at the shoes on the garson, look, wee shoes on the garson, oh, and the grand stockings on him.' Mud-caked fingers would touch the wee shoes and pull at the grand stockings. Me, embarrassed and scared, would literally hide behind me Ma's skirt. 'Be out and leave the wee garson's clothes alone', me Uncle Peter, a rod of iron and a tongue of pure Kilmanham broken regularly by Anglo-Saxon as were the cousins', even the wee'ist. 'You'll be getting shit all over your fine shoes, Mag [me Ma]. See, the woman's [his Ma's] old fucking pigs have been out and shit up and down the road here all day.'

As the first day passed and the grand clothes gave way at least to sandshoes, ney socks, an aud pair of khaki pants and a shirt. 'Sure he's a grand garson for the games' marked me out as an innovator of wild games up and doon the Kilmanham Road and far ower the fields to the Blackwater. An aud deed crow hung up to scare off others of his kind provided a set of headdresses; broon mud from the stream, war-paint. Bows and arrows, spears, along with a couple of other related tribes recruited from the scattered cottages, and we had ready-made as savage a team as to stand off the whole US Cavalry. Wild running and hunting of bulls and cows up and doon the fields, leaping from the trees, ploughing through the streams: mad, mad games that would run you to exhaustion, leaving you face up flat on the green hills, panting with squinting eyes at the summer sun and cementing a bond across the Irish Sea until the next return 'home'.

In Granny's cottage the bedrooms smelt of damp, and dark lofty shadows threw strange shapes across the tall ceilings, reflected and refracted from the oil lamps carried like Wee Willie Winky up the dark stairs, shadows rushing to follow on behind. Ten thoosand holy Jesuses stared down from walls, from shelves, from inside glass cases and china grottoes. The legion of the saints—plus a few who never existed and were only exposed in the great Vatican purge of the 1960s. Who could feel scared, dark and shadows or no dark and shadows, when Jesus and the entire cast of the heavenly host shared every spare inch of the bedroom, and in any case after the nightly prayers the staircase and bedroom and four corners of the bed had been blessed with holy water?

A little burning night-light encased in a small red globe, flickering like the light on the altar that told you Jesus was at home in his tabernacle. This room and the downstairs were full of cures. 'This one', Granny holding up a small white box, 'is a piece of blessed St Martin's nail; it's a cure for headaches.' Another was 'blessed St Jude's bone, powerful for backaches and sore bones'. A piece of hair from a long-gone pope, a lump of rib, a corner of nose-bone, every one especially powerful magic for one ailment or another, all of them blessed. Enough material at least for a pious Frankenstein to reconstruct a totally new saint with a collective immunity against just about everything going. The relics and cures were backed up by an armoury of herb cures and wild plants, remedies passed on through generation after generation of Celtic experience, like the stories, tales carried in whispers and burst of voice and rolls of eyes and gestures and strokes on the stone floor to attentive open-mouthed attention, ears poised like an

Alsatian on alert, eyes flickering to every flinch and movement, memory and imagination ablaze, a celebration of words.

'Hawk Maguire, see him down the road beyond, these nights.' Memory flashes to the hobbling old character with a crippled shoulder,

'Sure, he was took; took from off the ground in front of his house there. Ar, an' his poor mammy, sure, had just gone inside when a huge hawk came screeching out of it, down and out of the sky and picked him up. Picked him right up and isn't it after flying away up the hill beyond. An' the wee garson crying out of him, an the mammy shoutin': "Oh, God help me, oh, God de yee hear me, the great burd's away wid me child!" An' didn't God hear the pleas from the desperate and force that old burd to drop him? Sure, the poor wee lad was crippled ever since, but the nun up the convent says he's gifted, sure the poor and inflicted that's come to the doors of deat and had them closed again by the Almighty has inner grace.'

With nights as black as pitch, wild wind ripping the canvas sheet, which served as a door on the netty, you run through the dark from the cottage door, at dead of night, eyes on rapid patrol vigilant to all movement and sound, drawers down, inch backward in the vague direction of the wooden structure covering the hole. A sudden encounter with a scaly, bony, living moving object behind cause's heart-stopping seizure of your vocal cords as the Devil's hand tries to grab you into hell. Me head swings round in mortified fear while the big turkey using the bog to shelter from the wind takes off with a gaggle of indignant disarranged feathers.

Back inside, sticks burn and sizzle in the grate, full of red glowing turf and logs, oil-lamps throwing a mellow glow that barely reaches to the corners of the room, which is etched in semi-darkness. Sitting just within the safe borders of lamplight, me Ma, me sisters, the old Granda crouched, nodding his confirmation or grunting his approval, Granny standing in the middle, a tiny speck of energy, relates the tale:

'The banshee ... sure ... like the howlin' of the wind there, but a low old moan, then "Wheeeeeeeee", she'd come to the Fosters, over the hills there we heard her "Wheeeeeeeee", and Johnny said, "My God, it's the banshee!", and we run to the door and over the hill with a veil a-flying out! "Oh, shut the door, Johnny, she'll see us, shut the door for Jesus, Mary and Joseph, she'll take us too, shut the door will ya?"

Every object held a story: a big jar full of medals on the dusty windowsill, Granddad's medals, and out come the photos, the greet lang regimental picture, the Lancers! Granda was a lancer, a fine man with a dashing moustache, in his glistening uniform. Granda was a 'little Englander', a man who fell for the recruiting sergeant's tale, who fell for the English lie. Many an Irishman would fall in the field having previously fallen for the tale.

'This is a war in which Great Britain is engaged along with the other civilised countries of Europe to ensure that little Belgium is not suppressed by bigger nations. This is a war for the right of small nations, all small nations, to be free. Ireland can rest assured that if you fight at England's side in this endeavour and establish that noble principle that small nations shall be free, then Ireland will claim her freedom.' Off they went, and while he was away fighting England's war the English soldiers came up the Kilmanham Road shooting suspects—including Granda's racing dogs, not cos they were suspects but because they were Irish. They came, they dragged womenfolk by the hair, demolished the middle of Dublin, they came and would not leave. So when Granda returned he wondered why he had been fighting

Germans when it was the British state which had invaded and tortured his country. So the medals stayed in the jar on the windowsill.

'They were fool's gold, so they were fool's gold.'

'Come on, come on now, and Ah'll show ye', and Granny would lead us out the back door and point to holes and gouges in the wall. 'There's where they shot at the house and the poor dogs, just come up outta the pub, mad roaring drunk. They came one night an me alone with the childa, and Johnny away over in England trying to find work, they came kicking the door and cursing out of them: "Open the door, yi dirty Irish B's." Oh, God help us, the English soldiers have come; go away and leave us alone will ya; we're just women and childa, that's all, women and childa. An they kicking on the door, then smashing the windows and sticking their rifles through at us, "Come and open this door, you Irish bitch", an' they come in an' they throw me again the wall'—she falls against the wall —'an' the big feller, "Where's your husband?" says he. "He's in London," say I, "seeking work." "He's in the IRA", says he. "He's no such thing," say I ti him, isn't he only after leaving your Lancers an' fighting them old Boars and the Kieser for yi?" An they take all me poor childa and get Mag be the hair'—she gets me Mam by the hair—'and pull her tithe wall, and they set them all up to the wall, and kick poor Peter, and they go through all the drawers and pull the clothes to the floor and break every bit of delft in the kitchen, then went up the road laughing out of them. "Oh God", Ah said'—she'd throw both arms wide then brought her hands crashing together to form a prayer—"Oh God, send the English B's away, bad cess ti them and bad cess on yor dorty old queen."

This was the greatest of all the little plays the Granny would perform. It involved much re-enactment of the parts and aunties and uncles perform their various roles as they recalled them, the memory of that evening passing from them to me as if I had been there, in the way that the Celts had always told their stories and carried their history and bonny legends.

The fields and rolling hills round Rathfarnham and me Aunty Mary's provided brief incursions into Irish football, with the local garsons from round the doors booting the ball high in the air or catching it dramatically, running like Rugby players though never quite knowing the rules. Sitting up on the tree-covered hill overlooking the lines of tree-basked houses with their yellow hedges, letting the spray of the pounding waterfall soak us, and talk of the bold IRA, the bold boys of the IRA, writing in chalk on the surrounding pavements 'UP THE IRA!' Me Ma's aunty was in the IRA', she was too, as Kells midwife she had a permit to break the imposed army curfew and travel the length and breadth of Kilmainham in her little car, which she used to great effect right through the English occupation, ferrying materials and food to hidden IRA fighters in the countryside.

Oh, confusion on confusion at the matinee in Rathfarnham, a German subtitled film with the subtitles barely visible and only the German gutturals for guidance. 'Ah, for God's sake, speak English will ya', came the shout from the balcony, and my young brain thought, 'English? Why the hell should Irish people wish the film to be in English?' The Dublin dialect so pronounced in me Uncle Cory's brogue had never struck me as English. While me Ma oft told horrific tales of nuns bashing the Gaelic into them, which history and the effects of the British Empire had long expunged from their communities and speech. Back in England, while the father was oot on the neet shift, the Ma would iron, and as she busied in the kitchen or worked the hand wringer the haunting air from childhood ears carried via the Grandma and the bog:

We raise the old cry anew
Slogan of Conn and Hugh!
Out and make way for the bold Fenian men.

Sung softly in kitchen, sung loudly at ceiidh and when the Da was in one of his patriotic Queen and Country tirades—for despite his impeccable class credentials he was a patriot—sung face to face defiantly, legs astride and hands on hips, with her head deyin the Irishwoman's wag of temper:

We've made the false Saxon yield
Many a red battlefield
God on our side we will triumph again
PAY THEM BACK WOE FOR WOE
GIVE THEM BACK BLOW FOR BLOW
OUT AND MAKE WAY FOR THE BOLD FENIAN MEN!

At other times—at weddings, wakes, christenings, or funerals—the *Kevin Barry* lament reduced all to tears regardless of the occasion.

At the Jarra Irish ceilidh, which me Da enjoyed with me Ma— great dancers both of them—he'd resolutely refuse to stand at the end for the playing of *The Soldiers' Song*. Me Ma 'Get up, will ye, you're showing me up', and Da, 'It's a bloomin IRA song, Ah'll not stand.' But then at the British Legion Club dance, when all would be upstanding for the queen, doon would sit me Ma.

'Stand up', me Da would loudly whisper, face going red.

'No, you wouldn't stand for mine, I'm not standing for yours, she's not *my* queen.'

2
New Estate and Old Wardley Ways

Most of the Ellen Wilkinson was built, but the Leam[7] was still by and large fields and woods, and green banks up the ancient Viking ways to Windy Nook were clear of houses. Before the motorway, when the main Sunderland road was like a double cycle-path, the farmers' fields of waving gold, and the wild oasis of swamps fed by streams, and little dens of free grass unchained for several centuries, were a voyage of wonder for treks across the wilderness from Wardley to Usworth. Between the deserted, once house-lined, Bill Quay Road and the river stood granite banks, volcanic red hills like the Rockies, and rolling dales till the edge of Hebburn was touched. Despite the municipal socialist invasion of the new estate, Wardley was still a village bounded by green and river and rock and the Felling.

The new hooses brought non-pitmen, people whey dinnit clump oot to work in helmet and buets but left for buses at half past eight with the skuel kids. Black and often bloody pitmen striding oot from the pit gates at lowse to the background shriek of the steam-whistle brought the stamp of generations to new concrete pavements, hobnails sparking on new municipal estate as clogs had done on Jarra cobbles. The stride of the pit lad bending and lang, a rolling stoop, an' reed reed lips with ice-clear white eyes, a dozen black men roll their black hyme past new redbrick hooses and non-pit kids stand and gawp. The pitman's baggy pants wave a motion of their am, their jackets pulled tight ower bait tin and kneepads making a hump on the back. A dozen black humpty-back men, their dialects from two thoosand feet nearer hell and several centuries of striding back to the surface, sting the air:

'Huw many tha gettin' th' day?'

'Brockwell panzer wes knackered aal morn a greet wailer fast i' th' jib!'

Me Da, a strict Methodist of the Ney Swear, Ney Beer, Ney Smoke, Ney Gamble variety: capitalism the exploiter, the earthly tyrant, had injected an evil means to its own continuation in a fixed craving by its slaves for booze and baccy, a contempt for education and self-learning seen in the foul mooth, the Saxon four-letter and langer-letter words. Never so much as a 'bluddy', an 'arse', a 'bugger', or even a 'damn' passed his lips then or ever. But riled to quick temper—fierce, all consuming, massive, violent temper—, which could be expressed in physical force withoot the need for any preliminary swear-words. Or, if the situation was such that it could not be expressed in that way, like the time in later years some fool came roond collecting donations for a monument to the miners' hated class enemy, Churchill, Da reached a crescendo of 'Flippin' bloomin' heck, be doon that path, see yi, Churchill is it? Muurdrr, bloomin' golly, a muurdrr like him, be doon an oot of it 'fore Ah shift ye!'

Colliers' kids come running down the lane at the soond of the pit buzzer and the zudderzudderzudder of the compressor and clouds of steam, running to meet me Da. A knot of black men with the swaying gate, and Da, the smell of the pit on his clothes, bouncing alang, chattin', yarpin', an Da: 'Whey aye?' 'Gaan on?'

Black and humpty-backed pitmen from more distant reaches boarding the normal service bus en route to the toon fernant Wardley Post Office huddle beneath the stairwell of the double-decker, crooched in a nightness of blackness, multiple eyes peering out from belaw the stairs, or else sitting on the stairs and crowding out the platform until the next stop is reached, whereupon they all exit and wait until the clean and surface folk board unbesmudged before returning to their quarantine, the crack and bold laughter taking the bus by native storm and at once setting all trekkers with a light bubbling heart and cheerful 'Eeeee!'

Soon the lines of new council houses were ready to sail, clouds of steam rose from pipes, gratings, overflow systems, drains, and rose billowing from bathroom windows. Black bodies immerse in steaming water, and red lips part. The choir strikes up. Me Da, a fine tenor: 'Up with the Jolly Roger, boys, and off we go to sea....' Dozens of Mario Lanzas and from across the gardens a baritone:

'There's heaps of fun when the Jolly Roger's hung....' A rising volume of voices from row on row of hooses, joining in their parts, harmonising, no conductor. Steam and choir voices, two baths for each body before it is clean again.

Lang walks, lang walks, the pitmen was great walkers, meking up tha sunshine, meking up in air and oxygen, walking off the mine, walking off the cramped space muscles. Waaks doon secret paths of history, doon little winding lanes past lang-abandoned industrial sites.

'Nuw that was the aid Goose Colliery, whey the pump-hoose pumped millions of gallons o' waater oot the pits, ower yon'— pointing across the river to the Wallsend end side—it's all worked oot under river so all the pits' waater gets drawn inti here. See, La, aal the waater, Ah wes telling ye, we've gettin at Wardley comes from this shut pit and all the others that sump into it and from the river, the surveyor says the waater coming into Wardley is tidal!' The waaks were history lessons, illustrated guides to the heritage:

'The pitmen hid here wi'n guns when the sowldjers come to evict them from the hooses.' Doon the dilly line tithe staiths, 'in name Pelaw Main Staith', all the coal of the region shootin' in a greet black waaterfaal into the ships belaw. Doon the dillies the tubs reach tha destination, into a metal tube and torn heed ower heels and emptied, tub after tub, neet after day, a black stream from a vast underground ocean, all from the point of the pick.

From the distant bank of the Walker Yard, a young shipyard worker had jumped aboard a skiff with the ease of one whey meks ney big deal of something he knaws, takes a single oar astern and skulls at great speed across to Bill Quay.

Tyne River running rough or smooth meks breed for me and mine;

Of all the rivers north or sooth, there's nen like coaly Tyne

'An' that what we sang at skuel, did ye not learn it?'

In clarty paths along the river, past abandoned hooses and closed pubs, scenes of early nautical adventures filled me imagination together with the history lesson.

'Ah mind sixteen ships all tied up oot there'—he points out over Bill Point to the river—'waiting ti be loaded from these staiths. Fower tied up alongside the quays, the others at buoys. Dutch, Swedes, Danes, Greeks, the lot. Us colliers from Hebburn would take a blae on the riverbank here, win the sailors of the world, th'id oft as not have a squeeze-box and wi'd all hey a bit sang.... Whey aye.... Chinese sangs as weel, whey wi'd just mek a noise that soonds summit like.'

We laugh. I look into the man's face, a tiny hand held in a big hand, listening to the tales. His eyes moist and lost in time, he gaans back into the past and I gaan too.

'All them sailormen tied up at Pelaw Main and went shopping up to Bill Quay, a vorry busy place then, ye knaa. See, all roon here galloways and horses and flat carts fleein' aboot, laden win tackle and food. See tha, doon there wi'd all gaan swimmin' as lads, aye, nowt on, mevie a bit cloth like an Indian. Mind but dinnet thou gaan swimmin', the waater's poison nuw, anyroad Ah cud nivor swim

Ah hope ye learn, though.'

His eyes were sometimes angry in their memory and the memory that went before his time and carried on in anger. Then he'd squat like a pitman squats doon the pit in the la' and talk earnestly, passing the link.

'There stood the gibbet: a greet iron cage. In it they had hung a man, a pitman, a union man. Aye, hung him, covered his body in pitch and hung his black body oot there, covered in waater at high tide. They paraded that gibbet and the body all roond the pit villages on the back of a cart, then they stuck it oot there, to warn the pitmen not to struggle, not to fight back! If ye struggle we can kill ye, and then take ya dignity by hanging ye like a deed craw.'

His Da had telt him, my Da telt me, and nuw Ah's tellin thou. The gibbet was no langer there, but the spot is fixed in all time like a granite mountain. 'It was there!'

From the new estate the folk would walk back to Old Wardley to the Welfare ground, for sports days, or the Miners' Hall for 'Go As You Pleases' and gala days. The kiddhas would stage their own boody concerts, the cost of admission being a piece or two of the precious commodity, bonny bits being mer valuable, though not as much as the strange hard bright shiny blue stone found in the surrounding fields from time to time. What was it, and does any remain?[8] Wor street was Laski Gardens. No less than fifteen kids lived there.

Often we would set off across the fields to Old Wardley. It was here the tip, so dark in the imagery of the middle class, stood so magnificent to us. A snow-capped peak to climb, a dusty desert with clumps of gorse where cowboys dived for cover and cut their knees and let the blood run right doon ya sock, where Indians made war-paint from blackberries and wet coal, where abandoned pit-tubs were the entrance to gold-mines. The pit tip in later years, the lang grass providing cover for uncovering pink and gentle bodies, but now providing cover for hidie and waiting with baited breath till piss forced itself free in small drops as ya heart beat enough to deafen and eyes watched for the slightest movement or sound of the searcher: 'Keep in, keep in, wherever ye are, the rats and mice are at ya door!' The tip where sugar on bread and bait and a bottle of waater set the scene for picnics beside a fire that always got oot o' control, set the whole tip ablaze, and spread to the railway banks as we took flight in all directions, watching the blaze from afar.

Dave and Dad (1960)

The pit pond, a great ocean, rafts made from empty barrels traversed its depth, catch the strange dinosaur newts, or hurl greet wallers in an avalanche of shale and dust, sending cascades of twinkling waater up a height and a mist of blue and green slime jumping reluctantly into the air and splatting back again.

Corrugated sheets or lumps of cardboard with the front pulled up made excellent sledges regardless of the weather, booncing doon the black ski-run from the peaks of the tip, turning just short of the pit pond's shore, or else defying death and a soaking or a skelpt arse to plough straight into the dark depth of the pond and feel the water soak ye through and the quagmire under ya feet try to suck ye doon.

But we were foreigners now, we were from the Estate. The native inhabitants of the old village regarded the tip and the pond as their own and such interlopers as us as invaders. Sitting on the tip side, a fire of broken wood beams and dried grass, laid aboot eating the sugar on bread or golden syrup on bread, and suppin' waater from the bottle, your heart freezes, for doon below charging over the little railway bridge to the pit, armed with catapults and sticks, come the Owld Wardley Lads.

Catapults fired iron ball bearings or marbles, shields made from giant paint-drum lids from the river paint factories, bows and arrows with the ends of darts stuck on, and airguns. They were hard bastards. You were dead if they caught you, or you wished you were. Your best bet was to hold them off. Outrunning them never seemed to work, you got spilt up and isolated, and your lungs always give out before their buggers, leaving you in a remote spot to be kicked and punched, or have them cut your hair off or shave ya pubes, them that had them. So ower the bridge they'd charged, fanning all oot at the bottom of the tip, trying William's trick, spreading round the back of the heap to get behind us. Catapults wanged metal balls upwards but at this stage the advantage was wors. Greet rocks of ironstone, one between two of wi, launched ower the top toward the climbing foe below, lumps of metal scrap, bool the ancient iron tub wheels doon the tip, hoy the spears, wooden dowls with nails hammered into a metal point, or iron axle-bars. A well-aimed ball-bearing crashed into the head of the lad next to me, and the dark blood oozed between his black hair and ran in a stream doon his face and round the crack made by his open speechless voice, his eyes ablaze with pain and horror.

In a previous battle three of wor arra lads, with their improvised lang bows, let fly in beautiful symmetry the arrows all in flight, brass darts in their tips, arcing toward the upcoming raggy lad, transfixed as if outside the event, watching the arrows fall rapidly toward him until, too late, he dived to move as the brass dart on the end of the bamboo stick sunk with a punch like thud into his shoulder.

Dragging wor wounded away, the rearguard still spoiling for the fight lets fly with the glass pop-bottles we had carried

Liverpool Lions handball team with Captain Dave, bottom right (1960)

for wa waater, scoring a direct hit as another small face loses its menace and becomes just a small face again, erupting with a gash of blood and snot and tears, while I feel a sudden, excruciating pain as an airgun pellet hits me in me knee and a sick dark feeling comes round my eyes, capturing my attention and putting me head into a swimming near-faint until another pellet burrows and burns its way into my ear and I think my head is on fire and my ear is as big as me foot, canceling out the pain of me knee. They take me running off the tip, crazed like a herd of small animals fearful of capture, but wor adversaries likewise are slinking away save for the few revenge-seekers still breaking down their air rifles and firing at us.

A year or two later the arms race had reached the Age of the Bike, as the Owld Wardley Lads staged an attack on the Estate Kids. With little pennants on bamboo sticks, like the 7th Cavalry they swept along from Old Wardley. We rallied the warring factions of the Estate and even some mercenaries from the Leam and staged a spectacular ambush.

Lying in wait at both ends of the steep bank of Kirkwood

Gardens, they came, about twenty-five of them, handlebars glinting, whooping like redskins, one hand riding the tubular metal creature, the other holding the lance or holding aloft their 177 Diana's, picking up speed. Then we struck. Sticks shot out like javelins into the spokes of the front wheels, flattened paint-tin tops spun like giant shurriky and the disaster began. Bodies went heed ower heels as front wheels came to a deed stop, bikes crashed together and heads, gobs, and faces made contact with distorted bicycle-handles as the massed gangs of Labour council estates pitched in. A chair-leg wheeled around a head and brought that sickening thud and a falling boy and the drip of red on newly laid pavement, rushing head down, staggering to the refuge of home, his eyes see blood, blood, blood, NW on the paving stone. NW don't step on the lines, NW and great splots of blood, his legs getting weaker, then the kitchen sink filling with blood. One would remain toothless from this moment on, while another would keep his eye only at the price of being henceforth cock-eyed.

Battles were not always so undeclared or so violent, and most fights were small-scale, reaching a peak in the weeks before Bonfire Night as raids on everyone else's bonfires for wood often broke into battles involving teenage gangs and sometimes real big grown-up people. Bonfire Neet, in the old village, in my years, before pleurisy, was a great community affair. The whole village had a role. Men and boys scoured the surrounding hedgerows from Usworth to Hebburn for wood and boxes, whilst a women's militia, me Ma included, stood guard, often all night, to prevent thefts. In later years on the Estate the hollow at the bonfire's heart was used as a den in which young uns themselves kept watch or slept on guard, not expecting the latest development of the post-Teddy-Boy era, which was not to steal the fire but to set it on fire prematurely. A young local lad burned to death in the cause of the communal bonfire, and a local gang claimed a battle honour it hadn't particularly sought.

Alang the bottom of the estate ran the North-Eastern Region railway trains, trains to the coast and all points to London, a train spotters' spot. The Mallard, streak, blued metal, red-glowed, black-faced fireman, head sticking from the footplate cabin to catch an ice-cold draught of air, sweating another man's day's moisture in a fraction of a minute. The blinkered metal monoliths, a steel thunderstorm, clouds of steam and smoke, showers of bright sparks; man-made comets roaring along wor estate, on the hoor, ivory hoor. Steel-rail percussion scream, blur of iron spokes, first fast-spinning on the track then slow and deliberate, turning to throaty muffled roar, the early morning 'coffee-pots', endless wagons in tow, rattle and shunt for tension, friction, hegemonic adhesion, steel against steel.

Through the smoke and noise, tall cranes along the river, those swarming banks of effort but yet tranquil, rake the skyline. We knew them all: the biggest, the strongest, the nearest, the furthest, and every yard on which a ship stood astride the stocks, and we felt the rush of excitement when launching was due, riding pell-mell to the river's edge to catch the scene. We knew the riverbanks, and the ships, warships best of all, their size, type, firepower, class and age. We knew the cargo boats and liners, straining to make out the nationality of the distant fluttering national flag. We were experts on flags of all nations, partly from the river trade, but more concisely courtesy of PG Tips cards.

Lying abed, my darkened room flashed blue across the ceiling as welding torches down on the slips lit the night sky, the windy hammers and riveters distantly thudding, the 'lectric train adding a periodic shower of colour and rhythm.

It was reassuring somehow: all these folks up and aboot carried you into sleep while somewhere off in the distance of semi-consciousness was the dull clump, clump and scratchin' of me Da's pit buets on the pavement outside, then a chink of light through the mist of sleep, a black face and pink mouth knew then Ah was alreet; the coal wagons did their clankityclank clickityclick clankityclank times table ower the points, ower the points an' away off deeper into the neet.

From Windy Nuek, the land belaw was a patchwork of industrial humanity. Railway lines, goods yards, little country stations with blazing coal fires and polished wooden waiting rooms, vast engine-sheds. Major lines filtering off into small veins and colliery sites. Dillyways cut northwards while endless lines of wagons tramp and clank, often unaccompanied, towards the staiths. Colliery headgear and riverside cranes stretch for the skyline against factory and colliery chimney. In moats of green and brown bracken, the clustered villages, circles of houses, embrace the mine.

Surrounding fields of snadgies, snadged and eaten raw, grass-covered ditches, hidden by elderberry dens and secret places smelling of hay, crushed grass and the white, broken shafts of elderberry bushes, the bricks and mortar of a thousand constructions.

A circle of wise ins, assembled during the morn of Saturday, gathering at Jonty's pigeon krey, sitting on the tarred wooden veranda which served as the birds' flight path or squat with a fence post doon their spine as they would doon the pit. The bords wheel la' then swoop off in a breeze of wings off ower the tip. The crack was easy, non-laboured. It covered all subjects in the slow, methodical manner they used to turn ower the soil, deeply trenching, in a relentless, painstaking motion. Soil: these were men who loved its feel, loved the sight of growth, brought forth great forests of bushy green, leeks broad-girthed, beaming white, fine-flagged and stocky, great boulders of vegetables, kaleidoscopes of colour, filled the surrounding air with smells of vegetation, celery, scallions, onions, strawberries, apples, cherries, and tomatoes, great powder-puffs of big-headed colour and wee night-scented stock, oceans of potatoes wave upon wave, allotments as big as parks without the sight of a weed; they had worked these plots so long that not a pebble invaded the sanctity of the soil.

Jonty, the tracer of things, squatted doon in the corner, pointing an arm tithe sooth with a flat hand, spoke of origins: 'Wi were th' Brits, cousins of the day's Welshmen; whey wi wor all Celts in them days, we wer' all 'Welsh' anarl but the Irish and Scotsies were no Brit Celts, they were the Gaelic Celts, wi wa like distant cousins. Mind, the Brits wornt the forst, the aud Celts were folk afore them, though they didn't much like this land nor them doon yonder.' The finger of the still-extended hand points doon sooth. 'Them folk were th' Picts, some stayed in Wales, tha knaas, John?'[1] His speech would move from one listener to another as if to involve them personally in the tale. 'Though the most had sailed reet th' way up ti Scotland and reet oot on th' wee islands up yon.' His back straightened, head looking north as if the better to see Orkney and Shetland, and the witan crood followed his gaze north. 'Wor folks were part of the Brit people, the Brigantes.' He stands and looks afar to the west. 'Ower there where the built the geet waal from Shields, through Newcastle reet away ower tithe ither coast, it was supposed to stop them gettin attacked from up north, but the got attacked from both sides by the Brigantes.'

'Whey where's them Angles-Saxons from, Jont'? Jont' inhaled nasal phlegm and turned curiously to the questioner, ruffled that his picture had been spoiled but anyway pleased to answer a question.

'Denmark', he snapped. 'It wes Angles that cum here, the both of them came to put doon the Celts and take away tha lands, there was massacres done, them Brits doon sooth escaped into Wales and Cornwall and ower the Channel to a new land tha called Brittany after thasells.'

He stands up, looks again to the sooth, spreading out both his arms and drawing them back in again.

'All the Brits started fleein' north to mek a stand wi the Brigantes, whe wa the most fierce of the Brits.'

Suddenly his thought catches and he is sidetracked by an interesting aside.

'Wi had queens them days yee knaa, Mat? Celts allis had queens, them others whe come couldn't stand that, not the Romans, nor them Angles and Saxons. The Celts loved magic and womenfolk were possessed of magic, they knew things then the men didn't knaa. And men always bein' off fightin' mevies didn't live lang enough to get clivor. Mind, the women fought an aal. Boudicea was a great fighter.'

He stops talking, his eyes scan the past, then he lights upon his thread again.

'Aye, them Romans stayed a lang while, hundreds of years, and better than fight wi the whole time wi lived mer or less alongside each other, wi copied things off each other, but wi didn't try to wipe each ither oot. But them Angles....'

There was a calm like a chill cloud passing over the sun and all froze like shadows, each to a place. A darkness came over the ancient Tyneside shaman's face.

'But then'—his arm bent across his eyes and lang legs in a low crouch, his hand a shield as if to save his eyes from the dive of a great bird—'cum a blae that rocked the Celts from the throne of Britain, nivor be wasells again. The Angles had been fighting tha way north, piece by piece, till they stood in a greet horde at the Tees. The northern Celts had ridden inti Scotland ti ask the Picts and Scots and ower ti Ireland

and doon Wales to rally their ancient kin to stand wi wi, and they did come, Cadwallon from Wales. Who clashed with Edwins army at Hatfield and slew the Angle king and doon from the ancient Celtic kingdom of Dalriada, though that wes years later, when the King of the Angles was a butcher called The Destroyer! He set aboot what they call gen-o-cide, te wipe the Brits oot allthegither, so wi stood alain.' Jonty's 'wi' covered wi all, for hundreds of years aside it was as Celts not Angle that wi followed the yarn, if yarn it wes.

'The battle when it came was fought on a front from Durham ti Northumberland, from North Sea to Irish Sea. The Celtic furore, that mass battle cry that had put Roman legions to flight, rose again, and naked painted Celts swept doon again, but the Angles kept coming, pushing further and further north, till the Brits made their stand at Lindisfarne, an island sacred in Celtic myth and religion. The Angles blockaded it, till Brits died in their hundreds, of caad and starvation, and were floated off from the island, to be washed ashore in heaps alang the beaches of Bamburgh and North Sunderland. The sands wa reed, the rocks wa reed, the sea itself washed reed ashore. The Celts was broken, the Angles established their kingdom, and set aboot destroying the aud Celt ways and religion, built a Christian church on the sacred earth island of Lindisfarne, Ironically a branch of the Celtic Scotia church and called it Holy Island. Dazzled the beaten Celt eyes with magic tales of God and his wizard son and made them Christians, Destroyed the spoken twang of the North Brit, so Celtic speech would be heard ney mer in the lands of Northumbria, but the Celts hadn't gone, wi still lived here. Ida Edwin's son claimed his Angle kingdom on the greet flat rock of Bamburgh, and it would be Angle rule and armies that governed but the Celts, the most of wi Geordies se called, Northumbrians, Tynesiders, call us what ye will, remained Celt folk and still are, though be nuw wa mixed up wi all kinds of ither folk anarl.'

A brief silence falls. Fifteen hundred years of ancient Picts, Brits, Gaels, Angle and Roman invaders, the distant battle scenes of rock hill and mountain, moorland and dunes, drift through me mental screen. Billy speaks:

'Them's geet bonny frogs in the pit pond, Joss.'

'Aye, there's twe lope ower here iv a morn an sort the 'lotment oot, great for the garden ye knaa?' (*See p.315*)

As afternuen breaks so does this cooncil o' the wise, my wee head ablaze with knowledge of the men with the ler'. Teachers didn't knaa such things. Time travel like Jonty? These men knew the past as if it wes the day.

'Ye knaa, Da, it's like that Jonty wes alive during them aud days.'

'Whey, he wes son, in a manner of speaking, did ye feel yee wes alive in them days when he talked.'

'Aye, Da, Ah cud see the ancient Brits fleein' up north and the Saxons burning them out and killing them.'

'Whey, he seen it like that, when his mother telt him. Ah mind him tellin' is, it wes her grandfather had telt hor.'

'An' is it reet and true, Da?'

'Whey, Ah divin knaa, Son, mevie neybody dis ti be reet, but if folk heh telt the tale lang enough, then mevie it began wi the ancient ones thasells!'

The walk back to the new Ellen Wilkinson, through the old Wardley cottages, and the scenes of history as yet not truly unfolded to me, with the colossus, the Co-op, standing tall and wide and all-embracing over the line to Pelaw, the clothes factories, the big chimneys of the polish firm, the furniture factories, the ensemble of municipal socialism über alles. Hundreds of young women and wives walking arm-in-arm from the Co-operative empire. A future hope of breaking the chain to the mine, an opportunity for the young lasses, to me Da a bulwark of moderated socialism, our patch, the bit we, he told me, owned. These were the labour factories of wor class. To me, these folks were the non-miners, another people, the ones you selt yer mashed up flower perfume tee with the lasses, as we mounted the weekend stall at the end of the street. They held not the fascination of the ancient ones, the tellers of all truths and answers to all mysteries.

'The Co-operative movement, David, was much important'—me Da talked clear non-dialect when making the point—'in an attempt by the working-class people like worsells to bypass the gaffers and make things for worsells. You would dee worse, La', than to work in such, an not gaan in th' pit, where Ah wadn't like ye ti gaan, it's an awful place.'

But me brain was absorbed, absorbed with a time before, and Ah lueked at the fields, an' seen the camps of the north Brits. That evening the street kids, under my design, made cardboard shields and with me Ma's help emblazoned them in Celtic scrolls, rolled paper swords and maces made from nylon stockings stuffed with Plasticene, and fought all the day Laski: Gardens versus Baker, translated as North Celts versus Angles.

3
Up Ti Willowgrove

'St John's, not Willowgrove!' This was to be the last period of school. It stood on a bank, rolling, raggy, rock-covered and snatched with grass in a little plateau, over the end of which a steep drop of mud to an area unseen from the staff room, picketed by the footballers and athletic collaborators who would still give the siren of approaching teachers. The scene in the swallie, of all things unallowed: crime, pain, sex and self-abuse. It was through this bow we, the young uns, trekked to the secondary modern, so-called 'years'.

Here was the coming of tribes, the young St John's, the young St Alban's, now together as the new intake—the third-year 'big lads' now the fourth-year gaffers, last year's first years now the kings of the roost, we the knaa nowts, all of us. How had this all come about? In later years, I learned that the legendary '11 plus' was the cause. It seems I had a choice. I had had the chance. How had that gone?

When had 'education' ever had owt ti dee wi gaanin ti skuel? When had skuel ever had owt ti dee wi education? Suddenly, on the verge of puberty, of which I knew even less—well nowt, actually—here I was a victim of it. True, the daft lads were allowed to walk around the pipes on the wall of the class at the 'bottom' school, while we did colouring and sums, the daft lads couldn't take reading-books hyme and I could, but school had never seemed to be owt mer than the playground and a lot of grown-ups shouting.

How did I learn to read? Ancient memories revive still the colourful *Three Pirates*, letter-by-letter recognition before that, me sisters reading tiv is, reading back and having a hug, dressing of the little book in me mammy's spare wallpaper to make a cover, but a system of sitting and consciously learning had never been on the scene.

Dave — 12 (1960)

When the bus left little St John's and the tower full of bones and armour there was ney divisions, we were mental, we dived from seat to seat, we fought on the floor, we fired catapults from the windows, we stamped and sang until the bus driver went on strike, then we 'sat-in'. Teachers brought in cars, demanded we leave the bus—'I want you boys off this bus now!'—and the hard Felling lads would sing bare-faced 'Gaan yem yi bums, gaan yem yi bums, gaan yem yi bums, gaan yem', to the tune of *Aud Laang Syen*. One by one the struggling boys were dragged from the bottom deck of the bus, until all were dancing and singing on the pavements, then the lasses upstairs would start.

For all that, prior to the sacred exams, somehow some people got special red forms to fill in and to work on in classes while the rest of us just got on with the *Three*, *Four* or *Five Pirates* books and colouring in, and endless chanting of the tables.

SMACK, on the desk with the cane and the class in line from the front:

One two is two
Two twos are four
Three twos are six
Four twos are eight

And in rhythm nobody, it seems, had taught us we went on:

Eight twos are sixteen

Nine twos are eighteen....

But the red forms were elsewhere. They weren't in the table. They were old 11-plus exam forms. Some kids had been chosen; none of us, not even the chosen ones, had ever been in an exam before.

The exam day was a special day, special clothes day, but not like the confirmation, where nobody fails. But we had that to learn. The air in the classrooms hung heavy, the teachers' expressions were drawn, the school in semi-silence and your mind runs back to years before like a funeral home.

YOU ARE REMINDED THAT OLDER PUPILS ARE TODAY SITTING THEIR 11-PLUS. SO THERE WILL BE NO PLAYING OF NOISY GAMES TODAY.

Now it was us. What we did determined where we went, but most kids went to Willowgrove, there surely wasn't anywhere worse?

Doon wi sat.

Handed clean sheets of paper and folded pink exam papers, which sat, closed on the starting line. At least Ah cud read, though ah nivor knew huw.

'Right—on your marks—you may now start.'

English paper.

English comp-re-hension

Compre-bloody-hension? What the hell wes that? I'd lueked aroond, aboot ti jest, but the teacher's eyes caught mine. 'WORK', came the simple word of command, but not before Ah had seen the heeds shek in disbelief, or faces transfixed in the stare of blissful ignorance.

English comprehension....

A little bit of a story. In me haste to understand, I noticed not the list of questions beneath or thought them another part of the test.

The idea, Ah concluded, was to continue the story out of

your own head. Ah was good at stories, so away Ah went, page after page after page until the bell went and Ah swaggered out feeling Ah'd done well. It was a good story....

When the class reconvened, we were more at ease, until the papers came: maths, maths? Up till that day, wi called them sums, whey Ah cud dey addie-ups and tek awa's wesn't bad ... but this this wes maths, it might as well have been double Dutch, pages of strange squiggles, odd alphabets, the object surely was to find the missing object among the random type? Ah found a few ducks and something that looked like a gatepost, but that Ah anly did to pass the time on, Ah nivor wrote it doon. Elsewhere in the class, the raggy lads spent their time trying to make the people who were writing laugh. Mind, some kids were writing: these were the well-dressed strange kids who somehow had had old exam papers previous. On reflection they had been ofttimes ushered into silent corners of classrooms because they 'could work on their own', or so it wes said.

Failed, of course, but that wasn't too bad to bear, so had all the kiddhas, only the odd specky Willick had got through, and besplendit in badge, blazer and briefcase, they were now Grammar School Kids, poshies stroke softies, being posh and soft were synonymous to us.... Kelvin Garfy had got through. A source of endless bullying amusement, he was a 'mammy's lad'. Never sweared, until, that is, the day we all surrounded him in the yard:

'Swear or wi'll belt yee! Swear or wi'll belt yee!'

'Err!' the wriggling asthmatic poshy groaned. 'Swear!', the grips tightening round the unfortunate's throat. 'Pump, pump,' he yelled in the same instant as his eyes enlarged in the full consciousness of the foul vulgar sound of the dirty words which had come from his mouth, we buckled at the knees and generally collapsed over walls in silent body-shaking manic laughter. It was to bring years of mirth, the sight of a blazer bringing the instant response 'Pump' and renewed piss-taking and merriment.

Mind, some must have been bothered about that exam, since kids had been offered bikes, suits, or roller-skates if they did well. Doing well meant the grammar school, meant the first rung out of the working class, meant a step to the private house and not the council estate. But few went, so for all but the kids gifted enough to be allowed to work on their own, issued with the past exam papers and force-fed the educational equivalent of the queen-bee nutrients, it was not to be.

The maelstrom of the secondary school, a cacophony of puberty, past friendships, big boys, elder brothers and sisters, and the grip of expectancy. Bunched in the new school yard, boys dived about cocking each other, hand rammed hard over your own balls, the other cupped in a crab, grabbing out at another suitably defended; for those not so on guard the unexpected grab from an assailant impacting on the testicles, then squeezing them out of their bag, was excruciatingly painful.

Sex in figures, 36-22-36, it was at once the presentation of big tits, little waist and nice rounded hips. It was true, the ideal figure shape of older women. Those in their late 20s and 30s the 'pin ups' the film stars. Older people's jokes revolved around 36-22-36. Personally, in the older women department, in the film star 'sex queen' department, Bridgette Bardott was my ideal although she was an 18" waste.[9] I recall me and John Norman a sexual mental analyzer student of mine at about eleven trying to figure out what tits were for anyway, we, meant in a sexual sense. We had already long ago worked out the genitals part and what that felt like, even childishly with girls. But tits? They were 'rude' and 'naughty' and we were supposed to want to see them, but then what? We could not quite figure that 'tits' thing into the equation. Just a couple of years later they were to eclipse the inside the knicker bit, really, we would move up a notch so that any little female crotch wasn't as pressing as 'TITS'. But then after pubescent tits came the scary rediscovery of the 'bottom bits'. This was when you left childhood and became 'mature' we reckoned you got there according to experience with the bords at maybe 14 earlier if you were lucky. This was far distant, exciting, unknown, and debatable territory yet.

Young Teds hung around, shouldered walls, dragged at Woodbine dumps held in a safety-pin to extract the last drag, little eyes screwed tight against the acrid smoke. These were the days when the sweetie shop would sell you one tab, and the manufacturers made packets of five.

At last the bell for the start of this first day went. We were all marched into the assembly hail, packed, us at the front, eldest at the back; the rest were lined up in classes. We were as yet classless, we packed together in a knot of excitement and terror, unsegregated, we didn't know but in a second we would be graded, some of us destined to become thick, others bright.

Names and grades were read out.

'IA, Ken Lowes.' Up till now we had all thought wasells pretty much the same as each other, as good as each other, 'John Norman', 'Paul Murphy', 'William Bell', and so it went, to the end of the list. My name had not been called. I counted every line in the wood floor; I'm not one of the best, not one that the thin-faced headmaster had called 'bright'. The voices of people congratulating each other drifted around, blood rushed to me face, friends were drifting apart, people in different classes rarely were to mix during the rest of their school lives. The tears weren't far away.

'Next.'

'IB, Johnny Trainor, Michael Bailey, Tom Doyle.' Me heart was racing, eyes ablaze with tears, head bowed low, Ah wasn't there either, sick with indignity, loss of pride, my quiet opinion of myself as being quite clever.... Finally '1C'. The 'C' stung like a back-hander across the face, it would be a badge of shame at school, it would be carried afterwards, it would be repeated to interested-looking personnel managers who until that point were clearly impressed; then they would do a little cough or laugh out loud. 'Michael Quinn, Kathleen Mulroy, David Douglass, Thomas Dafter'—laughter, 'He's in the reet class'—and the rest, at the bottom of the heap, the abandoned ones, the dunces, thickies, knaanowts.

As the newly assigned classes milled and, confused, marched off to their new status, a shrill teacher's voice rang out: 'Right, now the rag, tag and bobtail ... quick march. And that', he said slowly, 'means walk fast over here.'

In normal circumstances, the ring of the bell meant release, it meant outside. This time it was the signal for protracted agony, as groups gathered in the yard to interrogate each other on which classes they were in, sorrowfully hanging me head, blushing with shame, greeted with sneers, the bottom of the whole school. Gaanin' hyme, lads yelled from the turned-round positions of the front seat 'Yee kid, what class yee in?' and the admission needs must be shouted too. 'Aa, he's a "C" walla.' Walking towards the door, up the street, wives hingin' ower the fence. 'Aye, wor Kevin gonna "A" class, yee knaa, eeeam that pleased. Ah'v telt him yee work hard at the skuel and thou'll not hati gaan doon th' pit.' Sobs started to break before Ah got the gate open; the folks were waiting expectantly for my first-day return from the seniors. I had considered lying.

Earlier, as we were drawn into the big assembly hail, I had made a mental picture of me flying through the back door and shouting:

'GUESS WHICH CLASS?' I had almost rehearsed the scene ... now it was set for a different play. I slumped through the back door, swallowed against the sobs and announced my public stupidity. Nowt wes said, though I sensed their disappointment.

I had let them down.

We had been told in the hall that at the end of every year kids could be moved up a class or down a class. Every year in that assembly we relived the horror. Though the indignity had gone, your heart still pounded at the roll-call, 2 'A's, 2 'B's and of course us 'C's. First year, second year, third year and, misery of miseries, as the fourth year began: 'DOUGLASS 4C.' In an age of scant work, the secondary school offered little enough recommendation of work, the 'B' stream kid was going to find it tough ... but a 'C' class lifer? As teachers throughout our school lives were to remind us, 'What employer is going to take you scruffy, ignorant lot?'

What indeed?

All alang the river communities, a guerrilla struggle raged from the age of 11. Resenting the creeping invasion of houses smothering the space, crowding oot childhood, folding in the acres of imagination, we- attacked the invaders. Wa secret walks from the Felling, alang little used routes. We had a greet drum of yella paint. This was the magic substance. The kiddhas gilded their wooden rapiers in the thick yellow magic substance, lines of new square red bricks piled in house-shape columns spreading oot; breeding, woke up to find the secret smear of the yella squiggle. The wooden frames awaiting door frames snapped under the guerrilla raids; hand- grenades fashioned from river clay, hardened, intact with pins, primed, pins oot and a hail of broken glass shattering the neet, aud gadgies screamin' and air blue and splintered, 'haway the lads'. Heart thumpin', hot pursuit by bobbies on bikes, 'Come back yee, come back'. and away like hell through the dark, rolling doon th' banks, crawling through the shite, Geordie guerrillas back safe and sound.

But the fields still died, still struggled to keep a face upward to the sky, to keep a head of deep grass to carry the lone rangers and Zorro, and catchy kissy young 'uns, but the suffocation continues without respite, anly the sanitised, crew-cut green of the poxy golf-course remains, a useless deed piece of tame ground bought and sold out to endless miles of bricks and new suburbia.

Across from Bill Quay, ower the North-Eastern rail lines to the cinder path through Amos's fields, stood the giant wooden railway bridge smelling of tar, pitch and various railway oils and greases. Atop the lot stand rows of signals standing' picket ower the lines. Fernant the bridge a wooden cabin straddling the line, a box festooned and hung with pendulums, chain-ropes, and weights. It heaved and snapped, rolled and watched, changed the lines and paths of steaming streaks and blinkers. It halted the mighty steaming monoliths or it ushered them through a holy place, in which you could pass hours of fascination and wonderment. Blackberry bushes abounded at the edges of the lines, the wooden fence was gapped and you could sit on the edge of the lines and watch the multiple movements of pulleys, signals, points and blinking lights, amid the smells of steam and oil and pitch, Mallard, Scotsman or 'coffee-pot' regularly consuming the whole tarry wooden edifice with billowing smoke. It fell victim to some other raiding party and burned like an inferno: stupid.

As the Geordie guerrillas doon endless miles of dilly line, greenhouses fell to the nightly attacks, lang-range lobs arch in destructive symmetry, landing with the smashhh gripping ya belly with excitement, gas-lamp panes speared by Zulus, building-site machines tipped and fired, oil drums busted, shrieks and screams:

'GEORDIES. MENTAL. GEORDIES MENTAL.' The *nouveau* Norsemen back again, setting' the night on fire. The pitman stands, his greenhoose shattered, his caring work rendered to smashed glass and uprooted plants, looks for a reason: stupid, aye, stupid; senseless, aye, senseless.

Doon away from Bill Quay, past the inhabited areas, doon past the empty derelict houses where the childhood explorers assured our young skulls were cupboards full of toys ... and shit, but sometimes a man would come wiv a geet cock and chase yi with it. Doon the abandoned docksides and empty harbours, where history had once poured the black blood of the county into keels and tall-sail colliers. Now lapping quiet and black the river, deep and inviting; where was the gadgie with the sack? We never seen him, but knew he was there, ever lurking, the gadgie.

There were few 'pure' Irish in the school, but one that we had as a classmate became forever the butt of teachers' jokes directed at her native brogue. Her rendition of Giant as Joint had brought 'joint of meat' jokes *ad infinitum*, a few vindictive laughs from thickos in the class, but overall the silence of solidarity, for we too didn't or couldn't speak the Queen's English. 'Geordie' had to be beaten out of wi, or this clown of a teacher would stand before this C-stream Geordie horde giving elocution lessons, repeating baby fashion on pain of the stick:

A king whose Christian name was Poo -
Was stopped by a cow
Which did say moo.

Serious, this was supposed to be. The balding, bug-eyed teacher would form each word with his mouth contorting and stretching, the spittle forming at the sides of his thick lips. We copied, imitating the bug eyes, with aching sides and blood-vessels nigh to bursting in an effort to suppress the volcanic eruptions of laughter, pain in your sides and a grip of fear in your belly, for to be caught earned strokes with the cane, yet from time to time ya body would stand it no longer and a full-bellied guffaw would let loose. Others, heads on desks to avoid detection, would shake silently, tears streaming doon their faces. For this self-opinionated grown man pouting and slavering, swaying and spitting a nonsense English verse, it was we the Geordies, the Irish, the hybrid Celtic plebs, who were stupid, stupid with wrang speech, cross-hobbled like a sheep.

'How on earth you lot will ever find work I don't know.' Sometimes it made us feel guilty, but what for we never kenned.

4
A Class War of Sorts

Without exception, the teachers hated the 'C' stream. We were a stupid, illiterate, violent, stubborn and sometimes dirty morass of rudeness. From the first week on, we would don the armour of thickness. They called us thick. We would show just how thick we could be. We became expert at the blank, non-comprehending stare, the painfully slow turn of the head, the deathly slow walk; the aura from head to toe that would henceforth reek of resentment. Teachers were aggressive foes, or else soft shites whom we could bait in retaliation. Once or twice, a silly bastard would drift in and out of wa lives who actually tried to interest us in something. Whenever they got us, actually collaborating the other teachers hated them, resented them, publicly argued with them, and blocked the thickos getting anything, which might appear too good for them.

The Headmaster was a small, wiry, non-dialect Geordie who at times could look searchingly into the dead eyes of feigned ignorance and keek like a detective for a clue of intelligent life. At other times he was capable of monumental violence—a show trial, before the school, girls and teachers alike, four boys dragged from the ranks, guilty of theft in the Felling, dragged by the hair, one boy slipping on the floor, the Head grabbing at the struggling body, cane in hand, dragged to the stage, pushed to mount it, falling against the wood edge, cry of pain, air charged with sick violence, the anger of injustice, the big thick woodwork teacher dragging two others down the hall, one fighting, the Head flaying like a cavalry officer with the stick across the legs, dragging hands out, whacking with fearful thrusts, smacks across the sides of the heads ringing throughout the hail, girls crying out loud, and mild-mannered female teachers hiding their faces in their hands. The thug woodwork teacher gripping a boy's lapels and shaking and shaking, 'Hand out, Quinn, hand out, take your punishment'. The lads stand, impotent and shaking with anger, tears of anger, fists clenched, 'Bastards, bastards', a collective anger, us and them, 'Bastards!' Windows would feel the edge of the vented anger, as would buildings and machines on sites, the bastards!

They were senseless: stupid, aye, stupid.

The Cane, number one instrument of control, stood on top of the blackboard, or lay exposed across the top of the desk. It was used day in day out, twice a day, three times a day. It fell with a 'swoooooo', the barely audible sound of a wicked stroke accompanied by the lick of sadism as the teacher's tongue slid from the slit of a mouth as his cane found its mark. Offences? Who needed offences? You were a thick child of the grubby working class; they were the masters and mistresses of a detention centre. Yes, this must surely be a place of penal correction. Lads would get the cane every day, lasses less regularly, for the capital offence of 'talking'. What monstrous crime is that—talking—that you hit another person, a much smaller person, with a stick for it? Or 'chewing'. Chewing? Such an abomination that you beat a young boy's hands to a swollen red pulp with a stick?

In later years, I was to hear a self-proclaimed Felling teacher announce that, yes; he used the cane because the pupils wouldn't listen to him.

'Whey the bluddy hell would want ti listen ti yee?' I asked? 'An' if Ah divind are ye gaana hit me with a stick?' Of course, no such outrage would be tolerated, not least cos out of schoolteachers can find themselves spread over pavements.

Talking, and laughing.

'Who laughed? Come on; own up, the boy or girl who

laughed.' Nobody laughing now. Eyes flicked from side to side.

'Right.' The punishment: the whole class caned, line on line, girls and boys, marching down the aisle, while the adult lashed out one after the other, the first encounter with solidarity: you don't tell tales.... Us and them.

Eager to learn—but not at the skuel. Whe'd be a sneak?

At Jonty's krey, the huddle of birds swoop low, bunch and jostle then soar off as if gone forever in a huff....

'Did Edwin and Ida always crush them north Brits?'

'Whey nor, La'. Nor the British began to gather for a counterattack, hid oot allower the Cheviots and attacked back eastward time and time again. Neybody can ever crush folks that want ti fight back—it cannit be done. Nor, what thi dey is, th' try ti buy yee off.'

Mind flashes to the football wallas, full of hatred most times, but even the most hated teacher had only to come down the corridor bouncing a ball and the stupid gets sit obedient and docile wagging their tales in expectation at the ball, the ball! must play with the ball! knocking thasells ower wi collaboration for a bliddy football, hated football and collaborators ever since.

'But later another Angle king, Oswald, he brought in some magicians ti dazzle the Celts; for ye'l knaa, La', the Celts love magic.'

Magic ... magic ... like Merlin?

'Nor Merlin's magic worked ... whey, mind, so did bliddy Oswald's magicians. His chief wizard was a man called Aidan, ye'l knaa him as Saint Aidan, a bluddy Celt too. He come ... and made the sacred Celtic island of Lindisfarne a Christian island— even called it Holy Island. Tried ti give the Angle king the air of an earth God or somit of the sort[10].

'Whey, bit by bit, th' Celts got ti accept the Angle rule, though they stayed Celts thasells, in fact the Angles mer likely than not come mer Celtic than th' other way roond.'

The school of the classroom was one of sullen resistance, or else electric struggle, clashing the desk-lids, fifty at a time. Instantly, one after the other, the sneck which held them in place was whipped away by a sudden movement of the ruler, and bang, bang, bang—before the teacher could even turn round. The teacher, leaving the classroom, abandoned the tigers to their own devices:

BEDLAM.

The nib of a wooden pen was a deadly weapon, especially fitted into the inkwell terrorist armoury: the straw. We received third-pint bottles of milk as part of the legacy of the 1945 Welfare State. The straw, filled with ink and fitted with a nib, delivered a sting and five inches of ink on any target. The air is thick with missiles as the softy teacher walks back through the door. A second of restraint, then back with the bedlam. 'STOP IT!' Stop! Words meant nowt, the pens still fly, the girls pelt inkwells, the walls are splashed, the teacher runs back and forth, grabs here and there, the kiddha throws the offending arm off, 'GERROFFIS'. Teachers from other classes invade the class, cuff, belt and drag the pupils, the struggle continues. Kiddhas out of their seats wrestle and mock, roll on the floor ... the softy teacher in tears ... the class is triumphant, the Head is sent for. The punishment is hard and cruel, but as the class subsides to leaders being thrashed the heartbeat continues—one for us. The softy and the cruel bastards knew if the Head was sent for, they had failed; we had won a tiny victory. A flogging might follow, but we never succumbed. They thought us little bastards. They still look back and think that.... We were, too!

Geordie, a credential of resistance ... it was a mark of wa resistance to authority and to all attempts to anglicise wi. Replying to teachers' questions in 'slang', as they called it, was cheek and instantly punishable.

'Bone, come out here.'

'Whey?'

'What did you say?'

'That's reet.'

The teacher grabs for the cane and makes to go down the line toward the risen militant, who leaps to his feet and puts his fists up in a boxing stance: 'Dinnet thou touch me, mind, Ah's warnin' ye, dinnit touch is!' Walks up the line looking towards the door and flight, the teacher grabs him by the collar, the lad whips round, teeth gritted, eye narrowed in fury amid a continuous 'MASSAMBOOLA 00, MASSAMBOOLA 00' chant from the class. A flaying hand catches the jaw; the jaw both fell open and leapt back of its own free will. Boney, a flash of black shirt and greased hair, going through the door and out down the corridor to temporary freedom. His return to some terrible fate, a day or two later, was greeted by a hero's welcome, the lads of all classes lining the fence and cheering. 'A' class kids had received the news of rebellion within minutes through the kids' jungle telegraph: 'Hey kid, that was great', 'Weel dun, kiddha!'

Spontaneous collective resistance was the most exciting playtime a multitude of different games, quite independent of each other—kingo, football, horseback fights, tuggy—out walks the teacher and blows the whistle. Nobody stops playing. He blows the whistle, which is echoed by the kids round the yard, but nobody stops playing. Teacher goes back into the school and returns with reinforcements carrying canes. Individuals are dragged off their sport, cuffed, caned and slung along the corridors until resistance bit by bit collapses and the lines sluggishly form up to be marched off.

The 'Ted' march, arms doon straight, heed stuck aheed

but dropping at a Neanderthal angle, all the while that menacing bounce, bunch o' grapes dancing on the foreheed.

A race against time when one of the meedmen left the class to gaan th' netty (although enforced English meant asking 'to leave the room' as if you could bring the bliddy thing with ye), sneaking up outside the open window of the marra's class and waiting till the teacher's booming voice was in full flight.

'How, Baldy-heed shut ya daft hole!' Consternation from inside the class, Baldy-heed trying to climb onto a hot-water pipe to see who his assailant is while the class camps up the laughter to the point of hysterics, young Teds laugh 'HAAR HAAAR HAAAAR!' Meantime away like hell back to ya own class before being sighted.

In winter, it would be a snowball lobbed through the window, in summer a clayball, bursting like a scatter-bomb on table or floor before the shocked teacher. Most 'C' class wallas kept ti themselves. Lack of communication with teachers extended to other classes. They were the hard lads, faces you could chop sticks on, heads you could nut all day without making a dint. Their weak spot was sport. Non-co-operation, hatred and outright violence against teachers could be diverted by holding up the bone of a football or handball match. They hated being inside, hated the indoors, hated the lessons, such as they were, peered out of the windows like captive birds. Some would be illiterate on leaving school.

'A' stream kids came from smaller families, although to be reet me sister Veronica was an 'A' class girl. They had damaged her brain somehow; she liked school, this school! She liked the teachers—well, the blokes anyway—she was a 'good Catholic girl', she cried when she left! 'A' stream kids' dads tended to be craftsmen, engineers, welders. They actually did some schoolwork, even some homework, tended to be brainier, cliver. No match in fights with the thickies in the 'C' class, though certain of them give as good as any could give them, in general, cliverness meant also softiness, hard Geordie meant hard lad, lack of accent meant softy. Geordie, a badge of hardness, taalkin' posh or properly or English meant collaborator, sneak, crawler, softy.

'B' streams were a mixture of both, straddling the other class alliances. For years I thought the class war was the battle between 'A' streams and 'C' streams, about snobbery at the secondary modern. It is a mind-blowing experience to learn that above grammar schools are private schools, middle-class private schools, and upper-upper-class ('Mind, ya croon's slipping, ya Lordship') schools.

'C' class wallas had problems stopping their noses running, had problems wiping their arses properly, had difficulty getting clothes to fit them, but were first with Ted gear handed down from older brothers. 'C' class wallas got in *real gangs* with big lads, got hammered, had knuckles like guerrillas, permanently exuding the smell of melting marge and inner resentment.

Charlie Brown was wor folk hero, not the later Peanuts character who was, I was told, well observed but was just a drawing of a dog thinking non-understandable things. No, wor Charlie Brown was a Ted, a US Ted, true, but we imagined him bejeaned, drain-piped, the home-sown variety, the shrunk-in-the-bath variety, the lap a lang length of jean material and buck-stitched like a Frankenstein face into the 12-inch-bottom variety.

Who WALKS IN THE CLASSROOM, cool and slow!

Bliddy hell, hear that??? Hear that—'cool and slow'?

The thick-wedge, walk-a-million-foot-high, bounce-on-the -heel, swivel-on-the-bridge, but slow variety.

Who calls the English teacher Daddio!?

'Dafter's' head turns, like a 78 rpm zombie, transits slowly all the class, eyes bouncing like the wedges, up and down, side to side, corners come to bear with the outside of a teacher's face, ower low, up the heed, slaw, deed slaw, eyes come fixed with the teacher's eyes in the stare that reads mutually 'THICK PIG'.

'Eh?'

Charlie Brown ... Charlie Brown...

He's a clown.

'Clown.'

Trainor, the art teacher swiping at the six-foot boy, whose neck would stand the weight of a gorilla's swipe, a Mrs Doyle swipe, a loud waap aroond the skull. Ignoring it like a mite bite, the clown carries on.

He's gonna get caught, Just you wait and see.

Why is everybody always picking on me?'

'Gerrofis.' Tommy Bone, son and grandson of Heworth pitmen, probably great-grandson and great-great-grandson of colliers, Heworth pit lad speaks defiantly in the village twang, 'Dinnit thou call 'is coward', with a direct punch ti the Headmaster's face. Throttled by the deputy, crashed against the wall, up kicking and fighting.

Who's always goofing in the hall?

Sneak up playtimes or dinner-times; give the staff-room door a kick or the buuuurrrrp fart sound with a stiff finger we had perfected as the 'gang' symbol. Then away ti fuck, screaming down the corridor, the call shout trailing ahint: 'Meeeeeed.'

Who's always writing on the wall?

Who's always heading for a fall?

'This is them, the cynics.' That was what the Deputy Head, a woodwork teacher, called us, rounding us up for the first time, class by class, dragging us out of desks, identifying our strange inter-streamed relationship.

'Failure of any one of them to volunteer for the school

sports—'

'Football?'

'Na.'

'Heeders?'

'Na.'

'Bag race?'

'Na.'

'Cricket?'

'Na.'

'Rounders?'

'Na.'

'Egg and spoon?'

'Na, na.'

Sport was collaboration, games were collaboration. Ney collaboration. Run roond daft and let the teachers think they had yee, ney chance, ney chance. Instead to stand and gawk at the hard lads, running roond daft, chasing a ball up and down their cage like a set of budgies, while teachers twittered 'well done'. Not for the meedmen.

He's gonna get caught,

Just you wait and see.

This lad Morella, Italian probably, some of their roots were laid in the Felling, his name meant nowt, one o' the leyds. Discovered sex, with his ma's tits hanging oot of a neetgoon. Shocked us all inti laughter, saying how he'd come into his ma's bedroom and she leaned ower and her tits fell out, first he'd seen, said tithe leyds: 'Ah cud o' jumped on her and shagged her!'

A quick mental résumé of what wor ma's were like revealed that nen of us what wad shag them, but Toni's ma wes young, very young, the tits, he assured us, dinnit droop but stuck up from all clothing and attempts to hide them. A delegation was arranged to allow inspection of Toni's Mam's tits, whereupon all were agreed to a grand conspiracy to have her screw the whole gang, We were halfway through the plan, with a couple of the lads already 'inadvertently' exposing themselves with 'colossal' teenage hard - ons, they must have been, since they took up 90 per cent of our consciousness; we assumed they were 80 per cent of our bodies— when Toni got nicked for stealing fireworks in Felling Square Woolworth's. Never mind, the plan would be put to good use with someone else soon enough.

Why is everybody always picking on me?'
Who walks in the classroom cool and slow?
who calls the English teacher Daddio?
Charlie Brown
He's a clown
Charlie Brown

He's a clown
He's gonna get caught
Just you wait and see.
Why is everybody always picking on me?
Who's always goofing in the hall?
Who's always writing on the wall?
Who's always heading for a fall?
That's me
Who, me?
Yes, you.

The meedmen, where did they come from? A slow process of initiation led by Ben, the leader, who gathered in those who were ready for the part. He picked you out from the playground throng, he listened to ya crack, he watched ya style, were ye cool enough, were ye meed enough, did ye mock enough? We dared together. We weren't the hardest in the school, though some were hard. We weren't the thickest. In fact, we were probably the most intelligent, though we aspired to hide it from all but worsells, we aspired to the thickness of my 'C' stream marras, and we perfected and bettered their sullenness. We were soft, really, most of us, though we hardened wasells almost to the point where we removed feeling—in the daytime, wi the gang. What we became was the best screwers in the skeul, the advice centre, the set-up crowd for shags, the friends who had friends who could tek ya heed off if necessary, amang wa ranks would come the heed men, but for a mock herbit mock, meedness and herbitmock, wa twin slogans of wa puberty and resistance.

In the teenage sexual ritual of audio, talk about it, hint at it, joke at it, the aud wifies' dandlin song ('clap ya hands for Daddy') became:

My lad's a canny lad
Works doon the pit
Nivor comes ti wor hoose
Unless he wants a bit.
Axed him ti marry is

Ye should ha' seen him wince
Ah, think Ah'v lost me canny lad
Ah'v nivor seen him since.

And the girls would whisper: 'What's long and thin, covered in skin, red in parts, goes in tarts?' Responding to the response in mock shock: 'Nor, ye dirty bugger, it's rhubarb.'

What's the definition of an American bra? Everyone chorus: 'One yank an' it's off.' What's the definition of a glass bra? Chorus: 'A smash and grab raid.'

From thirteen, a surge of tingling itchiness under the skin, a visitation of erection that wadn't gaan away day or neet, wank vornie throttle it, three times a day, four times a day.

The Lady of the Manor was dressing for the ball
When she spied the village idiot wanking off behind the hall
Wiv his geet big kidney-wipers and baalls the size of three

And a yard and a half of foreskin hinging doon belaw his knee
Hinging doon ... swinging free ... hinging doon, swinging free
And a yard and a half of foreskin hinging doon belaw his knee.
She wrote ti him a letter, and on it she did say:
'Ah'd rather be shegged by yee, kind sir, than me husband any day
Wiv ya geet big kidney-wipers and baalls the size of three,
And a yard and a half of foreskin hinging doon belaw his knee.

A vision of girls, the look of girls, the smell of girls, even the word 'girls' did it. The things they wore, the way they wore them, the little bangles and purses and rings, and hair-grips and socks and everything they had and did, the way they stood, leaned on one leg, bent one knee, the shape of them, size of them, sound of them. Wank? Wi wanked each other off, wanked wasells off but thought of 'girls', and the girls wanked us off—nowt personal, wanking the lads off wasn't personal at all, a steady boy-friend didn't mean ye couldn't wank his mate off, lads needed wanking off. That was friendship, not sex. 'Wadn't be seen deed gaanin oot wi yee lot', Doreen said as she wanked Pete off under the Bridge. And dogs, aye we wanked dogs off and cats off—not me, though. I thought it was cruel—'soft shite'.

He rode up tithe manor, tithe manor he did ride
With his knob alang the horse's neck and a baall on either side.
Wiv he's geet big kidney-wipers and baalls the size of three
And a yard and a half of foreskin hinging doon belaw his knee
Hinging doon, swinging free, hinging doon, swinging free
And a yard and a half of foreskin hanging doon belaw his knee.

He shagged her in the kitchen, he shagged her in the hall,
He shagged her in the parlour, stuck up against the wall
With his geet big kidney wipers....

The girl sits on the desk seat, throws the skirt oot so it drops behind her bum. Sits, bare knickers on the wood, for the purpose of lifting the edge of her skirt up, ever so gentle while the lesson continues. Her skirt is lifted up to expose a lang and bare thigh, lace-edged knickers, legs right doon ti her little lacy socks. The lads sitting beside in the opposite aisle cum in their jeans ... come in their jeans ... cum in their jeans, and the girls turn and watch them dey it, smiling sexually, sticky and smouldering, sex hormones coursing through her pert pouting bodice and bursting in an aura all around her so strong you could touch it.

The lasses lean ower and grab the boy's cock in his jeans, the lads drive tha hand under the skirt, down to the knickers, up the side of the knickers, down over her thigh, the girl writes or looks attentively at the teacher while the little stubble hair of puberty is fetching the lad off via his exploring fingers, and she starts to pant.

Playtimes: the priests would have had a heart attack and yet might, at the playtimes in the classrooms. Nubile tits thrust oota the sweater that Mam bought just the other day and never thought at 13 it would be pulled up by the girl in the cupboard sanctuary for the lads watching. Or the girls picking, on a toss of a coin, which lad they'd drag to the corner and subject to mass uninhibited petting. Under the desks, in the deserted classroom, on wa knees, Irene with her blouse pulled over her brown nipples, her hand down the front of me jeans.

'Ler is shag ye.'

'Not here.'

'Come on, it'll not take long.'

'Meet me.'

Gateshead Sea Cadet Corps (1961): nautical Dave (third from left)

My fascination for all things nautical: a walking naval encyclopedia graduated through a Bostik, plastic Airfix flotilla. The Atlantic fleet sat on my sideboard top; I could call up lightning responses to gun sizes, knots, overall length and beam. A day-to-day recollection of major naval battles from Nelson to World War Two.

Such exhaustive curiosity led from the junior section of Felling's library to an adult ticket and access to a whole shelf of naval mustiness. That smell of books and wood polish, the hidden stories it enshrined, the things you could know about—not just the pregnant girth of the steel Goliaths ploughing through the grey depths of the Atlantic; other books seductively stood, a wink of hidden knowledge, a title or cover which week by week slowed the advance to the naval stuff and bade me linger elsewhere. Unknown worlds of unknown things: Nessy, does the loch house a secret? Do flying saucers come from another planet?

We sat in the garden, me Da an' me, and discussed UFOS.

'Ye knaa, Son, it says in the Bible: "There are others, not of this flock, but of another, those also I must bring." Ah'v nivor seen one mesell, but theors mony say th' hev.'

'Di ye think there'll be men put on th' moon?'

'In your time, Lad, not in mine, Ah'm sure they will.' As it turned out, it was in his time and mine and a thousand space journeys and expeditions in addition.

By thirteen, I was on the track of unknown animals, a work which left an undying impression on me as we foraged the thick text for Nessy, misnamed a monster, and the unicorn, and the Orangpendec, perhaps the legendary abominable snowman. Or Big Foot.

I was fascinated and thirsty to know, but also perhaps trying subconsciously to get a fair start, start from square one, none of their special pink forms start a subject from nuw and see if Ah'll trail ahint. Subconsciously avoiding their weighted curriculum and developing one, which they wouldn't participate in, or spoil. Their reaction to this rival study, which was really no rival since we were only required to shut up, was one of bitter hostility and resentment, while I, its student, was 'cocky', 'arrogant' and 'superficious', a word I never did ken from then till nuw, and I think the thick bastard made it up, but it conveyed a certain impression, accompanied as it was with a clout roond the chops.

Like the groping for political knowledge, the territory had to be grappled with and held, and waved as a challenge. Every drawing, composition, paper aeroplane titled Mig 15, contained some sneaked-in reference or hint of the emerging ideology. The teachers' contempt for the ideology was second only to their contempt for my face, ever swipeable, ever having to 'take that expression off your face, Douglass'. The flat hand was not the favourite weapon, but it was the one, which better carried their resentment.

The strange alliance of dissident 'A' streams with a thicko from the 'C' class was an oddity of common location, and a secret rarely exposed. The meedmen were *thick* but not dense. Not being dense and being in a 'C' stream was an immediate point of conflict with the 'C' stream teachers, who saw any spark of intellectual ability as an assertion of 'cockiness' and an act of 'cleverness'.

A fascination with naval history and ships had taken me to the adult section of the Felling library to browse in awe at the shelf full of Navy books. Having adult books and being a 'C' stream walla often required me to hide the books from teachers' eyes. As teenage fascination in the weird and unexplained took me to the shelves of flying saucers, sea monsters, man apes, abominable snowmen, mermaids, the Loch Ness beast and other phenomena, so the books grew thicker.

'DOUGLASS!' the red-faced Deputy Head we nicknamed Double Dan, because of his habit of saying everything twice in his excitement and anger, bellowed down the corridor as I walked within striking distance. The book of monsters is savagely snatched from my hand; the corridor is full of inmates streaming into classes, watching, listening to the spectacle.

'Whose is this?', holding it like a dirty sock

'Av borrid it.' A mocking, scathing twist of a page, flick of a leaf, his ever-cynical sneer. -

'Who reads you this?'

'Ah read mesell.'

'Oh, and who taught you to do *that*?'

'Not yea forra start.'

That's it, book drops to the floor, to lie abused with its spine spread down the open leaves, death-like grip on me hair, a forearm across the face to ram me into the wall. The titters from the fellow inmates, enjoying someone being shown up, now stop, grudging shuffling off down the corridor, staring in hate at the class enemy. Other teachers:

'Get moving', 'Mind your own business', and sprawling, pushed and cuffed, I am precipitated to the Head's office. It was always like that, a showing up for trying to be clever, for having a book.

We rode to and from school on wa bikes. I had two fluttering flags on me handlebars, two miniature white ensigns I had got from some stone frigate, on a boats charge course, I thought pretty cool at the time, me handlebars were turned upside down like bison horns, and I had removed the mudguards. Other lads had edgy racers with dropped handlebars. Roads, pavements, cliffs, beaches, pit tips, dirt tracks and open fields: we rode anywhere, bouncing and ricocheting over everything.

Ben and some of the others had jobs delivering groceries and rode the huge Desperate Dan cast-iron bikes with the metal basket-holder on the front. Not only was there the question of its weight; when full of vegetables it took some holding up, so stopping and starting were trials of balance and strength. Steering was another thing: you steered, but the basket sort of stayed where it was; you turned, and it carried on. The impossible gradient of Felling High Street was an out-of-control roller-coaster going down, especially since the brake was on the front fixed wheel, designed to give perfect trips over the handlebars with the vegetables and bike landing on your head seconds later. Cycling back up the hill was like biking up Everest. Ben, ever the talker, the persuader, the lad with the personality, could have sold ice to Eskimos, was good for business, old folk liked him, trusted him. A breakaway grocery business operating from Pelaw was keen to recruit Ben, which it did, but no more heavyweight deliveries on a 1930s bike made from old girders, these would be pick-up-size boxes, he would be given his train or bus fare and travel in comfort, often he'd just keep the fare and walk with the delivery. The money was rolling in; so were the very interesting consignees.

Ben's precocious nature hadn't gone unnoticed and not only by the aud, biddies that squeezed half-dollars into his hand and kissed his cheek or ruffled his hair. He had landed a delivery to some newly build apartments round the back of 'The White Cottage'—just a box of cheeses and wine and posh chocolate—but there was something more. She was single, very posh, stayed in most of the time, lounged about, phoned for her groceries, and Ben brought them in. He had been delivering there about two weeks, and started to tell me more and more about her, how 'sexy as fuck' she was, how 'her nipples are as big as *that*', making a big circle between his first finger and thumb. He rubbed his hands together and did that ecstatic giggle of his: 'Ah'm gaana dee it, Ah'm gaana dee it, she wants it, man, it's deed fuckin' obvious.' We would both have difficulty walking as he talked. I rolled about the bed all night thinking of it. About six o'clock one night he shouted for me. He'd been round again. I shot out of the house and we ran down the street, me whispering loudly and panting: 'Did ye? Did ye?' He grabbed me arm at the end of the street, fair bouncing with excitement.

'She wanked is off.'

'What? Honest?'

'Aye, man. Ah, God it was better than fuckin' them at school, she stripped is, wanked is, rubbed her tits on is, Ah spunked on the settee, on the floor, on a' tits.' This was a secret—supposed to be a secret—she was scared shitless of anyone finding out. But the story spread roond the gang, then we closed ranks and would tell no one. The deal was, though, he had to get her to dey us anarl! We pestered him for weeks, till one winter night as the snow began to fall, and we wandered aimlessly through the slush, Ben, me, Pete and Simon, he said: 'We'll gaan and see Sarah.'

The snow was falling in thick sheets as she opened the

door and saw three drainpiped boys with their hands in their pockets and greet bulges in their jeans, led by Ben beaming his big happy grin.

'Ee, no', I heard her say. 'Man, people will see', and Ben's persuasive 'Haway, man, just for a minute till the snow eases up, nowt will happen.' She brings us in, and we are soon in the living room, with a telly, and the curtains drawn and a huge white settee. Soon Ben has his arm round her and they look kind of awkward, he keeps trying to unbutton her blouse, and we drape wasell all round her, along the arm of the settee, standing behind her head, sitting at her feet, leaning on her, rubbing on her, lying on her, then suddenly it was starting to happen, she started rubbing my cock through me jeans, rolling her head on Pete's crotch as he stood behind her, that was it, the blouse was open, couldn't move her, to undo the bra thing, yank it up, great full, huge tits roll out of her body and my cock is out, her long painted finger-nails expertly round it, and not a scratch. She did all of wi, at times two at a time, leaving one, going to another, playing a vibrating organ of thrusting organs, caressing our bare arses, letting your cock rub on her large stiff nipples, letting the spunk run over her manicured fingers, and keeping hold until it had stopped, not shrieking 'Urrgh' and letting go just at the wrong time as the girls at school did. We were a sensation, we were *the* lads. Half the school would have chopped their arms off to come with us. It was a one-off though, whether because of that or what we didn't find out, but she moved and the house stayed empty for ages, we still got a hard on though just standing outside and looking up at the empty windows. Soon after Ben got the push from the deliveries too, seems he tried to reinvent the adventure with a couple of women who didn't appreciate the favour.

At times in my last year, my hidden intellectualism broke

out of the sullen defiance, the ancient Headmaster, used to pouring his eyes into the head of an empty pool, the still waters of perfected and socially engineered non-comprehension, when from the deep of the hidden cavern it would rear, uncalled, but the violence of words and innuendo found its mark and the wee unspoken thing of verbal and intellectual challenge would rise. Aye, rise and say something, challenge something, say something.

So it was with the books again. So it was with the insult, the thicko with a book again. At 14 things started to come together, the *atom bomb*, the *H-bomb*, the *Soviet Union*, at once controversial, at once the subject of news and papers. After my exhaustive use of all information on the Bismarck, a favourite ship of mine, I discovered *Russia, the Atom and the West*, by Hugh Gaitskell. I borrowed it, in an endeavour to see what this would say. I stood in the assembly rank and rank, the rubbish of the prayers before the forgiving Christ, in a non-forgiving school. Happened to be at the edge of my line, at the back, Form Four, when the ever-malevolent woodwork teacher strolled and snatched the book from behind. While the whole school stood in silence, he shouted: 'I've got a book here', and thrust it back into my hands. 'What does it say?' he demanded. I read the title quietly to the woodwork teacher standing at the side, then he walked slowly to the front of the hall.

'What do they title that book?'

I read: *Russia, the Atom and the West.*

'What class are you in?'

'4C', I replied quietly.

'What class are you in, Mr Douglass?'

'4C, sir', I replied, so the whole school could hear. Then he took the book, walked down the giggling lines of first-through to fourth-year kids and handed me the book, saying:

'By the time you know what that means you'll have run up a fine. Here, Douglass, stick to things you understand.' The blush covered my body from head to toe. I had not even turned the first page, could not yet have answered a single question on it, thought it would be heavy even when I took it from the shelf. I had intended to struggle with it and get something from it, on the understanding that I could read, and if it was printed I could fathom the words later, I never believed at fourteen there was a book I could mek nowt of. But it didn't end there.

I was sitting at the desk; we were doing a rare assignment set by a young teacher to ease her conscience, on what we thought of capital punishment. She asked us things like that, we had a point of view, but if you got caught by other teachers, you'd get ridiculed, so it was a secret, and the conspiracy thought-provoking exercise worked, for we all had views and wanted to write them down, bad spelling, ink blots an' all. I was into my theme of World War Two a' la Commando comics and a few other references about Hitler etc. when in strode the Headmaster.

'Did a boy in this class have a book about Russia?' he asked. Only one boy in that class had ever a book about any bloody thing, Quietly I put up the hand of subservient surrender.

'Come out here', he said, whip hand ready for the fast draw of the cane (although he didn't carry it).

His eyes peered the depth, the drawbridge didn't go up in time, a spark was still inside from the Commando comics and capital punishment. He drew me outside the door and asked confidentially:

'Who gave you this?' The conspiratorial implication was clear: the commies can 'get to kids' as the bogyman of earlier years would carry you off in his sack or 'interfere' with you.

'Nobody, sir, I took it off the library shelf.'

'But who told you to take this one?' 'Nobody, I just fancied the title!'

'So what do you think of Russia?' he asked, smirking.

'Well—' I began a half-finished philosophy not yet formed, in fact only the rudimentary outline of the first thought had formed. 'They were on our side in the war, and they fought against the Germans, now people have turned against them.' The smirk left his face.

'Who told you that?'

'Nobody, I read it.'

'Who gave you the book with that in?' The interrogation had started.

'It wasn't one book; I read a lot about the war.'

'Is someone older telling you these things?'

Eventually the dialogue ran out. I didn't know who Gaitskell was, my ideas on the bomb were confined to wanting to know how it worked, and my opening line of philosophy had been used. Eventually it was:

'You leave that book with me, Douglass. I'll see the library gets it back and makes sure you don't have any more of them. You'll be getting the wrong impression and turning away from your religion.'

When I went back in the class, I put both hands under my armpits to create the impression I had been caned for something. A political discussion with the headmaster would not be understood.

Disasters abounded, all in the month of May, the month of labour, the day of marches, the red flag, and the Red Square parade! The 'room', now we were middle class, now housed—apart from the thick-piled carpet, the china cabinets full of vicarious Holy Jesuses but few having the grandmas' cures—a black-and-white telly. May Day, the day to roll from bed as dawn was breaking, while the house slept, to watch the Red Army, the guns and tanks and bombs, push their glorious way through Red Square; an event not to miss.

In the skuel, the title was set in art—we got art, but because of the multi-coloured powder-paint-bomb fights, exploding with geet cloods of red and black smoke to the improvised POOWSHH explosive noise, we had been banned from most painting. The title was to set a scene from May. Great, Lenin's mausoleum topped with the red flags of labour, the geet tanks and mobile rockets, nosed large and shaded in black across the paper, Ah was there, amang it, in the Square, drivin' the tank, muttering the tank noises, as plated metal skidded ower Moscow cobbles. Then crack! the clip shot me heed forard se hard me chin booncced from the desk-lid where it had been hovering in concentration. It was the wiry Heed.

'OBSESSED.' He spat the word. 'OBSESSED' and spittle shot from his lips. A dumb stare to left and right revealed the Blessed Virgin in splattered and smudged water paint. The holy altar covered in flo'ors. May is the month of Mary, not the Red Army! Interest or softer childhood memories would have reminded me that the young girls of the village took part in a venerated pious beauty contest to be the stand-in for Mary, Queen of the May. Flowers collected and strewn at her feet, she mounts the pulpit to be crowned in a garland of flowers and brown freckles over her nose.

Oh, Mary we crown thee with blossoms today,
Queen of the angels and Queen of the May.

Ah guessed the T57 hadn't fitted into the scheme.

The Christmas party of the third year, still more of the fourth, was the event, and the Christmas present had graduated, from colourful boxes of bright-coloured plastic or oil-smelling metal aids to fantasy, to smart Italian suits with added meedmen extras. Two link buttons—'when ya jiving, yee can had ya top finger in there ye knaa, lueks geet edgy'—red satin lining, roll collar, double inside pocket, length not ower lang ti be drape but far away from bum freezers, which were soft. The fascination with style, an instant battle-front with the practical choice of the Ma, who kenned not that a tartan hood in a duffle-coat meant ostracism by the whole world, that roond-toed shoes were the mark of the mammy's lad and a sure sign of being a pouf. So the winkle-picker and chisel-toe signed up with the slim-Jim tie to hold the gang as 'smart', 'edgy', and show we were in the league for sex. We wore the badge of teenage.

This fascination with suits coincided with projected images of work and a job. Tailoring was the joint ambition. We knew of the cutters and the fitters, and the good coin and cheap top-quality suits that went with the job. A sliding scale of job hierarchy, Jackson's top of the tree, then Burton's and gradually downward to the Co-op. For the time being, to be a tailor's apprentice or a cutter made you a respected man among men.

Being a hard man, one of the gang, was a duty. I failed, as Kathleen Mullroy made a pulp of me face in Newcastle Haymarket. Amang the lads on the bus, Ah telt hor: 'Shut thee hole', she wez mockin' is skatin'. She mocked on. Off the bus Ah grabbed hor ti warn hor of the lip—sister of hard Irish brothers, she'd been warned of the lip a time a' twe afore, and be bigger blokes than me. She give me a flat hand to the left lug which deafened, stunned and vornie tuek me heed off, then punched me full in the face before walkin' off to join the jeering females. The meedmen stood, shamed, and left me, crying, 'Yi'd best dey that again.' I shouted, 'Ah didn't feel nowt'—and staggered sideways to a helpful railing.

My oldest sister Marina had been a frequent inmate of hospitals, sometimes taken in the night by ambulances, sometimes visited by strange doctors. Always my poor Mam would look desperate and Da would be doleful. I enjoyed the hospital visits. Queen Elizabeth, General: she had stayed in most from time to time, the earphones, and sitting on the bed, the music of the carousel two-way family favourites. The stacking of the green chairs, visitors from the ootsides—but she was frequently back with us, and dancing, and courting, and reading to me. Some distant thing in the back of my brain was kept distant. Then I heard what I should not have heard. It was dark, night-time, there had been creeping around, it was raining, I was sleeping. I heard a stifled cry from my younger sister, Veronica, and the mumbling of my father's voice; the distant sob of my mother, I was left to sleep and pushed the dreadful noises away from my head, but they lingered. Next morning the curtains stayed drawn and my Da, red-eyed, pushed the bedroom door open, I feigned ignorance for ah-divikna what reason, and kept the image and consciousness far from my thoughts even as the house filled with distant relatives and reverberated with Irish and deep Geordie pit accents, even after the funeral.

Later, the memories of trips to the seaside, outings to town, unused presents of soap I had bought for her, welled up into an uncontrollable wretched sense of loss. I was tortured by the realisation that she would never again hop and skip to the music, nor yet play two-baller on the wall. Ironically, the loss itself never leaves you; it remains like a barbed token of the things, which can never again be, and the total irreversibility, the everlasting knowledge that it can never change, fans the flame of desperate loss.

It was years later, that leukemia was diagnosed as a by-product of the nuclear bomb; this knowledge drew me inexorably into the anti-bomb movement and the Youth Campaign for Nuclear Disarmament, to door-to-door evangelical sales of Sanity, a hundred copies at a time, but the personal rationale was too personal to use in doorstep argument with the neighbours.

I can't recall just how I learned of the whereabouts of the YCND meeting, but I was still a shiny member of the Sea Cadets and had tracked down the address of the Young Communist League meetings, though had been unable to find it. Forbye, to the musty old Labour room and small YCND meeting I went. Together with the rest of the meeting, we descended on the Bridge Hotel, where I actually met some YCLers.

Being in the YCL was a great act of secrecy. The badge was kept in a little box lined with cotton wool, much as I had earlier carried a much-prized RSPCA 'Animal Defender' badge. A log was hidden in my room: date joined, date badge bought, date first pamphlet bought. At school it was the first break from the gang, something I did without them. Me mates joined the conspiracy of silence and referred to it as 'the laughy'.

'Ah'll not see yi the neet, lads....'

'Oh aye, its laughy neet.'

The highly prized CND badge was a mystical symbol, an act of defiance, a mark of intelligence, a link that joined the skinny 'C' class kid to a haunting culture emerging on the TV screens. It was worn on me jacket, transferred to the jumper when the jacket was taken off, transferred to the shirt when the jumper was taken off. Taken off altogether when the wiry, twitching Head—'What's this? What's this, Douglass?'—saw it, though he confided his agreement with the cause, but not 'the cheek'.

Having become a communist, I had to read the relevant texts. Entering the Felling library, I requested *Capital* by Karl Marx.

'Would that be *Das Kapital*, sir?' the unruffled librarian asked.

'Yes, that's the one'.

Heads turned, and eyebrows rose as I was led to the desk where the Reference Section books could be read, for these were not for loan. Presently the weighty tome was brought and placed before me. Heads still peered in the youth's direction, anticipating a showing-up. I turned the heavy cover, Gothic writing, the first page.... Good God, it was in German! I couldn't send it back or just walk out after it had been brought to me, so sagely I read, or pretended to, turning this page and referring back to that, nodding in agreement and smiling here and there at a shared literary jest by Karl. Thirty-five minutes later, I felt I had covered my mistake and left the library, saying 'Thank you' to the puzzled librarian.

The roller rink was wor regular forte: speed, a laugh, collapsing in a multiple, prearranged pile-up with eye-drawing middle-class girls in pleated skating skirts, luscious thighs, a wriggle of the posterior as the pleats bob off on tutored skates. The ice-rink was for real skating. Nearly all the girls wore skating dresses, and not otherwise having had much opportunity to inspect pubescent female thighs and posteriors at close range, we drooled fit to melt the ice. But divind get caught; there was a way to act in female company; drooling was oot—meks them think ye've nevor been wi a lass before, play it casual. Taak ti them nice, divind swear or thi'll think ya thick, but drop in the sexual innuendo all the same. 'He might be little but ee's got some energy'—Ben boosting me up in front of a tall, long-legged girl balancing on her skate tips as we tried to get off with her. Danger at the rink, as the speed skaters cut by in a shower of ice and a flash of steel. 'Ah'll get you on the ice!'—a deadly threat.

A tall, gangly kid, posh English accent, soft looking, having the piss taken out of him by a couple of the likely lads: 'Ah'll get you on the ice.' The crowd waiting to get in fell silent and a murmur went through the throng as to the soft-luekin' kid's credentials. They were not long coming as one of the likely lads, suddenly finding himself exposed on a quiet patch of ice, looked up in sudden recollection of the threat, too late. The tall, gangly kid looked soft ney mare, as two added thrusts to the gleaming skates sent him close through the narrowing gap like a shark, a twist like lightning, a shower of ice, and he was in reverse on collision course at 'ain miles an hoor, greet lang legs and blade extended. The impact was silent but for the gasp as Likely Lad One, in a genuflection of pain, had the wind forced from his guts, and knees, head, and ice came together in a weighty thud. Gangly smoothly in the crowd before Likely hit the ice. A test of time, as his body is dragged from the ice, his marra tries to find a way to the ice exit, head turning this way and that, eyes in a panic, then an instant of speed flashing through the crowd, tearing up a wave of ice in a spectacular hockey stop, felling Likely Lad Two with one foot and rasping his head with a back kick from the other.

The street-hard lads met their betters on the ice. Later years of unemployment would transform the city unemployed into gladiatonal skaters with skill born of daily practice through a lack of much else to do. The meedmen watched, gabbled for weeks about it, and learned to keep wa place. The roller rink was less crowded, we convinced wasells.

Getting up the speed to TELSTAR, we quite cut a dash at the roller rink. A couple of the lads could rumble by backwards, switchin' forwards, wheels rotating like castors. Some of the young professionals showed wi up with jumps and spins, but we didn't resent them. We had learned to respect skaters who knew their stuff, even the posh ones could mek a wally of yi on the rink, and that was a bad image with the lasses.

On trips to Shields market with me Da, the link with the past, the smell of the sea, and the sounds and the occasional barefoot Arab trader selling his wondrous items from the pavement, magical and foreign, strange Sinbad writing on the oddly designed tins and jars. 'This one, metal polish, very special, very special', and it was, too; the brasses on the webbing belt and gaiters shone like beaten gold after one application. Here and there, down the sea road, Arab cafés, chip shops and bars.

'Ye knaa, Son, Jonty says the Arab folk have always been here.'

'What, afore the Brits?'

'Yes, they were here when the Brits first came, trading here in Shields. This was like a market stall for all the tribes. The Romans and the Vikings too, they came here to trade and, like, dey thi shoppin'. But the maist of them, ya Granda always said, came as seamen, strang men, strang union men, fierce fighters. Ye'l no see them lads drunk roon the toon though, or using foul language', me Da said, making that swing of his head and nod to the side with a wink, which meant 'Think on that!'

'All together like the folks i' Shields': that's the saying when people get packed up snug thegether, the sand-dancers, the toon folk call them.

'Is that coz of the beach, Da, or coz people get dressed up as Arabs ti dey that sand dance?'

'Ah'm nivor se sure son, mevies a bit both, but it's ainly in fun anyway.'

When the meedmen went ti Shields it was in cowboy hats and sunglasses, to hang aroond the corners of the Waltzer, bop to the Everly Brothers, or spin with the bar thrown down like it didn't bother yee how fast it went, arms nonchalantly alang the back of the waltzer, knuckles white in an unseen iron grip to hang on, while the big lads spin the carriage faster and faster, trying to make yi scared.

The Everly Brothers and smell of chips, the pretty girls screaming and posing, pouting, chewin' gum like chewin' the cud, slow and rhythmic, looking you up and down. The gang lay on the beach. Pedro and one or two mer swam in the sea, the laughter drifting back and forth like the tide. Forra mock we buried his shoes. Later, as he searched high and low. Ben decided the game was up, so we sets off to dig up the shoes ... here, no here, then it must be there, till vornie half the beach had been unearthed an' ainly one shoe turned up. A devastating, dumbfounding' mystery, which became the spark of adventure. Pedro was not in a disposition ti gaan yem, havin' recently been bought the shoes. We decided to run away. The meedmen on the run. We pooled what money wi had, and, with a towel wrapped roon Pedro's foot, set off ti gaan as far north as we cud. We ended up, God knaas how, in Blyth, hoping ti break inti Leo's folks' caravan, found the site locked up and a guard on patrol.

Evening was turning ti night and the sea air bit through the bones. First attempts to sleep on the beach, huddled in a heap, jumpers ower the heads, proved abortive as the cold rose through the freezing sand and rocked wi wi' shivers. We next headed to the holiday chalets, which we raided like commandos, scaling the sides and up onto the veranda, creeping alang the top deck while a security man's torch swept the walkway, stifled giggles and murmured 'Roaring twenties, roaring twenties, come alang, Ah'm taken' you to the roaring twenties'. We fancied wasells as hoods on a jail break. But huddled on the concrete, hiding from the sea wind, even with the clothes on back to front or inside out, the cold was deathly.

Back at Wardley, parents swept from house to house in

anxious cars. By midnight it was obvious the whole gang was missing. The police on both sides of the river had been alerted, but we were off their beat, at least so far. At last, the cold proved too much and we resolved to head back to native territory, find a hiding place amang the woods and walks, which we knew weel. As we clambered down off the chalets, the plan was elaborated. Using my cadet skill we wad mek a big bivouac and camp in it, nick from Woolies such food as we needed or raid the fields for spuds and snadgies, and sign up a couple or three of the likely lasses to live wild wiv us. Excitement abounded, and the hum of plans took us to the roadside to hitch a lift. Oddly enough a car, well, a geet car, stopped and we all poured in.

'We were on the Duke of Edinburgh award scheme, but this lad lost his shoe so wa playin' safe and headin' back ti base.'

'What part of the course?' the suspicious driver asked, but he couldn't fault me.

'It's the Bronze. This was an initiative test. Ah reckon hitchin' back after losing a shoe is showing the right initiative, isn't it?'

We were dropped on the outskirts of Newcastle, the wrang side of the river and directionless, headed for Walker. As we got to the end of one street, two coppers on the other end spotted wi.

'Hey, yee, stop there!' Instead, wi were off like a rocket, bumping and sniggering. 'Roaring twenties, roaring twenties.' We were hoods again.

'Ye want us, copper, ye come and get us.' As we reached an apex of streets, a squad car skidded to block wa path, the path of 'absconders'. Absconders? What was that? Pedro's towel tripped him up and he went down first. Leo ran into a lamppost and vornie knocked himself oot. Ben got grabbed by an interferin' gadgie watchin' a hole in the road, and I got trapped down a side-street with Spud. Gradually the bedraggled bandinos were rounded up into the cop shop at Walker. The bosh still believed us ti be another gang, someone they kept calling 'absconders'. At last, it dawned: they thought we'd escaped from an approved home or a Borstal, 'nor, anly wa' ain'. When the parents were sent for, the air was blue and so were we. It was weeks before the gang reassembled and cut lowse again.

Toy boats, which had become cracked and damaged, could be given spectacular funerals on the river, large plastic liners, or some once magnificent aircraft carrier, would be sailed off into the swelling tide, with a lit candle placed inside its hull or dropped down its funnel. You could watch from the bank as it slowly descended beneath the waves, slowly listing to port or by the bow, simultaneously melting and breaking into flames. Added drama could come if the vessel with shot up by air gun pellets or marbles fired from catapults. One such fusillade, totally misunderstood by a gang on the opposite Wallsend side of the river started a cross-river war, which raged intermittently for over a year. Juvenile ingenuity fuelled an armed race. I think it was Larry who first designed the handlebar cannon. Finding a relatively straight length of bicycle handlebars, he first hammered home a cork in one end, drilled in a touchhole, then filled the bar up with gunpowder from fireworks; neatly into the other end, he stuck a small ball bearing. The raggylad musket was ready to point at the big doomed plastic liner now almost mid stream., weighted the canon down with rocks, charged the shot hole, lit the match and ...bliddy hell, everything shot up in the air but the ball bearing cleared the river and landed with a thud on the other bank near a group of Wallsend lads'. Within three weeks an arms race had begun and two teenage tribes on opposite sides of the river were firing a veritable battery of pipe guns at each other. They were thankfully hopelessly inaccurate and seriously more danger to their own side than the other. It was odd how things seem to pick up their own momentum and arrive at unexpected and wholly unplanned conclusions. The meedmen, were something like a working class teenage Tyneside Secret Seven or Famous Five, well not really in composition or in outlook but ye'l ken the drift. The river banks were still unexplored, still untamed, still in many places untouched by human hand, granite rock ranges, and sand hills merged into abandoned industrial landscapes from langsyne ages.

We ranged alang the Felling Shore, looking for what we would discover. On this occasion, we found a huge industrial tyre, with much heaving and perseverance managed to get it standing up, and balanced. It towered owawi as we set off booling it alang, slowly and laboriously at first, especially up the wee brays and hillocks, where we heaved like the final stages of rolling a near complete snowman. Suddenly and all of its own, it got the idea, and some ancient inanimate instinct locked in, as it gathered speed. Now it was running ahead of us, and we followed on cheering and waving, suddenly doon a steep swallie and up a steep bank fernant, then unassailed sped toward a little picket fence which it cleared following a smallie hillock and lowpt clear into the air, seeming to stay air borne for some moments then dived like a stone reet ower the edge of the drop, which happened to be above a moored twelve foot dingy tied up at the quay belaw. It splatted straight into the hapless boat which sank like a stone amid a greet sploot speared to the bottom of the river by the tyre, left just a keek above the watter line, a monument to its freedom. Well if that boat owner ever gets to read this, and if this is any consulation, it wasn't mindless vandals who didn't like ya boat, mer like a conjunction of freedoms and sods law. By Christ did we laugh, and then get serious and sorrowful then fell aboot laughing again and sometimes both emotions at once, it still impacts me that way now, decades doon the line. Ah mean, bliddy hell?

Between childhood and teenage comes a mix of loss and excitement as the happy kid's things give way to needed teenage things, but the transition was over with the fidelity record-player, all of me own. The world afterwards was filled with electric music and drums, and young men pacing stages. I learned to bop courtesy of me sister, who for some time had sported the ponytail and regulation flop at the front, the bobby-socks, pastel cardie over the flared skirt and wide elasticated belt with brass fasteners. Her bop was one of the best around. She was a Tommy Steele fan. Tommy Steele! This weird sister, she had 78s. *The Only Man on the Island*: there was a part in it where he said 'Huh' like a wee laughlet. She sat for hours turning the needle back to the *huh* part. Huh, huh, huh, squealing strange squeals and hugging herself in a strange rocking manner.

As me and record player met in social conjunction, skiffle had given way to a nightly profusion of rock bands: The Sinners, The Saints, The Devils, three guitarists and a drummer, same coloured black or red or bright yellow shirts. An indescribable thrill of identification, bright bobby-socks, drainpipes, an edgy feeling in ya belly. Buddy Holly provided that beat and impulsion, which sent the floor of the Palais bouncing, and me with me sister's crazy bop. In them days, lads could only get away with dancing together by pretending to be the band. US Bonds were a favourite, singing in unison, a multifold of microphones and shaking heads, while Pedro was always Daddy Gee, who we imagined to be tubby. The Shaddas provided the best forum. The school yard here and there seen patches of lads practicing the new 'walk' in readiness for the bop. Shadda walks could be done in a line, with other lads, without lookin' soft.

You tell me that you love me, Baby,
Then you say you don't,
You tell me that you'll come on over, Then you say you won't.

In a magic moment you were Cliff, sideways looks and lisp, while the meedmen Shaddas walk behind in support.

The TV and films told us were a café culture and so we tried to comply. We always went to the cafés on the Felling High Street for wa dinners: big plates of greasy chips, bottles of Coke, a piece of cake or two, three pence on the jukebox. You could always buy one cig if you wanted one; some of the lads thought it increased the image, together with the raised collar. The fag was always smoked beneath the hand, to avoid detection. It was a pattern. Learned in the schoolyard, it had the added advantage of looking hard. Looking hard was a series of tricks, as opposed to being hard, which many of the Felling lads were. For wor part, Ben advised a slight limp when walking. It looked hard, like you were crippled in some God-almighty rumble, a slightly hunched shoulder, like a permanent Billy Fury doing his sexy shoulder bit, 'cept it wasn't meant to be sexy, it wes meant to imply a battle-hardened body. If ye couldn't dee nowt else, try a slightly bow-legged walk, hands hovering near the thighs as if in readiness to fast-draw the Colts. As we advanced toward some other such assembly of lads we assumed wa hard postures, hunched shoulders, slight limp, bowed legs and narrowed eyes, the aura of hardness pervaded the High Street. We must have looked rather like the junior Quasimodo fan club, saved only by the fact that other 'gangs' hobbled and crouched their way around in the same fashion.

As image and ideology, behaviour and desires, whirled in

maelstrom, clashed with adulthood, Helen Shapiro was wa advocate, fourteen and mature we mouthed along with 'Don't treat me like a child.' her instant top of the charts hit.

Dragoonies Café at the head of Felling Square, with espresso coffee like the pictures, stood host to a mass motorbike gang garbed in identical black leather and string ties the Rockets. The shining machines stood in the lamplight, line on line, waiting for the next explosion of exhausts, kick-starts, blue smoke, and the roaring convoy takes off *en masse*.

The smoking potency of wild teenage freedom represented itself in the Tiger Cub, a tangible vision for bikers at the more youthful end of teenage. The meedmen seen thasells riding off in a flash of nickel-plate and studded leather, walking round the evening glow in reverend, hushed tones. Yet here and there, the thunder of the Vincent and Black Knight, fat-girthed 1,000 cc invincible monster of the road, existing only on the very rim of reality.

The Palais was *the* place, standing on Felling Square, Peggy Sue rattling the windows, shadows of bouncing bunches of grapes, to the old folk a cauldron of fear, to us a sign of coming of age, though we were on the young end of the clientele, we 'mased at girls from wor form with the older lads. Inside, the Wardley and Felling lads eye each other from respective corners, young miners or unemployed; they had younger sets too, with lads from twelve to fifteen, usually brothers of the older sets, while the sprung floor catapulted wedge-footed dancers, stiletto dancers. Groups of lads walk in single file round the perimeter; another group walks in the same fashion in the opposite direction, the two columns passing each other with a fraction between their shoulders. One bump and the dance floor would erupt in violence. The cool kid sits down while his girl jives, one hand turns her, the other sups the drink. The music, dancing, pounding, the air charged with violence, stomach knotted in fear, penis seldom flaccid as whirling skirts and laced underskirts reveal bare legs, thighs, knickers and belly, all part of Friday night. Sometimes local fights caused the police to raid, then it was a scattered battle right through the Square; in one such running skirmish, a polis was stabbed to death with a bottle. Inter-town rivalries and sexual jealousies sometimes gave rise to vendettas, in one of which a young miner was stabbed in the belly down the pit:

The Ted he came from the Drill Hall dance,
Through the streets so dark and narra,
And there he spied nine Fellin lads
Come to dey him in, in Jarra.
He wrapped his belt aroond his fist,
But thiv beat him ti a shadda,
An' there he lies wiv he's heed caved in,
In the dowly streets of Jarra.

Near Christmas, we wandered past raucous door-holes of the toon pubs, resolved on a Christmas booze-up. Previous experiments had been restricted to parties where the main object was to provide enough booze to give the lasses an excuse to say they couldn't remember whatever it was they had done.

Overlooking the stinkin' Lonin' doon ower the lanes, three of wi had got paralytic on three bottles o' broon, Ben drinkin' the residue of the wor two, and staggering off doon the Lonin with his shirt tail hingin' oot. This was different; this was the meedmen, best Christmas suits and raglan overcoats, off forra proper drink in the toon. The trick perfected, we hit the Black Boy in the market: one of the hardest hard-case City Centre Big Market pubs, one therefore unlikely to be ower-frequented by polis. With Ben gettin' the roond in on a huge tin tray, the heaving, smoke-filled noise-filled hole ably camouflaged the likely lads suppin' the beer:

'Sup it sla, ye knaa, ye divind swig it'—a sure sign of immaturity, but whe'd want to swig the foul-tasting poison anyway? We next moved on to the lang-gone Brass Man, a rough hoose pub, up the side stairs, and to a table parked off the beaten track. We took turns to gaan into the bar and come back with a geet tray flowin' with glasses. They were on their third unsavoury pint, while I was genuinely three sheets to the wind, having given up drinking the soapy-smelling dish-swill beer ages before, leaving the glass in front of is for appearance sake, had been secretly quaffing doon Babycham, bottle after bottle. The late-night bus rocked ti via antics and singing.

'Oa gud neet, Mister! Gud neet, Misses, happy Christmas, happy Nuw Yur! Gud neet!' the only time we had ever really sung carols with gusto and boundless happiness.

Protestant girls were a latent source of sexual desire, being protiedogs they divind believe in God, not like wor lasses, so there's nowt stopping them getting shagged, protiedog lasses aal dee it. So went Ben's theory. Days doon at the coast engaging the youthful teeny-boppers, standing linking each other, giggling and chewing.

'Ye gaan ti skuel across the road?' In unison: 'Is that a Protestant school?'

What nonsense! Whey cud be randier than wor lasses? Skuel in third and fourth form was a hive of sexual frenzy, amazing more didn't get caught at it. In the sloping field hidden from classrooms, lang grass hid many a grouplet or couple, it was here where at twelve I was dedrawered by three of the fourth-form girls, who sat astride is, amid rustling net underskirts and some manipulation, a warm, wet sensation around the lower regions whilst a fluttering, almost anxious, feeling pervaded my chest and heart. That was IT, I thought, Ah never was sure it was and it didn't seem to have all the sexy other bits, and naked things, that other lads told of in their encounters, so I never let on to Ben or the gang, just sort of let it sit as maybe I had, maybe not, maybe I had some mysterious encounters I wasn't letting on about, after all I wasn't sure what exactly I had done, they had done; it was my first ejaculation. As we progressed, months and years, through the school, lads would make the grand announcement that they'd done it. Leo riding his bike pell-mell up the bank, jumping off it grand style while it was still moving, letting it carry on on its own, till it ran out of momentum and keeled over near the wall, while he was bounding up to the meedmen who stood watching in a huddle.

'Done it, Ah've done it, done it, Ah've done it!', and everyone throws their arms around everyone else in a single gang-hug. bouncing up and doon cheering. Then the details. He and an older girl and one younger than him sat in the cab of an old abandoned lorry doon Stoneygate, touching each other up, exposing more bits then the older girl:-

'Whey, gaan on then, put the fucker up is.' The gang roared as he told of his plight trying to pull his skin-tight jeans off 't'dey it reet', falling on the floor of the cab then finally throwing all abandon to the wind, gets out of the cab and pulls the buggers off, before diving back between the open legs of the rather plump fifteen-year-old with her feet resting on the dashboard, pulling her bra and jumper up in one go. A hurried, not very long, encounter Leo admits. But as soon as he came, he had a hard-on again.

'Fuck her as well, you've got to fuck her now', and the younger girl clambers over her large mate to position herself as she had, this time, Leo telt wi, he nearly snapped it trying to get it in. We all roared again as he related how he had to keep checking that he hadn't missed and was trying to enter the battered old leather of the driving seat, at last his second ejaculation saved the struggling, wincing girl from further penetration. 'She had a bare fanny, ye knaa, tight as fuck', was his concluding sequel. Later Ben rather jealously told wi all he could have fucked them two ages ago, but Bet was too fat and Pam too young. He awarded Leo a shag, and a part shag for the partial penetration of little Pam.

The classroom itself, even during class, more usually at playtime, housed couples groping under desks, and at every chance to get into a huddled groping encounter. The class cupboard, although exposed to all other class members, was hidden from the teacher's view, and just as weel. Unsophisticated grabbing, hasty contact, breasts grabbed through the clothing, while lads were nearly disembowelled by girls suddenly grabbing at the bulge in skin-tight jeans as they passed by. More effective sex could really only take place on the way from school, in the disused empty houses, or at night lying on the railway banks under the tunnels, fudged and confused but in a fashion managing to expose enough, let enough out, see enough and feel enough to keep a bounce in the wedges.

Since childhood, I had preferred my girl contacts to have knickers and ankle socks, no technology; however, as the girls became fashion-conscious and bestockinged, so too came the damned suspender belt, a fiendish construction of finger traps, meaningless buttons and strangulation elastic. Today's fetishism over the miserable object is surely born of masochism, or else this generation's sense of sexual navigation must be greatly improved.

After weeks of distant desire, I finally got to 'gaan oot' with the 'B' stream girl from Conistan. Being oot meant walking; awkwardly holding hands, an arm on her shoulder was oot since she was a foot bigger than me, working it around to Learn Lane Park just as darkness fell. Ben would be proud of me. Finding the secluded park bench and gettin' started. Necking, breasts through the clothes, resistance, a little, that's normal, more necking, long deep snogs, back to the breasts through the clothes, no more resistance, on to step two, breasts underneath the clothes, hardening nipples, shiver, bra, no problem just howk it up, oh aye, nice shape, sticking out there all of their own, cup them gentle, squeeze her nipples, then onto the borrums. See, it was a contradiction really, these wonderful sensuous breasts standing out pert and ready, graced by the white lace of her bra, should have caused me to linger long and savor the tender brownness of her, but then you'd never know how far you could get. And the further you got the more cool and experienced you were at it. So, having just exposed her breasts, it was canny! Reet, now on to the next objective, cold hand on belly, disaster! Suspender belt, me hand on its creeping juvenile voyage none too certain of routes or even ultimate direction for that matter, having only recently believed the source of my endeavours lay about level with ya hips, somewhere near where a boy's cock was. First I encounter an elastic strap, negotiate that, wrist stops tight by the strap, try and manipulate me fingers up the top, elastic waistband, sounds of twanging from the nether regions, me nearly on the path, writhing off the seat, blood totally stopped in me wrist, drive me fingers down, and emerge—at the first elastic strap. A cool look of contempt from the 'B' streamer, rapping her fingers, me heavy breathing, sweating, gangrene-laden hand and blood-pressured arm, pain-wracked and confused.

'Ah'm not used ti these.'

Shit, a bigger showing-up than Katie Mullroy had given is. Not a story to tell Ben, no, definitely not a story to tell Ben. How did the darn things work? It was three years later

I discovered you didn't need to undo, untie and remove the object, by which time, confused, I had untied little decorative bows, knitted elastic cat's-cradles with me fingers and twanged me way through a number of fiascos.

Communion, still a Sunday obligation, wasn't possible without confession on the preceding Friday. Confession meant sins: sins of the flesh. After one of the more daring sorties ahint the class cupboard door, and after missing communion for a week or two, much to the notice of me Ma, for fear of receiving the host in an unblessed unforgiving state, courage was mustered. Me idea, as of aud, to slip the real sin in amangst the regular misdemeanors and hope it went unnoticed

'Bless me, Father, for I have sinned, it is three weeks since my last confession.... I have been bad-tempered, I have back-answered my mother and father, I have told lies, I have been immodest, I have missed prayers, and I have not had communion in three weeks since, Lord forgive me and by Thy will I will never sin again.'

All the while the priest whispered: 'Yes', 'yes', 'yes'. Not noticed? Then, in a deep resounding Galway voice:

'Tell me now, son, and how was it you were immodest?'

'Well,' I felt myself getting hot, 'I touched another's body, Father.'

'Now, was it a girl or a boy, my child?' Me lips were getting dry.

'A girl, Father.'

'And where did you touch her body, my son?' I hadn't banked on this.... The courage all gone now....

'Her stomach, Father, her stomach.'

'Is that where you touched her?'

'Yes, yes, Father, her stomach.' I thought of somewhere lower and thought God would think my sexual navigation was out of order again and tried to conceal the thought of that thought, in case he seen that as well.

'Well, son, if this is a good confession, you must say five Hail Mary's and four GlorybetotheFather' s.'

A sinner, I left and went to the rail, to reason that it was a farce. Marx had said it was opium. The Little Lenin Library, from which I intended to be a little Lenin, explained the world in material ways: you were in a clutch of fear, now was the time to break it. I walked from the church, no longer clean, Gabriel kept his pad intact.

School's out... 3C: Dave on right(1962)

The row at hyme came later.

'Ah'm not gaanin' to church, Mammy, 'I dinnit believe it, 'Son, oh—have thought to your immortal soul', and clasped her hands with a clap, and looked to heaven. 'The ungodly shall have a great claw come from the floor and drag you down to hell. The bed will split open in the dead of night and tumble ye down to hell.'

'I don't believe that superstitious nonsense, Ah'm a materialist...matter, this earth, body and blood, no more gods.' I advanced in wicked defiance; still, I slept on the edge of the bed, in case it should split and precipitate me downwards into hell, or that I might catch a glimpse of the claw as it broke from the floor grasping for my immortal soul. Yet I told myself: 'what nonsense, for I am a goodly person', just in case God was listening, not that He was there anyway....

So ti Jonty at his krey, minus the witan this time, just me and him, me walking roond the field of vegetables and flowers that so filled you with earthy, nutritious smells while he flung out handful of pigeon corn crying, 'Ha'way, ha'way', and as the birds soar in to land or sit crooing in the krey I get roon to test his wisdom against those of my new tutors.

'Lenin, lad, is not the first rung of the ladder, casting aboot in the waater as ye are, graspin' forra rung.... Neither is ya Marx or Engels, but suddenly ootaya depth, amid the waves of curiosity, ye mun grab a rung and work ya footin' oot later.' (That was right: I was often awash with new thoughts, which just kept rolling in. Before I had crested the last, another broke bigger than the first. How did he know that?)

'So then, Jonty, ye think the Marxists is correct?'

'La', the ladder is for them in the waater, Ah's on the deck', and his grey aud eyes from a millennium stirred a still well, and my virgin intellect shut it off as a chasm suddenly opened up beneath the ground I had just discovered and declared safe. Me mental drawbridge crashed shut with a force that made me blink. Jonty turned:

'But thou will knaa, despite theesell thou will knaa.'

5
Years of Rebellion

Sexual intercourse began
in Nineteen Sixty Three
Which was rather too late for me
Between the end of the Chatterley ban
And the Beatles' first LP.

Philip Larkin

We left school, for what good it had been, a little before 15 years old, this a one-and-only concession to the thickies of the 'C' stream, to give us three months' start on the other streams, who would leave in Easter. Geordieland was awash with unemployed youth, anxious to claim a first wage and have a job. Gettin' a start ... a start. Those who, like the tailoring heroes of before, had exuded an affluent confidence, hands - in-ya - pockets-and-feel-something-other-than-your-own-balls confidence. There was no grand leaving ceremony for us, or for anyone for that matter; but the Head took the time to write out references and in my case, while listing the string of 'C' class successes, did note I had developed 'a wide interest in general knowledge', ney match for bein' able to add up and spell, but better than nowt.

We signed on in a cellar under the Felling Council offices, young uns from school havin' ney stamps claimed ney coin, it was just in case a job came up, to get a card for an interview, and stand at the back of a half-mile queue waiting also for interviews, the same interviews for the same job. Staying in the toon, ti buy the first editions of the *Newcastle Evening Chronic*, diving on the jobs page, to be first at the place, and stand at the back of another half-mile queue and be told the job went afore the paper came oot.

I had new status, I was unemployed youth, I was a young unemployed worker as in the Young Unemployed Workers' League, I was part of the growing mass of unemployed working-class youth. I was, as the Young Communist League education class telt is, part of the reserve army of labour. If this was the reserves, I wanted to be part of the regulars—in fact went vornie to joining the Royal Navy, which still held a romance carried over from me tarry cadet days. But even after the interviews enthusiastically welcomed- me to the lofty post of boy bugler in the Royal Marines, even after the entrance test, and the days of day-dreaming of endless leagues of rolling oceans and mighty vessels ploughing the deep, spray breaking over the glistening turrets and varnished decks, I drew back, as political ideas began to fit the state's bodies of armed men into context. Somehow, I felt robbed, felt that if I hadn't asked so many questions, didn't think so much, I could be happily blowing sunset on the quarterdeck of a frigate while it swept through Shields piers and off to the Arctic, as I had dreamed of so many years before.

The musty, smoky room at the back of the People Bookshop, the centre of the Communist Party of Great Britain and YCL on Westgate Hill, with its fading encyclical fading on the outside brickwork, 'Read the Daily Worker, the People's Paper', embodies for a time the living image of socialist hot coals. Unemployed and quasi-Teds in Geordie twang and ageing winkle-pickers sat alongside mousy-haired girls in woolly cardies, or blonde peroxides in mock leopard skin coats like the films usually portrayed as pros or ladies of easy virtue at least, but were still quite fashionable for women in their late twenties and early thirties, no matter how tarty that image, beside the caucus of young workers in donkey jackets, work boots and overalls and the tall Nogbad, the bad character, the oldest YCLer in the country, the Stalinist über alles and organiser Stan Wilks.

His fingers supporting muscular arms with rolled sleeves, he leaned forward from the speaker's table, which in turn took the weight of Jimmy Hagen, the curly-haired shipyard worker who was the speaker. He too, in overalls from the yard, had come to speak and been 'honoured'. His spread fingers took the weight while his other hand formed silhouettes of shapes, or dug back into his own bosom, or grasped at his forehead to pull forward the ideas, his narrowed eyes seeing already the awakened proletariat and its quest for power. Then an open hand swept back in the gesture of return, to call forth again the pioneers, in much the way Jonty had described Celts regrouping north.

'And so Marx and Engels showed to the mass o' the workers that the boowazee wasn't some gaggle of ungodly, that is ti say evil, monsters but is a class, a class which acts at times of necessity and no' just at a whim but oot of the necessity of tha' development. Just as they in fact dig their own graves, and are forced ti give way tithe proletariat as the new revolutionary class, This new class, this proletariat, which oppresses neybody, because the social conditions which allow it to take poower divind necessitate it to oppress another class. And indeed, comrades, the proletariat bein' the dispossessed, havin' nowt, and takin' nowt from neybody, has neybody bela' it upon which it rests or feeds from. It is a class of itself, the comin' i poower of the proletariat is the end of class struggle, with the proletarian conquest ower the boowazee forst class struggle then class itsell will begin ti wither away to a society of people, not riven be conflicts and classes.'

This worker-intellectual, with visions conjured as if from oot the top of his heed, forst riveted yi ti' the seat then cast yi oot ti browse the musty shelves of the Little Lenin Library, and hours of often non-comprehending lookin' at pages on which words just sat and stared back blankly. A foreign language, which couldn't be avoided, tentative usage of which was often less than perfect. I referred to the dreaded enemy class as the burgosea, until someone took me aside and told me: 'It's boowazee, it's French, see?'

The day the Soviet missiles headed for Cuba, and the Yankee warships set out on an engagement course, the life of the earth swung in the balance, silence hung dark foreboding over the hoose, ower the streets. I like the others gravitated to the bookshop, surely we could dey somethin', must stop it.

Me Da: 'Where deyee think your gaanin', like?'

'M'gaana try and stop the war.'

'How can yee stop the war if its gaana happen?' he asked sarcastically and I felt stupid and futile.

'Ah divina, but Ah'm gaana try.'

Arriving at the bookshop, I found it already a hive of activity, people had stopped off work, women had left the dinners, the unemployed had drifted in throughout the day as the clock ticked by. I felt absolutely certain we were going to be engulfed in a sheet of flame and poison fumes. We improvised posters and slogans and set off to march round the toon, aboot thirty of us.

JAW JAW, NOT WAR WAR

JAW JAW JAW, NOT WAR WAR...

And the people on the pavements, feeling time running out, knowing that on the ocean war was approaching at a rate of knots, some joined in, shopping an' all.

One Two Three Four,
Cuba doesn't want a war,
Five Six Seven Eight,
America negotiate!

Crowds at the bus stops fell in behind us, talking worriedly, walking determinedly . . . to no particular place. It was a scene being enacted in probably every city in Britain, and Europe, and probably the world.

Hands off Cuba!
Hands off Cuba!
Hands off Cuba!
From cinema queues, from bars:
Jaw jaw, not war war!
No war, no war, no war!

We ended spontaneously, 2,000 strong, in a rally near the Chronic office, from which the press workers came out and joined as if in an act of petition. An all-night vigil followed. I went to bed, crying softly in a bitter feeling of betrayal, that my life was going to be taken before I had a chance to live it, the world would die before I could help it. In the morning I wasn't deed, Khrushchev had backed off—bloody coward!

The musty Westgate Road bookshop contrasted to pub socials in obscure toon pubs. Me chest swelled to songs of struggle, Les Cain, a world-wide rambler, picked-up his guitar in best Guthrie tradition and took off to the States and Canada, returning with spider-spinning fingers and a host of songs. Stan Nogbad, the Bad Wilks, of uncertain age in a heavy topcoat, the oldest YCLer in the business, with a deep, penetrating voice, and the young uns who'd gather like a clandestine resistance from the four corners of the city, called by word of mouth, cramming to the ceiling.

A little earlier, two well-heeled prostitutes had given the labour movement something they didn't know they had on offer and a terrible scandal broke, helping to turn the tide against 'Super Mac' Macmillan. Mandy, my fav of the two, had come while on bail to open the La Dolce Vita nightclub, and while a huddle of born-again Christians carried posters condemning her for her sins of the flesh and Babylon, a number of us YCLers turned up. Though doubtless the Party

Line was almost as moralistically critical as the Holy Rollers, we cheered her ootta the car like she was a conscious subverter of the hated Tory government, a Red fellow-traveler and anyway a randy bastard.

'Good lass, Mandy, bonny lass! well done!' The city kids, sharp to understand the visit, sang and skipped:

Half a pound of Mandy Rice,
Halfa poond of Keeler,
Ten bob ti put it up,
Five bob to feel her.

But in the smoky, guitar-strumming, knowing and shared environment of the low-ceilinged pub, movement people, the Reds, the leftists, sing (Twist and Shout):

Well. John Profumo, John Profumo,
He got Christine in the back roomo
He knocked her off,
So did Ivanoff, oh yeah,
John Profumo, Christine Keeler,
Spaghetti bollick-naked
Don't forget the fruit gums. .
Well Mandy Davis
She come up here to save us from the Tories
She wants a Longbenton'nt or Newbiggin
She got the cold war with the Heaton, oh yeah...
John Profumo . . . Christine Keeler.
Spaghetti bollick- naked
Don't forget the fruit gums.

Like me earlier cadet days, the YCL held frequent camps, deep in the woodlands of Hexham, once quiet little pubs swamped with a black-leather-coated, ex-army-clad YCL and long-haired fellow-travelers. An unobstructed under-age drinking sing-round provided the Dutch courage for even the youngest to sing, me included, sticking to the Irish rebel side of the family repertoire. Which was acceptable, and the banjo player and guitarist could pick and strum along.

Cider was the nectar of the Gods in them days and long sessions in the local hostelry left me severely over-indulged and near to collapse, the room was mobbed and heaving with bodies, so a back window was opened and me near-rigid body was catapulted out the window, to be collected at lowse. Harry the big guitarist carried me on his back and dropped me heed first into me sleeping-bag, except it wasn't, and worse, waking suddenly in the night with a gross feeling of impending sickness upon me, Ah'd struggled fruitlessly to find a way out of whatever it was I was in, ower late, ower late, as the sweet-smelling spew gushed into the foot of the bag and I, by revulsion and to avoid the flood, backed away, away and discovered a way oot. As I staggered from the tent, the night air rapidly folded the rest of the night upon me and I slept drunkenly beneath the stars. Meanwhile Black Tom, the sleeping bag's owner, back from a midnight caper, stripped off and dived feet first into the pleasantly warm sleeping bag.

How the North Was Won

'Fuck, this bag's been out in the rain', he told himself. Next morn the full horror of the cider-like smell in the night, which had kept him blissful with thoughts of apple trees and spring, brought the entire camp out in sympathetic vomiting as Tom emerged from the sleeping bag in big climber's woolly socks, dripping in spew. It was the last time I drank cider and the first time I was hit by a communist.

Other times, as we lay a dozen to a tent, the awkward little get ney mer settled in the Communist Party faithful than with the Popes, inhibitions hidden in booze, Ah'd challenge: 'But why did Russia invade Finland?' And Wilk's voice calmly cutting through the night:

'The world bourgeoisies abandoned the young Soviet state, when it asked for a common front against the fascists. They conspired in the hope that Hitler would finish off the fledgling workers' state, and then they could bring him back in line. So the fascists were advancing through Finland, the Finns couldn't stop them and they wouldn't take the assistance of the Soviet state, but the Reds knew they had a fucking big line of guns, like the Maginot line in France, pointed at Russia, and it could fall into the hands of the Nazis to be used against Russia, so the Russians went in to keep them at bay.'

'What aboot Poland then?'

'That was the same. The Polish government had collapsed. There was no government in Poland, and the Nazis were sweeping towards the Russian border, the Allies had done nothing to defend it, so the Red Army went in to halt the advance.'

Still in the musty back room with the bust of Karl and swirls of smoke, the awkward little bastard would persist in contradicting as he had in the classroom:

'But comrades, if the German Democratic Republic has developed so wonderfully, a purified German workers' state, and instituted a modern socialist state, why is that bluddy geet wall slap through the middle?' The balding worker in the sleeves and braces lowered his glasses in the fashion of the party intellectuals.

'Yee see, my young comrade, one canno' take the conditions of life that surround ye and judge the conditions of other parts of the world by that. Ye must knaa something of the formative backgroond tithe conditions of the GDR.

Before the wall was built, those on the American side of the city did nothing for the industrial development of the country, for education, whilst the GDR spent its meager resources on educating its people, elaborating training programmes, teaching workers skills. The GDR had a low standard of living, and food was cheap. The GFR seduced workers to work in their sector, paying massively higher wages. These workers were crossing back to the GDR to spend their money, and it was breaking the economy, the best-trained people who were needed for the reconstruction of the society were being wooed by good money and social position in the west and from there being taken to the USA and Britain. In addition, comrades, the country were being heavily infiltrated, and we suspected that saboteurs were crossing over to cause shortages and whip up unrest, so when the wall was built it was an action of self-defence, to stop the talent being drained from the country.'

I was hard-pressed to reply, and my discontent reached the stage where I styled mesell a Titoist, and wrote TITO on Newcastle walls, only to find some shit with another lump of chalk had added a couple of fs and a hyphen.

The folk social at the Bridge Hotel packed the upstairs room with songs and visions like I'd never dreamed of, collective singing by everyone in the room. That all these people were pledged to stop the bomb, moved me as nothing thus far in my life. Singing *We Shall Overcome*, with more depth and feeling than any hymn I'd ever heard, with everyone standing up, vornie brought tears to my eyes. I had nicked me sister's tape recorder for the night, it was a prototype with big spools on the top, but all the same that night I swept down the stairs of Castle Garth and over the Swing Bridge, to walk yem for ney other reason than to listen again to the sangs, and swinging me arms like I was at the head of an army.

The Bridge was to become a second yem, and at times a first one, from then on.*

On the trip to Holy Loch, the bus was shared with nice YCND people in zip-up anoraks. The YCLers had brought guitars, and one guy was a decent trumpet player. Beer-cans rolled down the aisle.

Och, och, there's a monster in the Loch
A monster in the Loch, a monster in the Loch,
Och Och, there's a monster in the Loch
And they call it the Polaris.
Tek the whole damn show up the river Alamo
The river Alamo, the river Alamo O, O, O
Tek the whole damn show up the river Alamo
For we dinnet want Polaris.

Edinburgh, where we arrived as darkness fell, seemed to teem with American sailors, and we were warned against wandering the streets for fear of attack, though the lang lanky striding beatniks, their Glaswegian beatnik inspeak ricocheting from the buildings, struck a note of fear and wonder in all. In Bobby's bar, the already developing Bohemian atmosphere was swamped with protesters from near and far, their banners in piles of rolled material and wood covering the floors. Sangs came from every corner, and the license to drink uninterrupted by polisis and the need to gaan yem were enjoyed to full measure. As blood rose full, we were a force, we were a tide of change, we were its anthem, old Scottish communists, men and women, grown-up beatniks, and we the youth, as the communists called wi.

Nuw the Yanks have just dropped anchor in Dunoon,
And we've had a civic welcome frae the toon,

As we cum up the measured mile bonny Mary o 'Argyle
Wes wearing spangled drawers below her goon.
But ye canna spend their dollars when yer deed,
No' ye canna spend their dollars when yer deed,
Singing ding dang dollar, everybody holler,
Ye canna spend their dollars when yer deed.

In the early hours of morning, two greet riverboats, their giant paddle wheels churning up the waves of the Clyde. A white dove of peace flying from the masthead, and numerous red flags from every masthead. Dockside slipways were lined with workers waving, and boats on the river sounded their foghorns. The decks resounded ti 'Excuse me comrade', 'Thank you comrade', while below decks the bar-room rang wi Scottish defiance:

He lives in the White Hoose,
Ah'm sure it's no' the right hoose,
It should be called
the—pooder room
Let's send the Yankees hyme
And its ANTI Polaris
ANTI Polaris
And send the Yankees hyme
Up wi' the rampant lion,
Up wi' the rampant lion,
Up wi' the rampant lion, and send the Yankees hyme.

'Excuse me, my young comrade. Thank you comrade.' On the decks, lang-haired beats in sandshoes and dirty jeans danced slow-timed dreamlike skip jives to trad jazz:.

Gonna lay down my sword and shield, Down by the riverside, down by the riverside.

Astern, the anarchists bombed every passing warship and police launch with empty beer-bottles amid cheers from the Geordies, until we were warned: 'Totally irresponsible, comrades, the polis is no carrying Polaris, and that's what we're here aboot.'

From the boat at Dunoon, a singing, marching, dancing, chanting tide of bodies clapped and sang its way to the sinister half-submerged submarines skulking in the bay, like guilty hippos.

Every Friday night while the Teds still bounced their way to the Madge and their girls' bouffant were stuck like glue, we went out selling *Challenge*, the YCL paper:

Aye in Newcastle was quite a stir, forta mark the closing of the year
For the Beatles on the front of the Challenge were, and we sold a canny few
Lassie cum a towroway.
We started sellin' at early light
And we sold inti the coming night
And we shouting Challenge with all our might
Will ye buy the Challenge nuw, lassie cum a towroway?
Me and Bob Vincent and our gallant band
On Jackson's corner, we took our stand
And the paper it was in big demand,
Will ye buy the Challenge nuw lassie cum a towroway?

On Saturdays, we'd penetrate the heart of trade union Tyneside with *Daily Worker* sales, into Heaton, or Wallsend where shipyards stood cheek by jowl with collieries, and the teeming proletariat stood back to back in smouldering readiness.

'What is it, hinny?'

'Want ti buy a *Daily Worker* ti help kick oot the Tories?'

'Whey bless yi Ah'll buy owt ti get rid o' them.'

'Whey's there?'

'Deyee want ti buy a *Daily Worker* help get rid o' the Tories?

'Me daughter isn't in.'

'Oh isn't she? Well deyee want ti buy a paper ti help get rid o' the Tories?'

'We already voted, hinny, ah dinnit need a paper.'

Aldermaston: veterans of the movement were distinguished by their number of Aldermastons, this year's was to be the triumphant breakthrough from moral minority to mass movement. When the big bag of details arrived in the post, I laid the lists of instructions out on the bed, the colour assigned to the north-east region, our place in the march, our orange baggage-labels, where and when to drop off rucksacks and how to pick them up, minimal things needed. I had had such instructions before my journeys to distant Royal Navy outposts for week and fortnight courses, but this was different, this called for more initiative than any course, and I was basically going alone; as I packed my kit, Dad looked on with mixed cynicism and respect, me Mam fussing aboot with more tins of food and sensible things like toilet rolls.

'Mind the nettles don't sting you down there', she joked.

Aldermaston was indeed a rolling mixture of currents of humanity, but it was the rolling nature of the young marchers which the press had focused on and set me stomach tingling with anticipated 'gaanans on'.

Correct gear included a blanket-lined combat jacket, to which I pinned the campaign medals, Holy Loch 62, and 'Youth Against Germ War and Chemicals'. Chemicals would have been handy, however, since the sister had contracted mumps, and I was avoiding her like the plague as the day of the march drew nearer and gargling night and day with TCP.

A line of coaches stood beside the Central. I sat at the front, amid a small group of YCLers and older CP men, all the bonny lasses in their jeans and leather jackets, with their hair tied in long red ribbons, with a garb and gait that increasingly spelt rebellious youth, political consciousness, shared involvement. Lads with flagons of ale, guitars and rolled-up banners skipped and mocked aboard the bus behind.

'I'm on the wrang bliddy bus', I thought. Still, that crowd had a foreboding exclusiveness and I was not yet part of it.

Dimmed blue lights of the coach, mile on mile of flashing lights and darkened fields, subdued singing of We Shall Overcome, provide a backdrop to deep, drugged sleep, and the sweat poured from me body as a thousand and one mixtures I had swallowed took effect.

In the early hours of the morning, wor bus in a sea of buses and bodies, we disembarked; I felt lousy and looked for a netty. I had been constipated for a fortnight; it was a waste of time. My face ashen, I staggered around half-conscious of crowds, banners, singing, and droves of roly-poly lasses skip jiving down the road. The studious intellectuals raising and flowing hands of plea and point. A girl discussing satire prompted a rush of intellect and me poisoned body rallied.

'Aye, it's good, that.'

'What?' she asked with raised eyebrow, 'that satire—which?' Which? I thought satire was *That Was the Week That Was*. I dint knaa any others.

'*That Was the Week That Was*.'

'Yes', she mused and curled her intellectual nose up, 'sort of, but I was discussing its classical form in *Gulliver's Travels*.'

'Is that satire, like?' The question went unanswered as a tall student interjected with historical satires, and a cloud of grayness passed in a wave over me body. At the first stop, I'd submitted to surrender, stood at a long line of folk seeing the people in the first-aid tent. Sore feet, crying babies, hangovers and 'Ah think Ah've got mumps.'

'Mumps? There's eighty-thousand people on this march', and they whisked me away into the rear of the tent. I was to be transported from point to point in a Land Rover, then packed off home at the end of the march. . . . But it wasn't to be.

Despite an interesting test of me potency with a student nurse, me glands in me throat continued to swell, me throat rasped red, me head was swimming and there was a feeling of rising panic in me stomach. I struggled from the camp bed, out into the dark of the landing; below, the wounded, footsore marchers slept or quietly strummed guitars. I staggered to the top of the stairs and feebly cried out: 'Will someone help me, please?' Then knees buckled and I distantly felt bump, bump, crumple, as I bounced down the stairs.

I awoke in Maidenhead isolation hospital, gills swelled up like balloons, eyes bloodshot, belly in a knot. A room of me own—it was just as well. In comes the nurse. Return of the starch, pulls down the bedclothes, 'Turn over' (turn over?), yanks up the nightshirt Ah'd been given, while pulling on long plastic gloves, then wham! she stuck her geet lang middle finger right up me bum and I screamed, then she crooked her finger and went 'Naa, naa, naa' and twisted it aboot as me heed vibrated in physical shock.

A bedpan was brought a little later, but they needn't have bothered. Later on I was allowed to the toilet with shaky steps, but I needn't have bothered. Next day in comes the starch, and starts pulling the gloves on

'Woh, woh', says I, 'Ah divind need that again.'

'Have you been?'

'Been? I was in all day, oh aye Ah've been, by God Ah've been.'

'Turn over.'

'Oh, no.'

Wap.

'Ahh!'

'Naa, naa, naa.'

'Ahh!' Nay problem this time, bedpan, bedpan, bedpan—oh, bloody hell. Ah really did think it would overflow. . . . I got to go to the toilet, every time Ah stood up and walked away, Ah had to rush back in again.

Lying in bed, throat red raw, arse red raw, jowls gynormous, and throbbing pain behind me lugs, listening to the earphone news of the march as it neared London, where groups of youths and 'anarchists' broke away from the main march and spread across the road, blocking the traffic. Stewards and police had tried to control the black-leather-jacketed and longhaired people. Me imagination was ablaze and Ah felt robbed of a place in history and thought these anarchists seemed much more fun than the grey studiousness of the YCL. Still, the local YCND came to see is and bring me books, even tried to get a grip with one middle-class lassie, but it was a bit incredible, me in a night-shirt in bed, weak as a kitten, her fully clothed in polo neck and jackboots sitting in the green chair, but I was awarded me campaign medal—Aldermaston '63—to add to the row of badges on the combat jacket, stuck out in a line like a medal ribbon.

Newcastle Bigg Market was closed off on a Sunday neet, a remnant of some ancient freedom, and the preachers gathered, each in a circle, the crowds of toon folk en route to pubs would tarry to taunt and laugh, then take the challenge and become engrossed in argument, the sky-pilots, various public speakers, the pacifists, wild and hairy, the anarchists, poets shouting the growing free-verse beat philosophy, and the Communist Party stand, a wee platform behind which stands the graying, wild-eyed communist seaman—and Black Tom, taking the platform for the first time:

'They say it's an affluent society. Look at the unemployed kids here, ney work, no' for the kids an affluent society. . . .' Then he froze, his big bottle-bottomed glasses steaming up. We thought he'd done great, said just what needed to be said.

'Ah, there's plenty jobs, just a set of lazy kids who don't want work', voiced by a disheveled bloke in a raincoat. This set the scene for me first public voice.

'Nonsense', in measured reply. 'Ah want a job. Ah,'ll dee owt. Tell me where there's a job, Ah'll dee it.' The crowd cheered.

'Ah'll get yee a job the morra, -the morra.' His face angry and determined, me feared.

'What aboot the thoosands unemployed, my mates from skuel?' The old CP shipyard worker tugged, while the raincoated job-finder thundered:

'Ye see, he dissent want a job, just uses it for propaganda. Brainwashed young 'uns. The commies brainwash these young uns.'

The aud CP guy: 'Forget the thoosands, ask him where's your job.'

'Alreet, alreet, tell me the job, Ah'll dee it, Ah'll dee it.' And Ah meant it. -

'Which job?' the crowd cried. 'Which job?'

'Ye be here the morra at nine, and Ah'll get yee a job.' Taking the cue, I followed it through.

"Aal reet,' I crowed nuw, addressing the crowd from the street, 'Ah'll be here the morn at nine, yee be here.' And, waving ti the crowd, 'And yee be here likewise.'

The crowd swept on tithe bridge following the session, the CP and the YCL glowing with Tom and me. And the next morn I dutifully turned up. Ney Mr. Raincoat Man, but a number of Holy Rollers who had come ootta curiosity for the showdown, and older unemployed tired of the argument, and a few of 'the youth', as they insisted on calling us, like a new breed or species. Raincoat Man re-emerged a week or two later and started again, but the old party Veteran thumped the stand: -

'Yee cheered the heart of a young boy, offering him the job he always wanted. That boy borrowed the money to get here where ye said yee'd provide the work—but yee weren't here! Because the guff in the paper isn't work, and though yee believe it, it can't conjure up work—not even for one willing lad.' It became a starting point for many a Bigg Market lecture, and I overnight gained an honest reputation: the willing unemployed lad.

As darkness fell, the crowds milled round the Holy Rollers.

'I have been a wicked, wicked woman, I have known of men, I have known of the drink, but now I've found Jesus, amen!' She's only twelve, and the crowd guffaws. The Sally Army wifies scolding the longhaired beatniks prancing and affecting a mime to her every scold of damnation. To her challenge that they are Satan's children, a beardy responds: 'Ye're a wicked, wicked old woman rejoicing in nowt but repression, gaanon doon ti see yon aud Stalinist there and get yersell laid.'

'Amen', saieth the crowd, stitched up in laughter.

Barney stands like a scene from the 1930s, his spot booked for a generation on the steps of the watter spoot, wearing a grey, crumpled, gabardine mackintosh, cap held in front of him as if at a funeral, head almost bald, grey wisps blowing oot fra' the sides, a speck of energy, undimmed by his years, a fusion of Jewishness and Northumbrian, of pacifism and radical socialism, he speaks for his party, long since gone from corridors of office, its heroes a distant dusty page of history. To Barny, obscurity was the price of principle. In his curling, burring Northumbrian, he berated 'the warmongers and traitors in the coats of Labour. Renoonce war, divind just march for it, divind tell ithers what ti dee, start wi yee, refuse ti sanction war, refuse to take up arms, hail all workers as wor brothers.'[11]

Beside him on the crumpling rostrum, in khaki shirt, belt and braces, his shirt tucked into his underpants so the white top keeked above the troosers, the inevitable haversack containing copies of *Sanity* and *Labour Leader*, the self-educated Douglas Kepper, a southern unemployed railway worker and keeper of the ILP's temple on Shields Road. Neither had yet met the barbarians whose hordes would break down the continuity that fascism and social-chauvinism hadn't dinted. Kepper berates the Communist Party for its record in the second war: 'And the CP members would sneak round London painting swastikas on the wall, only to be photographed the next morning for the *Daily Worker* headline: "Fascist Outbreak in London, Join the CP to Stem the Menace"— to shouts of 'Tommy-rot' from the lofty red-cheeked YCLer Rob Davies. The crowd choruses: 'Oooh.'

'They used to say, when I was selling my socialist paper, and that means of course my anti-war paper, "Still selling your fascist paper then?" The Communist Party, so-called, became as big a set of war-mongers as Churchill, urging workers to work harder and not to strike. They took the boss's side in a bosses' war.' Serious cross-arguments up and down the ranks, the speakers talk across one another, the beatniks in mock send-up of the CP: 'I'm against war. I hate war—and I'll kill to stop another one!'

The crowd drifts down to the Bridge, still arguing. In more serious vein, the vying contenders in public polemic now strike a more conciliatory guise, the arm around the shoulder:

'Now look, let's explain.'

'Oh aye, aye, that 'ud be reet nuw, but that's not what yee said.'

The musty backroom packed with mystery, ancients supping orange juice, explaining to a well under-age young anarchist: 'Nuw Ah wes with your Prince Kropotkin when he cum ti Newcastle, and a vorry interesting man he wes, tee.' The subculture of moppish hair, longer than seen in a hundred years, but shortish by later standards, corduroy jackets, fraying jeans. A becapped worker smelling of diesel oil from the railway, handing over smudged Little Lenins. Strumming guitars of YCL and Nogbad's resonance:

Once there were trees and a river,
Once there was grass where yi stand,
Once there was songs about rights instead of wrongs,
Once was the time of man.

The song mirrored the perceived union of thought. Despite what other badges they wore, all wore CND's badge. Despite other prefixes and suffixes, 'peace' was the word, and the passion now in all was to get rid of The Bomb, The Bomb. The word was enough to conjure up the annihilation of all, without fear or favour. But the communists knew and knowingly winked or cocked the head to a comrade:

Now they didn't know in the old times
That the lands and the seas were to share
They didn't know in the old times or dare.

Once there was trees and a river,
Once there was grass where you stand,
Once there were songs about rights instead of wrongs,
Once was the time of man.

Doon from Windmill Hill it came, a great torchlight procession of the unemployed. It was a Communist Party initiative. On each corner a couple of young communists hand out fresh lumps of wood, wrapped round on the end with petrol-soaked clouts, the air alive with smoke and shadow, flames and gawpin' folk. Had we come to burn something or other, to raid something? Was wor anger such that Newcastle and Gateshead had risen? No, it just looked that way. 'Tories oot, Labour in, Tories oot, Labour in, Tories oot, Labour in.' The chant became meaningless and the giggling rabble added to it: 'Tarrytoot, Lerisin, Tarrytoot, Lerisin, Tories oot, Labour in.' Fresh with me knowledge of pamphlets and lectures, at the head of me first Labour march, unemployed and angry, time for summit more daring: 'CAP-IT-AL-ISM', and a few responded: 'OOT'. 'CAP-IT-AL-ISM—'

A grip comes ti me elbow, it's Nogbad.

'Eh, Dave, it's good, good shouting, Dave, but there's a lot o' young uns on the march won't understand like you do, about capitalism and that, Dave, better keep it simple.' And, taking me into his much-esteemed confidence: 'You understand, comrade.' Ho, well, did I understand?

'But of course, comrade.'

'Tarrytoot Lerisin, Tarrytootlerisin', crossing the Swing Bridge, a burning dragon trailed Bottle Bank and right across the River. Passing the University area en route to the ITV Studios, a column~ of students joined in. 'Trots', I was told.

'Trots? What are they?' University Young Socialists—students. Ah think students are randy, me mind clicked, and me feet fell back to take a look at the randy student Trot people, but the girls were fat—I didn't like fat girls, not that way—and the blokes were all spotty Willicks. Still, it shook me, as out the gobs of the front 'uns:

'CAPITALISM OUT, CAPITALISM OUT!' Willingly joining in the shout, to show I knew, I knew. 'COMMUNISM': in/out in/out, the responses were mixed.

'SOCIALISM', they countered, and we all shouted 'IN, SOCIALISM IN' Not to be outdone, and fresh from me YCL lectures:

'IRAQI FASCISTS OUT—' the arm gets gripped. 'Dave' Nogbad is back.

'Ah knaa, Ah knaa, Ah forgot.'

Reaching the ITV studios, we caught the publicity and were planning to walk past and disperse. But some of the Bigg Market crowd were bunching up and stopping the march passing. Police started to get anxious and began pushing the crowd backwards. Suddenly burning comets roared overhead as the sticks started to burn through. The Gateshead raggy lads at the back were flicking the burning ends straight into the cops' ranks, one through the open window of an empty police car. An involuntary 'HAWAY' burst from me lips and the will to surge forward took me feet some steps in that direction together with one or two of the Bigg Market crowd, but the advance was stopped by Nogbad and other lofty characters:

'Come on, lads, we don't want this to become a bore, do we?' The flat open hands of reason. We've made wa point, comrades, this was our march, Ah'd ask nobody to spoil it. Come on, Dave, social down at the Nelson.' Ah, well. . . and in the narrow back room of the Nelson, Maureen Wood, an even newer and younger young communist than me, and first target of passion since leaving school, sang House of the Rising Sun. Everyone's mind's eye fell not on New Orleans but on the Doonbeat, even those who like me hadn't been there, a club of underground, sensuous, forbidden resistance and magic.

There comes a slow awareness of the Geordie beat poets. The big-bearded, prematurely balding beat stood legs astride to read, fearlessly . . . such words, unrhyming, just talking and swearing. .

We all laughed every time he said 'fuck', but we listened to little else. I asked the big red-cheeked farmer's boy, who was an illicit source of unconventional knowledge, how this was.

'Poetry, Davy, yee shudn't confuse with whatever crap they give ye at school.' Oddly enough, such memories of the tap tap of the brown sea rat, and I must go down to the sea again, were happy ones.

'Poetry is just saying feelings, like the blues I loaned ye, it's the things on ya mind, it needn't be rhyming, only if it comes oot that road. Listen:

I do not wish to drive a cart,
But walk on a lush pasture
And feel the gentle kiss of a summer
Breeze cascading from the sky.

'Isn't that poetry?'

'Aye, Ah suppose it is.'

'Nuw then, here's a copy of *Red Flag*. It's the Trots you were asking about. Ah dinnet agree with this group mesell but it's close.'

The magical paper fairly glowed, emblazoned with the words RED FLAG and the bold hammer and sickle. The words didn't make much sense, though, so I stuck it up on me wall at hyme, which had now ceased to be clandestine. Lumumba had been there since I was thirteen. My deep respect for the man had moved something in me dad, and he allowed the cuttings. Mind it must in honesty also be said pride of place on one wall was a Nazi German Submarine ensign. This too, resplendent in its own way, with its Swastika and Germanic Cross, was a much prized possession. I was within the catchment of that generation that had collected world war two memorabilia. Boxes of ammunition a great deal of it still live, 303 cartridges, mortar shells, bayonets, swords, gas masks and owt else. The Nazi stuff was unspeakably cool. I was just coming to the deep realisation of the politics of this force, in much the way and time as I had that of the British state. But at this time, war, navies, guns and flags were still mystical and magical. I would be a liar if I denied that the Nazi navel flag hadn't stayed up there along with the Lumumba cuttings and now Red Flag, but whereas these latter were part of my political awakening and choosing of a side, the former was a legacy of something else. It must also be said, a few of my acquaintances from the estate with a similar interest for all things Nazi and warlike and military , developed from the point of thinking it cool and 'edgy' as we would have said, and took the path to the far right as a political progression. A couple became young Nazis within the NSM then founder members of the National Front. There was a time when I used our closeness of association to help set up a violent confrontation with the Tyneside Nazis, an ambush if you like, the consequences of this were to be fatal and best left unelaborated. From that time on, me and these fellow young workers, fellow miners sons, and Wardley lads were to be irreconcilable foes. Despite the fact, they still greeted my parents with respect and civility when they met, and I worked down the mine with their Dads for a time. Gordon's Dad, a hugely comic man and solid Trade Unionist would scratch his head in utter bewilderment at his son's political trajectory. Mind, my Dad too bewailed the Anarchist in his house and the crazy kid who was emerging from the social democratic cocoon of moderation and stability they had tried to construct.

Maureen Wood, the first girl I fell for, and her mate had come to the YCL camp at Hexham in her denim shirt with black polo underneath, her jeans tight round her bum. Her eyes were like twinkling dark stars, her face always a mass of smiles. She slept in a tent with a lad—Mick, I think, Mick

Turnbull—she fancied coz he looked and dressed like Ringo Starr. I heard him tell his mate next morn: 'She says she'll ler is next time', and I was at once erect and jealous at the same time. She had noticed me, though, and I tried awkwardly to get to talk to her. On the bus back hyme she sat behind me, still with Ringo. I wrote the second poem I had ever written as the bus bounced back to the city and the comrades sang:

'Flying higher and higher and higher, Our emblem the Soviet star, And every propeller is roaring, Defending the USSR!' She was the first girl I had ever loved.

Walking back from socials and meetings, we would walk home, just to be together, me yammering on about politics, history, poetry, two nights running, walking, yammer yammer. On the third night, coming down the dark lane that led to her house, she walked over to a doorway in an office building and stood.

'What's that?' I asked stupidly.

'It's a doorway', she replied, sliding her arms around me. Thick? I was always so concerned at making an impression as a wise and thoughtful lad; I missed some of the basics, like actually necking with the girl I constructed my fantasies and poetry round. That night I wrote another poem.

But this would be a short-lived fling. Forra start I was scared shitless because Ringo, jealous and angry, was gunning for me, determined to get 'his woman' back. Then it was suddenly over. I wrote yet another poem.

A week later, I had discovered Pauline and written a poem to her.

The day I got an interview—bakery, Fewster Square on the learn—I was given the job. A baker's apprentice. How, lad, did I skip hyme that day? The 'C' class indignities were wiped aside, and me folks fair bubbled with happiness. To me ma (for Ah'd nuw stopped calling her Mammy as me sister urged it to be soft and square, a fatal combination) it

Young, gifted and Geordie (1962)

was in the family blood. Many of her brothers had been bakers in Navan and various relatives before.

It was the first job, indescribable as an achievement, though the 64 hours a week were long, the first pay's £3/9d to take home proved that Ah had really left school. Baking and confectionery's many skills and the pleasure of achievement started to find an awkward place in my soul. But it was not to last. Philosophizing ower the iced buns and preaching the forthcoming workers' revolution in a small family bakery didn't gaan doon weel. Neither did me odd disaster.

The new Olympic-size swimming pool in the Square had just opened. Through the great glass doors and up the stairs was a small cafeteria overlooking the baths. At the top of the stairs was a veranda directly over the baths. My task—quite Herculean, Ah thowt mesell—was ti carry a full tray of steak-and-kidney pies from the shop through the Square into the cafeteria. Bedecked in me full baker's outfit, including the white baker's bonnet, I set off. It was impossible to walk and carry the tray with two hands, so I adopted the style of the waiter. The tray aloft me heed supported on one hand, I walked nonchalantly up the road though secretly groaning under the strain. I had got through the glass doors and mounted the first flight of steps when suddenly the doors opened again and a greet gust of wind lifted the tray and propelled it at speed to the edge of the veranda, where, blocked by the bars, it catapulted the complete contents into the baths.

Pandemonium and hysteria below, some swimmers had been splattered by pies and heads and faces bore the runny broon evidence, some eagle-eyed swimmers had caught them in mid-flight and trod waater while enjoying the unexpected and gratis bait. The rest of the baths carried the flotilla of the pie fleet, some braving the waves, others in various stages of sinking, not a pretty sight and merry hell to pay back at the bakery. Ah wasn't lang getting the push.

Stardust

I came upon a child of God
He was walking along the road
And I asked him where you are going
This is what he told me
He said I'm going on down to Yasgur's farm
I'm gonna join in a Rock'n'Roll band
I'm gonna camp out on the land
And try and set my soul free
He said, we are stardust
He said, we are golden
And we've got to back ourselves
Back to the Garden
I asked him, can I walk beside you
I have come here to lose the smog
I feel like I'm a cog, in something turning
Round and round and round
Well maybe it's just the time of year
Or maybe it's the time of man
I don't know who I am
But life is for learning
I know we're stardust
I think we're golden
And we've got to get ourselves
Back to the garden
By the time we got to Woodstock
We were half a million strong

And everywhere you looked, there was song and celebration
That night I dreamed I saw the bombers
Up there riding shot gun in the sky
And they were turning to butterflies
Up above our nation
We are stardust
Come from billion-year-old carbon
We are golden
We just got caught up in some devil's bargain
And we've got to get ourselves
Back to the garden.[12]

6
Into the World of OZ

As in *The Wizard of Oz,* when I encountered the ILP Hall on Shields Road the world changed from the black and white, or grey, of the Young Communist League's brand of Marxism to a spinning-top of whirling Technicolor.

We had been, the YCL and I, to a Saturday-morning meeting of the Tyneside Youth Employment Committee Council at the Delector Hall in Raby Street. After the meeting, we sauntered over to what was becoming a stronghold of 'the progressive youth', as the comrades called them, the scene of the residue of the ILP, who numbered among them surviving suffragettes. The Heaton CND held their meetings there, and moves were afoot to found a Direct Action movement to confront the nuclear state.

At the end of the narrow back street, a strange youth in a big coat, with eyes like dinner-plates and a skull like a black dome, wrote DESTRUAM ET ARDIFICABO on the wall. He eyed me suspiciously and said it meant 'I shall destroy and I shall build', then giggled strangely. This was Dave Wallace.

Inside, the afternoon binge was getting under way, Spanish cittern, the language of debate and the street. Rhythm and blues: DOO DOO DO DUM ... DOO DOO DO DUM . . .

Wallace was a grammar-school boy but not at all like the 'pumps', the Willy-wets I had met earlier. Forra start he spoke in pure Shields dialect, heavy on Saxon. True, he claimed to be bisexual and berated all for repressing the homosexual side of their nature, but we only ever seen him trying to get off with lasses. His dad was a bus driver, his Mam worked in the chippy, his granddad was a retired, though still revolutionary, miner, and his gran smoked a

Tyneside Committee of 100

pipe, he said.

The Tyneside Committee of 100 was aboot to form. In me ignorance, like many others I imagined it was the ruling body of the CND and I thought I would earn me first promotion in the movement. In the evenings I attended the ILP meetings, where all the folk seemed to suffer from one facial deficiency or another: Doug Kepper with his spluttering twitch; an aud bald bloke whese gob stuck on the side; poor Mrs. Bell, a surviving suffragette and Heaton heroine who had rescued bairns from a burning hoose and suffered the loss of her beauty and vornie all her face, skin an' all. For all that and their slightly intellectual aura, their position on war and weapons was unequivocal: they were in essence pacifist socialists, with a body-and-soul anti-capitalist belief and a deep conviction for co-operation and fraternity. They were like people time had forgot: they were us but left over from the first time round.

The day that the Glasgow-to-London march hit Newcastle, a lang-haired, bearded, anarchic team strove forard carrying

Scottish Committee of 100 Glasgow-to-London March crossing the Tyne Bridge: (left) Andy McGowan, Doug Kepper, Clem Alford, Ken Sutherland; (right): unknown, John Samson, unknown, unknown.

a replica of a Polaris missile ambiguously labeled 'DEATH TO A MILLION CHILDREN!'. This fusion of the Bigg Market ILPers, (The Bigg Market was a sort of Tyneside Hyde Park Corner where speakers and tendencies, holy rollers and anyone with a rant to air assembled and let rip) the beats, the hip freaks, the pacifists and the anarchists carried a sacred glow of mystery and, with me basking in that glow, it was the day the circus hit town. It led me to the ILP hall on Shields Road, where the march kipped doon for the neet, and a social had been planned. While the Stones...

C'mon . . . ever since we parted
C'mon, can't get the car started
Laid up from my job and I can't afford to check it
I wish somebody'd come along, run into it, and wreck it
C'mon, every time the phone rings sounds like thunder.

Some stupid jerk trying to reach another number
C'mon. . . .

The beats prance out the bell-bottomed leg stride, hair in cascading waves, girls in denim shirts and polo necks skip and shake, jumping to the side. The music runs down undulating arms and breasts and off the pulsing hips. Harmonicas wailed and bass turned to full, doom! doom! doom! doom! doom! doom! doom! of the blues vibrating the windows in their frames. In corners on the floor people sat and philosophised while we swigged broon from bottles bought en route.

It was in this room that we formed the Tyneside Committee of 100, where I met the Geordie beat poet Tony Jackson, where the schizoid Wallace became the first secretary, having served his time with Jackson at Shields CND. It was here that the moon-faced character Dave Reynolds with his gadgets and transistor valves and squealing receivers constructed the peace radio.

Jackson, the beat poet, dark glasses on his fat face but beardless at this point, huge white knitted sweater, sandals and box-file of poetry, traveled back with him on the last bus from Worswick Street, philosophised, fantasised, felt the stare of straight proletarian eyes, felt the hostility of the Ted generation which was stagnating, felt a part of the bold, emerging beat red generation. A new world was emerging. A new set of configurations was growing somewhere behind me brain. Jackson opened out his box file, drew out a sheet and read without the slightest inhibition on the bus full of late-night drinkers returning home:

I want to make you a poem, my love
So as to hold you to me
Without you ever
Wishing to depart
I want to bring

Wild flowers
From the valleys
For thee
And shells from the sea bed
Both of which
You shall love
Unto extinction.
But I am with you beloved
To hold your hand
And to stroke your soft hair.

I blushed throughout in case the piss-takers on the back seat thought he had written it to me! I dared to think but not yet to write myself. My attempts were laboured if honest., on reflection they were shite, but the fact that I was writing, writing feelings, colouring words, trying to capture in speech emotions, was actually the launching pad of my intelligence ,it was the intellectual equivalent of swimming my first width.

Les H was a man who always struck me as a white Negro. His stiff wiry hair and rhythmic stride contributed, but he was obsessed with the blues, raked through from old 78s and obscure American LPs. His darkened bedroom overlooking the Heaton railway line resonated with the heavy bass turned to full and the treble vornie off. He carried the air of the Mississippi Delta. Blues, real black man's blues, was a cult on Tyneside among progressive teenagers. They raked through old 78s at jumble sales and in junk-shops, they traded stuff with the foreign seamen on the quay, they hoarded records, which had never seen the light of day in the USA and raved over black bluesmen few outside of their Native American states had heard of. Les actually had a multi-track 78 of Leadbelly reading kids' nursery stories. We all got to know *The Billy Goats Gruff* off by heart. There was a bond between the dispossessed and abandoned kids of the northeast and the lives and struggles of black people in the states. The Geordies were the white niggers! Their music would become body and soul our music. We didn't know it then, but something similar had been happening down in Liverpool, a radical hard city also abandoned by the southern ruling class and left to fend for itself since the 1930s. Scouses were to become soul mates too, as the beat attitudes of an emerging youth culture started to come together.

Mick Renwick, a Newcastle pitman's son, who's Dad worked at the Wallsend Rising Sun Colliery, introduced me to Dylan, changing and orchestrating my life. I was dossing at Mick's place, where we squatted on the floor and listened to this message, this revealing of wa souls' own contents, this spellin'-oot of yet unspoken urges. With his musing of long-suffering folks on a knife's edge, Dylan would remain the poet of the generation as long as he reflected it:

Mothers and fathers throughout the land
Don't criticise what you can't understand
For your sons and your daughters are beyond your command.
Your old road is rapidly aging
Please get out of the new one if you can't lend a hand.

The world was a maelstrom, swirling with philosophy, ways of living, testing all borders and barriers of reality. Ralph Robertson, guru of spirit, Vedantists, Buddhists, yogis, occultists; matter and strict scientific materialism shattered before moon-like blue of eyes beaming with wisdom and sympathy and permanent radiance of his smile.

Tensions at home caused no such gush of empathy, but rows and verbal fury as the young rebel clashed now with me Da, later and later nights, increasingly not coming back.

As the movement developed, a network became apparent, more a route of kindred cultures between Liverpool, Newcastle, London, Edinburgh and Glasgow. On the weekend of the Birmingham Outer Circle march we stood on the Newcastle side of the Tyne Bridge, four embryos of an awakening minority, archetypal; me in me denim shirt with black polo neck, me waistcoat, me black bells, me combat jacket; Les in his specs and donkey jacket with the already ancient Aldermaston '62 badge, ragged blue bell-bottoms and faded hush puppies, hitching a lift; Cathy, wild, passionate, sexually the vanguard of uninhibition, her blonde hair blowing across her headband, she skipped the Downbeat stomp around the tall thin banjo-player from Stockport, his banjo slung on his back, their hair blew together. We crammed into the big truck, a heap of dedication and newness. Stockport man struck out on the banjo

I am a wagon driver, boys, Delaney is me name,

You're in, your on your own, me boys, in the heavy transport game.

I keep me wagon rolling, boys, however tired I feel

I've been serving of me twenty one years behind a steering wheel..

This bemused the lorry-driver, already half-plussed by me and Cath vigorously touching each other up and raising the heat in the cab some degrees.

The Outer Circle march was part of the FALLX '63 exercise commissioned by CND nationally. Object: to show up the total lack of provision in the event of nuclear war. Here in Birmingham, we'd march roond the periphery of Birmingham's Ooter Circle Ring Road, mapping oot the extent of a small nuclear blast within its boundaries. Hospitals, fire stations, water department etc. had been contacted and asked what, in the event of such a bomb to this extent, were their contingencies. There was nen of course; in any case, hospitals, fire departments and sewage disposal would aal hev gone in the mushroom blast with the inner circle, the ooter circle, and the whole of Birmingham. Still, it seemed a worthwhile exercise.

Les and me stopped behind to find a job, slept in doorways, moved on by the law, dossed in bus-shelters till, totally skint and starving, we headed back to Newcastle. Hitching, walking, dossing by the roadside, we resembled the US bums we sometimes sang about, mile on mile, 'a-walking down the road, just walking down the road'.

Passing a snadgy field, we leapt the fence and massacred them. Sitting on the fence, wagging wa feet, gobs filled with turnip, we looked up to see, some thirty feet distant, a huge police station, and peering oot of every window was huge policemen, and crossing the road toward us were several more. Shit!

Arrested for stealing turnips! Sitting in the cold cells, we speculated on the prison photos of Trotsky, Lenin and the Wobblies, political subversives, revolutionaries and us two caught snadging snadgies. But after we'd coppered up the few pence we had between us to pay toward the cost of the turnip, they let us gaan. Shortly afterwards we were pursued by a police car but needn't have worried as the cop stopped and thrust oot the open window a packet of crackers and some cheese; wor confusion, gratitude and hunger rendered wi speechless before he drove off again. We didn't philosophise, just ate ravenously. We vornie walked the whole road yem. I landed at me Ma's back door, dust-covered, matted hair, starving and glad to be fed, slept for two days. Never liked Birmingham since.

Growing knots in me guts at seemingly endless

unemployment, queues for jobs which had gone the previous night, lack of money, led is to turn a covert YCL whitewash campaign into a virtual kamikaze assault on the city walls. While the teams broke up and spread doon quiet back lanes to paint END UNEMPLOYMENT and TORIES OUT, me and Val, a small dark-haired YCL girl in huge-framed glasses and a geet lang leather coat who always carried the seductive air of the stereotype of a Russian spy, set oot for mer adventurous targets. I carried the paint-pot and brush, Val was the toot. Me greatest coup was a huge YOUTH NEEDS WORK on the Ministry of (un) Employment offices near Gallowgate. This new prestigious office block, walled in smart grey slate, fair glowed under the new ornamentation. It caught the press as some passing photographer framed the slogan alongside the recently introduced parking meters and titled it in the local rag: 'NEWCASTLE TODAY'. Luckily, the paper didn't appear until after our narrow escape from the bosh.

We had progressed along Percy Street, past the Go Go and, while Val kept watch (she said), engaged a huge wall, with the mer interesting slogan MONEY ON JOBS, NOT ARMS. Unfortunately, the recently introduced parking meters had held Val's attention a little ower lang as the menacing step of a cop advanced toward is, though reet past her. She, seeing little point in a hopeless cause, took off, typical of a Russian spy really. I had got as far as MONEY ON JOBS, NO, when a voice fernant me neck went: 'How.... Picasso. What the fuck ye think yer deyin?'

Grabbed, dejectedly tellin' me plight, unemployed, end of road, didn't know how to spell 'arms' or was it 'alms', had ti dee summit, yes, it wes a one-off, no, I wes on me aan. ... He ler is gaan, cud ye believe? He ler is gaan. Mark yee, if he'd known several other Picasso's adorned the city and one was to make the local paper, Ah ha' me doots that Ah'd Iv been inside that night and not able to bask in the full glow of the comrades' congratulations when next wi met.

Still, the city commuters, the workers, the students, passed the geet waal and mused. MONEY ON JOBS ... NO. 'Ah ... it was obviously an ironic comment: no money for jobs', concluded the student leftist ... whey nor the worker, MONEY ON JOBS-NO! it was the growing Tory youth revolt which older Geordie workers warned of, the drive-the-scab-train syndrome not at all, dear comrade.... Spotty Willick student to bus-borne worker: 'The students are overwhelmingly conscious of the unemployed plight and are with you....' The wit: 'Yer aal wrang ... it's a Spanish emigrant, probably from the Civil War, whey's complaining his kid cannit get a job

... he's wrote luek, luek MONEY ON JOBS. NO?

I wanted to finish it, or paint it oot. Every day I passed it, but the cops always staked it oot. Ten years later they pulled the wall doon. Not the cops, the civic authorities. But anly me, and Val, and the benevolent cop knaa the truth and yee of course, nuw.

7
Keep Alec Great

We must have the bomb To give Alec aplomb
So he could look finer
Than
France or China In a nuclear seat at the top.

Forget all the tensions, Poor housing, small pensions,
Two thousand million is little to pay So Alec can have his nuclear say
In his favourite seat at the top.

And please don't complain
'It's immoral, insane',
You'll be put in your place As a beatnik, a red. just watch Alec race
For his nuclear seat at the top.

Just watch the crowd's cheers, As, with smiles and with tears,
They consent to the doom of the world To keep Alec installed
In his favourite seat at the top.

Following Mandy's and Christine's coup, Mac fell from grace, and Alex Hume the 'aud Man of Munich', as the CP called him was ushered in. His leadership debut was to be at the City Hall, the urban reds, the broad Labour movement and busloads of students gathered to greet him, me with a bag full of tomatoes and a huge red flag on a stout eight-foot pole. As the croods milled and heaved the busloads of toadies arrived and were splattered with volleys of tomatoes and toilet rolls. The CP faithful chanted: 'MAN OF MUNICH! MAN OF MUNICH!' We the youth: 'Gaan yem, yee bums, gaan yem, yee bums, gaan yem, ye bums, gaan yem.' Then a great black car swept forward and the balding skull stepped from the car to mount the steps of the City Hall. Nor ney comfort in this city, bonny lad, let the TV see Geordie Poower. A red surge of anarchists and weirdies took me in heedlang charge to the steps (alone, I later discovered) and I started to moont the steps three at a time, 'Tory bastards', the greet reed flag billowing in the evening breeze. A cop hastily bounces doon the steps to meet is, another takes a flying leap from behind and pulls is backwards just as the front cop trips and lands nigh enough on the end of the pole, which, wedged in the nuek of the concrete steps, winnit yield its fulcrum and, pulled backward by the weight of PC Boot-heed and gravity and my own seven stone, the cop is catapulted in a full arc heed ower heels to land with a lood 'crump' on the street. Pulled, dragged, carried, bounced, Ah'm precipitated to the meat-wagon. Three or four others are in the darkened van.

'On the floor, pig', a voice rang oot. My hair is grabbed, heed pushed down to the floor, ootside the crowd brays the sides, sings, shoots, but the van is led away slowly through the crowd. Cellmate is Sandy, one of the YCL lasses initiated with me, but she was sharp moved into another cell; later her mother, a hell of a strict woman, could clearly be heard beating the rice oot of 'a. The other three, the unemployed baker's apprentice and two students, sat musing ower their plight until we struck up loudly *The Red Flag*. We had got to the second verse when in strolled Sarge Brainbox.

'Ye knaa where that sang comes from?' (Actually James Connell wrote it, but why spoil his lecture?) 'Whey, where that sang comes from, if yee'd done there what ye've just dun here, where de'yee think ye's'ud be?'

We all shrugged.

'YE'D ALL BE IN JAIL', he pronounced. We looked at him through the bars then bust oot laughing. He didn't ken the joke; we didn't ken his message.

When at last we were hauled before the magistrates, Sandy was in contrite mood, having had all forms of parental punishment inflicted. Not I and earned a contempt of court alang with the fine. Course, it wes me Da's money I wes protesting with, but that hadn't occurred ti me at the time.

'And you, young man', the old female magistrate in the juvenile court thundered, 'if our prime minister wishes to visit this city of ours, you have no right to obstruct him. Don't you believe in democracy?'

'Aye,' I countered, 'Ah wonder whe elected yee?

'Take him from the court, take him from the court', passin' me Dad, who had one of those twitches in his eye which usually preceded him taking a swipe at me. While the students outside raised cash for their arrested comrades, no such funding was to come my way, snobby gets.

Ye see, part of the problem was at the initial hearin'. When all the lot of wi was herded into a big dock, aal the big lads, the student, a Liberal, believe it or not an anarchist an' aal and another bloke whey confessed ti just bein' awkward, whey wasn't at the demo, just gaanin' yem when the cops got in the road; the charges and what happened was read oot. Whey the other, auder blokes was all swearin' nen-violence, peaceful protest, ney projectiles and the like, me, whey the read such glorious things Ah'm supposed ti hev done it was ower good to miss. Threw a policeman straight through the air ... broke his arm! Flattened another one, cut his heed, smacked another wi' the pole.

'How do you plead?' said the beak in the geet court. A few moments while I jostled through to the front rank, pushing the softy's oot the road. Me? Knocking ower half the Newcastle police force? Whey, 'guilty', of course ... dey the same again. Course, Ah didn't really ... they and me was a victim of circumstances and gravity, Ah suppose ... that and Einstein's theory of relativity.

Anyway, it would look grand in the yarns in the movement, 'cept whey wad really believe I had dun all them things?

Whey all the softies and students got kept, me and Sandy were referred to the juvenile court.

My quest to ken the occult world took me first to yoga, to pranayama thinking about breathing ... when you've nevor givin it a thought afore, to find an inner equilibrium, to struggle with meanings of Vishnu.

Sitaar aar aaaar sitar aaar aaaar, the snake before my vision in coils through the asanas. I see before me the padmasana figure facing away... at the lowest vertebra Kundalini and the four-leaved lotus and the figure swivels to face with the six-leaved lotus over the nervous sexual Centre,the ten-leaved lotus Manipura over the nervous navel, anahata, the chakra of the heart.

Sitaar aar aaaar sitar aaar aaaar, 16-leaved lotus over the throat,in the centre of the brow AJNA two-leaved lotus and Vishnu Sahasrara of the 1,000 leaves.

In imagery, it was the sketch-plan for deeper meaning on deeper meaning, from self to planes of existence to levels of consciousness. Though I never really knew if the abrupt pieces of staccato on the sacred Ravi Shankar were a tabla or the record jumping.

Though I was now a shop assistant on Broughs' van, raja yoga took each aspect of the day as a spiritual homage not that all day was bad if all day was lang. My now shoulder-length hair, my beat attitudes and mock hush-puppies, assured me a fan club of pre-teen girls, an Old English sheep-dog with a hair style like my own, whom they dressed in a black polo-neck like my own, and a number of promiscuous housewives impervious to likewise randy daughters. The self-service van had its consolations; but, despite the raja yoga, the lang, lang hoors was killing me brain with fatigue, arguments with the boss, sexually precocious Jarra Girl Guides, hands-down-ya-flies housewives and complaints aboot me hair and dress.

In more saintly vein, went on retreat with Guru Ralph to the scene of the erstwhile drunken YCL camps.

Wilksie: 'Davie, you're turning into a crank like that Robinson fella, you're just not materialistic, Dave.'

'Aye, but Stan, look at the greet stand by the Buddhist monks in Vietnam.'

The Buddhist monks in Vietnam wouldn't spit on that fella Robinson.'

'We-ell, I think they would.'

Yer' says Stan, 'pwiit' like that!

There was to be a fast also. I started it on Thursday and had gone two days at work without food, trying to evoke the spirit, an aud borrowed tent, a primus for the waater, a couple of blankets, and loads of books on the assumption that not eating released unlimited time for study.

From Hexham we set off in driving rain and winds to walk the lang lanes to the burn. To be empty and weak, wet and now shaking with cold was anything but liberating. We set the tent:. ney groond sheet ... ney bliddy groondsheet and a sodden field. We struggled with the primus to try and warm the tent, the rain ran in rivulets down wa faces, wa clothes were soaked to the skin, we laid papers on the floor, the cold was through to the bones and I fell ill. Ralph, the yoga nature man, took me blanket, dipped it in the stream, crazy crazy bastard, he was gaana sacrifice is in some odd occult ritual: death by freezing. He swept all protests aside as he wrung oot the dampened blanket then wrapped me tightly, mummy-style, from toe to heed, not an inch to move. Minutes later the steam started to rise, the heat like a great radiator swept over my body swathed in heat. The sweat now took the place of the wet, and through the night in topsy-turvy sweating sleep and sweltering half-awareness, half woke to see the padmasana guru, a towel around his loins, hands open and laid on his knees, head erect and eyes closed, from deep in the tomb of his body as if resonated by the earth:

OWM ... OWMM. Was it sleep? was it dreaming in feverish twilight? but did his body float? did he not sit on the ground but hover a piece above it?

The morn brought fresh sunshine, a forest drying oot, and despite a lack of towels, we dived into the freezing stream, drying wasells on wa shirts and warming water in the pan ti sit cross-leggedy, sip hot waater, feel its warmth and let the sun warm flesh.

Dozens of joss-sticks circled wa squat as we sit motionless hour on hour, think nothing, nothing ... think of hands clapping slower, slower, slower, then stop clapping ... that instant thoughts stand still, the screen is bare, mind empty ... an empty instant: OOMMM OWM Madme Padme Sadme OWMMMM OWWM ... Tat Sat.... Suddenly the bushes and trees mek hostile rustle and through the holy aura two soldiers, rifles in charge position, bounce into the chanting saints.

'Are yee the enemy?'

Ralph's eyes, showing ney surprise, beamed: 'Anly in a manner of speaking.'

'This is the war zone, ye knaa. Ah'm surprised ney thunder-flashes have went off aroond here.'

By Sunday we'd agreed to eat, but hadn't anticipated the near-total lack of strength and energy. We set off on the lang march to Hexham but collapsed by the roadside a quarter of the way along and sat panting, unable to move until a passing car rescued wi.

We had it all planned: we would brek the fast with a cup of tea, then sit for an hour or so.... We could then graduate to a bowl of soup and gradually let the food back into our systems. That was the plan. Once in the cafe, temptation proved ower much even for saints. Soup please and double chips and beans and bread and butter and ice-cream and apple pie. The eye was certainly bigger than the belly which in wor case had shrunk ti the size of a walnut; half a dozen spoons of the soup later and wa guts wad tek ney mer. It was a sin, the plates full of chips etc. were brought but neither of us could touch it, bellies swelled ti busting. We waddled from the cafe and flopped on a seat. We neither spoke nor moved for two hoors, by which time wa bellies were rumbling empty again and we wondered if the food had been taken from the cafe table yet.

In the carpeted Victorian big hoose alang the poshy Osmond Road we sat serene, at least the others were. Fiona, the virginal sanctity of her body untouched, her elegant bourgeois cheek-bones so beautiful, her shining eyes so full of wisdom. A swaying, sweating Jackson, bells aboot his neck, toes curled up to the heavens, belly rippling with fat pranayama exhilaration, the dissident van-lad, killing all sound. Karen in constant blushing and confused state. The guru Robinson with his aan guru.

'Vishnu is the beaming fire and his brilliance constantly attracts Kundalini towards himself, coiled like a snake in the lowest vertebrae, waiting for the moment when she can climb up through the channel of the spine to unite with Vishnu.' Kundalini symbolically personified the goddess of nature, the coiled one ... but, like real jokes, nobody ever explained what was symbolic and what was metaphor, what was real and what perceived.

Somebody give me an electric shock, I'm heading for a fifth-dimensional depression ... echoes down the corridor of a clinical Marxist mind. A shattered illusion, a nonentity in time and motion, a dozen eggs and 21b. of butter but for God's sake gimme an electric shock...an orange robe ... a kick up the arse. And still it runs riot in the cabbage patch. Ever listened to your heart beat? You can't stop it only the listening; Don Quixote, Don Quixote! What's the matter, man, ran ootta windmills all of a sudden? Ya gotta adapt, man try a contest with the new Woolworths, all US pagodas. Write shit all you want, but folks gonna take no notice anyways.Anyways, it's getting to be a bore ... an' you started making me think again ... so get down from that VAT 69 and gimme my electric thing.

Night clubs abounded in the city: the New Orleans, Guys and Dolls, the Go Go and the Downbeat club. The Downbeat was the beats' blues beat, freak revolutionary peacenik beat, the sound was an enlargement of Les's bedroom: BOOM BOOM BOOM BOOM, BOOM BOOM BOOM BOOM, BOOM BOOM BOOM BOOM, the very stairs and walls rattling with gut-churning bass. The darkened warehouse swam in smoke and heat, bodies paced in the incessant doonbeat stomp, legs in a turkey trot me Mam said was like the Old Kent Road, the room paced as a body, bells flapping, hair a mass of waving corn; like a wind-tossed field of tossing, bobbing corn, Cathy comes screaming out of the air.

EEEEH, IT'S DAVIE, IT'S DAVIE, FORST TIME EH? A REAL BEAT NUW, EH? Then a dive away back into the heavy beast of continuous movement. Around the walls, people shooted in debate: art, poetry, politics. In the darker corners, two naked bodies writhe on the floor, visible as they roll from under a coat, which cannot contain the legs, and arms that escape regularly. Over there another couple under a combat jacket, the girl's thin naked arms encircle the back of a denim shirt, stroke a heap of hair still wagging to the music. On the walls, BAN THE BLOODY BOMB. Sleeping in a heap as the night wore on, coming to grips with a sweet-smelling person. Like a marathon, as a bunch flop on the floor another bunch are back up all night long ... all night long ... doze and sex and walk from there blinking in the Sunday morning brightness, having a breakfast of beans on toast at the Railway man's cafe with the sweet-smelling person, a beat with a silken scarf in her thick, bouncing hair and trying to find a way of asking her name without seeming too heavy.

The Go Go was more respectable. For a start, it ageistically separated into two parts, the young set and the other, which was licensed. You would find little more than heavy petting in either and, although it had moved rapidly away from Tin Pan Alley pop, it played around the fringes with the Rhythm and Bluesy sounds emerging from Liverpool and elsewhere. Still, they had the Stones, whey were very acceptable. The club was not beyond the pale and beats were accepted, even Jackson, in his bare feet and raggy shirt open to the waist, cut the occasional dash. The Go Go was also the scene of the Mod culture; ootside its narrow doors stood rows of gleaming scooters, their tank aerials tipped in mock foxtail, their crash-bars a mirror of lamps. Geordie Mods had emerged from the fringes of the youth culture. Most dressed in home-adapted bells until the manufacturers realised a new fashion had developed and started selling them, and various denim waistcoats or ex-railway waistcoats and the general assortment of Army and Navy Stores, street-spun, internalised fashion. Alongside the Mods there developed a group given to eccentric dress: Victorian collar, posied waistcoat and a walking stick, tie-pins through the shirt, metal armbands, and suit trousers tight-fitting and cut to end just above the top of the Cuban boots. The walking-stick spread and became as much a feature as the combat jacket. While Mods were dress-conscious many of them were also politically conscious, and the respective groups were simply two sides of the same growing culture.

The city streets, or certain of them, were soon marked by groups of beats and what the press called Mods, who spent the long idle days sitting about, sprawled in the sunshine, or propped up in doorways, watching the world run by. Sitting aboot, being laid-back, wasn't difficult with most of the youth on the dole. The underground (literally) coffee-bar on Pilgrim Street (the Palette) was a dubious sanctuary. Dubious, because the staff frequently hoyed wi oot into the rain or cold, and we'd huddle in the greet stairwell of the Keep unthinkable to gaan away yem, where we could actually get fed in a conventional manner else we'd camp in a swarm under the High Level, singing the sangs of the Geordie folk revival, while reveling in the anti-culture fashion of a growingly self-conscious generation.

On the fringes of the movement, moving through the mists of skip jive, sex and the blues were art students; they were a magical symbolism, a romantic character somehow at the core of the mystery of beat attitudes and anarchism. We lusted after art-student females in abstract and from afar. Art was hip. Being an art student provided a cloak of intellectualism not requiring actual knowledge, just a splash or two of paint on the anyway faded and ragged bells. With this in mind, and having been given the push from Boyd's, me an' Les signed on at the art college for night classes, eeee whey it wes anly a GCE course, but whey wes ti knaa as we strode the city, its river banks, the Central Station, and High Street, greet sketchpad under wa arm, and a battery of various pencils whey's lettered code suddenly tuek on meaning. Oddment pieces of hardboard were the currency in canvas, though oil was a luxury more stolen than not, wi couldn't paint God luv wi, though Les could draw passably.

The day the whirlwind from Glasgow hit the city, and Clem th' Scots git tuek up his seat in the ILP hall, he painted wild abstract things on odd shaped pieces of hardboard, carrying them doon ti the Quayside, to prop them up for broon money alangside Jackson's leaping poetry theatre. One delighted petty bourgeois rushed to Clem's horizontal reed abstract and, lifting it vertically, exclaimed on the wonderfully vivid bullfight scene. All blinked, not least Clem, as the horizontal whirligig of reed and black became a passionate vertical bullfight of swirling cloak and charging bull. Sold.

'Ken, Ah did start it that way.'

'Bollocks, Alford.'

'Aye, Ah did then changed ma mind, ken?'

'Knackers! Buy is a broon.'

The Committee of 100, back from all night at the Doonbeat, gathers up reams of Peace Pledge Union posters (no sectarians us, particularly where we could get antiestablishment material for nowt), buckets of paste, and sets off through deserted city streets, via Heaton, or roon by Jesmond, plastering oot any army adverts, any police adverts, any Tory adverts, any empty shops, blank walls, lampposts and the Tyne bridge, so the poster could be read by those on the upstairs of the double-decker bus.

Me Dad: 'Look at that there, I wonder who climbed up

there to do that.'

Me Ma: 'Ah think it was your son.'

Army recruitment offices were covered window by window, each slap of the paste brush with an incantation like a prayer.

The network of dissenting youth ensured a regular interchange between Liverpool, Glasgow and Newcastle, as well as doon ti the Smoke, of course. Runaway youngsters. Dropout youngsters, trying life without parental constraints. Runaways from bail and police harassment, runaways from boredom.

Quite a few of the Newcastle freaks now inhabited Finsbury Park in London. Wor Doug Kepper had meanwhile been promoted to National Committee of 100 secretary so he wes there too. Me and the schizoid Wallace decided to join them. In the early evening we stood at the Newcastle side, stuck wa thumbs oot, and headed for London and whey knaas where. There was some money via Brough's van, which I jacked in to mek the trek sooth and maybe abroad. We'd gettin passports because France was a good scene, they said, and we might all nick ower there. Most of the trip to London was in the back of a lorry, with flapping canvas covers. We sat in the back suppin broon and, singing *H Bomb's Thunder.*

Don't you hear the H Bombs' thunder? Echo like the crack of doom!

While they rent the earth asunder, Fall-out makes the earth a tomb.

Do you want your homes to crumble? Rise in smoke toward the sky?

Will you let your cities tumble? Will you see your children die?

Men and women Stand together do not heed the men of war!

Make your minds up now or never Ban the bomb forever more!

and *The Lambton Wo'orm:*

Whist, lads, had ya gobs, Ah'll tell ye's an awful story, Whist, lads, had ya gobs, Ah'll tell ye 'boot the Wo'orm.

and pissin' ower the side when the needs tuek wi, finally falling asleep bouncing on the bare boards of the truck, wa empties rolling aroond the floor.

In a previous time, a Geordie writer, Jack Common, had said: 'whereas the southerner comes north with the air of an intrepid explorer among the primitives, the northerner goes south with the spirit of' the barbarian.' It hadn't changed and, once sooth, we wasted ney time reveling in Geordieness, in dialect; in rowdy, drunken behaviour, that was the dominion of the Geordie alain. In Finsbury Park one afternoon, we manned three sets of row-boats and at once reverted ti wa Viking antecedents. Ramming each other, launching boarding parties, fleein' inti the other, wrestling in the boats, staff fighting with oars, boats careering, raucous dialects thrust across the park. We join battle with some Dutch whey join the fray, till at last all four boats sink and the Norse/Dutch wild men, hair spreading in geet circles from wa heeds, kick oot for the bank while the park attendant and a couple of pigs (an expression we had borrowed from our Atlantic cousins) set off ti cut wi off. Wet, barefoot, running, hysterically laughing, the forces of law in hot pursuit, taunting': 'Anarchy/Geordies. Anarchy/Geordies.'

We lay on the beds in the Finsbury flat, the Dutch, the Geordies, laughing, smoking dope, getting dried, Dutch reading free verse, in magic letters round the room WELCOME COSMIC VISITORS, so you couldn't mek it oot at once and as it slowly made sense the lips part in spontaneous smile and shared consciousness. In a South Shields flat one of the lads had fairy writing, roond and roond the wall from the skirting board ti the ceiling, fairy writing! He had, he said learned it from a rare book.

Welcome cosmic visitors. Dutch: BE KIND TO THE UNIVERSE.

But we weren't ower kind to London, bouncing onto the Tube, roaring oot *The Blaydon Races*. As a challenge? Surely not, for we aspired to non-violence and rejection of violence of the anti-social type. As a stamp of delineation: we are not from here, we are the north. THE NORTH, the Geordies! And it was to the Geordie pub we went, wherever that was, a place with wooden beer-barrels as tables ... a place doon in a cellar ... a place with sawdust... and Geordies ... and Scots, the blood brothers literally, often soaking up tha own blood in the sawdust from fighting, from being drunk and fallin' doon, from smashing the top off a wine bottle, too impatient to open it not movement people but Northern people, an acceptable fringe on the ridges of wa social 'near group'.

Here we sat, stomped, and sang the sangs aboot the pits and sangs aboot the sea, sang the songs of clogged and capped labour, us capless, jobless, intoxicated Norsemen Celts. Dutch: Lurn yesell Geordie eerster less.'

We rolled from the train at Finsbury Park arm in arm:
The Internationale unites the human race.
Then comrades, come rally, and the last fight let us face,
The Internationale unites the human race.

Viva la Quince Brigada
baroom baroom baroom baroom bara
Viva la Quince brigada baroom baroom baroom bar-ra

Doon darkened streets to the Dutchmen's flat. They confide:

'But here we have a surprise for you.' They pointed to the corner of a broad street where stood FINSBURY PARK CONSERVATIVE AND UNIONIST ASSOCIATION AND CLUB. We reeled.

'But you must look here.' There, in shining letters of fresh white paint: FREE LOVE ... FREE DOPE ... FREE ROCK MUSIC AND REVOLUTION. They beamed in pride.

'Ah didn't knaa they were in prison.'

'What?'

The Dutch?'

'Ya, we Dutch....'

'Geordies divind dey that wi Tories.'

'Nae?'

'Aae.' In one movement three rocks from the nearby kerb smash the groond-floor windows amid a greet shower of glass, like the whole wall was collapsing ... lights coming on ... dogs barking, people running, us running, bumping, laughing ... falling doon, collapsing in gardens, away ti hell. WA MENTAL ... GEORDIES ... THE MEEDMEN....

'What?'

'Oh, nowt.'

Collapsing in the flat ... sides aching with laughter ... and sheer bliddy joy ... falling asleep where we lay ... while the record player on repeat played the Stones ... the Stones ... the Stones ....

Night after night we hit the club, despite the bedroom lights on and a shout from the upper classes in the upper window: 'We can see you!'

'We can see yee an' aal.' Smash! Police sirens screaming roond the corners.... It was the roaring twenties syndrome again: disperse ... lie in a garden while the torches process the surrounding hooses ... pissing wasells ... fearful... ecstatic.

But the shared flat, arguments, fights even bloody inter-Geordie fights, daft, incessant, ney holds barred and ney mercy shown, which are the curse of the race ... the broon dog, the idiot broth, the journey into an unfriendly space ... even fighting in the sacred Goodwin Street, home of the National Committee offices ... even throwing up in Kepper's office ... even lying flaked oot paralytic outside the door while the printworkers stepped ower wi and tried to get on with tha business.

We decided to split. Me and Vim, one of the Dutch, would head oot for Europe in general, a couple of the others to Ostend, the rest for an anarchist camp in the sooth of France. We left ... bloodied and resentful, anything but carrying the sacred flame of peace but seeking to rekindle it.

8
Out for Europe

We hit the road for Dover and nowhere in particular, though the sequence of lifts was unusual. Aboot 30 miles from Dover we landed a female car smuggler. Not that she said as much, but every subsequent country we reached she changed her car and national registration, picking us up first with a Ghanaian plate on a German Audi. We crossed the Channel with her, us sleeping in the doss bags in the bar, her in a cabin. Our passports had caused some consternation since they were covered in black blotchy marks and the photos had smeared the result of wor Viking re-enactment in Finsbury Park. In Calais, we cleared the Customs ney bother, we were, after all, in a car; wor fella adventurers didn't get much farther than the beach since the lang hair and doss-bags and shortage of coin registered them as vagrants and they got hoyed oot fernant.

Vim went off with the smuggler the next morn and left me in a Paris market half a shift... but I was cool, sitting like the beats back hyme. Through pointing and grimacing and repeating the English word like I was teaching a baby, Ah managed to extract a couple of oranges and apples, and while the sun shone me heart danced. But it grew cloudy ... plenty people were staring at is ... lang, lang hair wasn't too common, not even on women. Paris girls seemed aloof — didn't knaa where it wes at, like. They pushed each other and giggled in a sort of Charlie de Gaulle laugh: 'Hu hu hu hu.' Later on, groups of young lads a wee bit younger than me started to swirl aroond in nearish proximity, like small schools of sharks, looking for a moment. Ah felt vulnerable, felt a bit daft, felt Ah knew ney key words like 'luek kiddha' or 'what yee luekin at?' Such guttural shots ower the bows at yem dispelled the puff slag of the lang hair and peace badge

... no here. They were coming closer ... standing in a strange Continental way ... like leaning on one leg with their hands on their hips, or resting on their elbows, which were placed on a wall with their flat hand supporting their turned faces ... that blood-curdling feeling ... like a sick feeling before you knew something was gaana happen....

When Vim, in he's daft knitted Dutch hat and blue bells, swayed in his sailor-style jaunt from behind them and, putting his arm around a French shoulder, was suddenly rabbiting away. 'Hu hu hu hu', arms waved and the turned-down French laughter was everywhere: but of course, aye, *mais oui*. Even better than the rest of his nation, Vim was a linguist *par excellence*. He was asking directions ... they were happy to oblige. I was still a fish under scrutiny. Ah didn't knaa what the buggers was saying, did I?

After walking the muddy flatlands outside Paris for mile upon mile, I felt the effects of nights of booze, ney sleep and ecstatic exertion of fear and fury. Speech ran oot, though me legs carried on. Vim said: 'A bit further only ... I seen on der map ... the girl driver she said *ja*, she had used....' As darkness closed, a greet juggernaut bounced the road, lit wi up like shadows, speeding to gigantium then back to black, but in that instant had lit the building, stood back off the road. 'The barn ... the map had said ... she had used ... and straw, *ja*, straw ... I smell.' I too could smell the straw. But without lamp or light we padded round the walls, tapping the floor with expectant feet—but fuck it, I collapsed in a heap, pulled the combat jacket ower me heed and slept like a deed man.

As an early-morning belly rumbling wakened is up, a stiff elbow, arse bone, spine bone, reminded is that I hadn't really been comfortable even if you in the brain department had slept like a top. The daylight revealed an upper deck to the barn, jam-full of dry, warm, comfortable hay—hay, yi bastard!

'Hay, yee bastard, back', responded a voice from above. Vim had foond the hay, foond the ladder, couldn't find me. Down the bit road from the barn, a French reg. Volvo, and the lass.

'Hi, some bread and tubs an' orange juice from the hotel, lads', she said. We ate, and felt sick, and I slept like a babe till I woke to darkness again, and miles going by, and felt a lang, lang way from yem, from what being a beat meant. What did all this mean oot here? Neybody knew what wi were supposed to represent, what the raggy badge of rebellion meant... not yet.

In Belgium, the girl took off and left us with the keys to the Volvo, on condition, it stayed parked down a little Dutch alley and Vim swore blind he couldn't drive, which he couldn't. Belgium was OK: Vim spoke the language like a native, though I didn't knaa why at the time. We walked roond the lively bars to a beer cellar, where tables of young uns and audens rocked and swayed and sang. One I thought was familiar, and, with the Amstel pils owber alles, I joined in full voice. 'Guinness, Guinness, gives you strength, gives you strength, gives you strength' went down like a bomb with improvised brass band impersonations, oompha oompaha, euphonium, praa praa hadawaycumback, melted into the swaying Belg Flems. The hokey-kokey, roond the roonds of table-tops and wooden stage, as bodies fell in maniac drunken mirth. We slept a piss-disturbed but crumpled sleep in the Volvo.

The sudden staccato early morning, jumped up to see a Gestapo agent with a gun through the front windshield, a gruff, urging, shooting voice, a grip on Vim's hair, and he disappears from the front seat before he could get up.

'Aal reet, aal reet', Ah shooted as the back door opened, and was thrown up against the car. A few pedal cyclists, beret-hated Belgs roll by the incongruous scene. The reality of the situation started to dawn as Vim reasoned, his shoulders rising and falling, his breath laboured. He mopped his brow, turned frequently to explain: 'Passport.... They want to know how much money we have...They think we stole the car.... They want to know who is the owner. They don't believe us....' (Ah! if it's stolen and she's part of a network, we're done for.)

'Tell them we can't drive, tell them we can't drive.' 'They don't believe us. They want to know if we are homos. They think we broke into the car to sleep with each other.

'Fuck off!' 'Ja, FUCK OFF.'

'Frau.' Now the Gestapo had me by the lapel of me combat jacket and rocked is against the car hard. The peak of the cap smacked onto me nose.

At last they took the passports and went back to their car across the street. They took the Volvo keys and locked us oot, then waited and watched ... and watched ... and waited.... At length, a bubbly dark-glassed Yankee, head-scarfed, skip-and-walk girl (the driver) carrying trade plates, breezing past the cop car as if it wasn't there.

'Hi.' The Gestapo ease out the car, do the gun slinger, hover over the big revolvers. She turns and, without words from us, seizes the situation or knows the situation. Skip and a little walk, an apologetic head down, a head thrown back.

'Hi, guys.' Then to the Dutch: 'Nae, nae wrang.' Then French ... cops from Walloon. She carries trade plates. A discussion in French. Vim: 'I cannot hear ... she says she must pick up the car ... last driver ... no international licence ... she has the trade plates ... is delivering.... She has an American passport. She had for sure', says Vim, 'a British one on the boat, then another ... now...' 'What the hell wi gaana die?'

'For we?'

'Nowt.' Vim was learning the Geordie 'eerste les'. Wi dee nowt. Some tossing of cop heads ... some scrutiny of papers without mirth ... then the walk ... both ... hands before the guns. Passports ... money ... ney further wo'ord....

'Get in, guys', continuing the Stateside. And away ... chat ... weather ... how'dya sleep? ... nowt aboot all that... we didn't ask ... she dint offer.

Through the German border.

She was *en route* via the Alps. We decided to leave and dropped off in a German city I think must have been Cologne, beside the border. Wet streets ... rain ... gangs of young 'uns, short hair ... wee mopeds and bikes ... the latest thing in Germany on a wet day ... and two lang-haired freaks.

It was rapidly growing dark and the rain was falling in a steady sheet of discouragement. The pubs were alight with a mix of martial brass and Germanic rock ... deep gutturals and much pushing and rough carry-on seemed the crack. Judging from the nudging bullet-heads propping up the doorways, we didn't expect a welcome, so press on ... to a mer remote, a less used, mer tatty if yee like, oot the weel-lit gaanins doon the way apiece.

At any other time the soond of the tinny whirr of a noddy bike was a source of amusement ... visions of a six-foot rocker in a winged helmet clearing the gate and fiercely kick-starting a moped. In Germany it was no so much a joke, it was the machine of the Ted's. Seven or eight of them, greased hair, leather jackets, Elvis Germans, incredibly astride the glorified moped. But whey wes in a position ti meg, for it was" us that was the gang's target.

Wolf-whistles, clicking noises: comprehension, which transcends language. 'Girls', 'Puffs', Transvestites', 'Ugly pros': Vim was translating the comments and laughing along with the big-faced greaser cruising alongside. They didn't appreciate the laughter. It was coming, me guts telt is, it was coming. A plan starts to develop, as they always dee on such occasions. Kick one off his bike then fuck off sharp and hide. They'd have to drop their bikes, Ah wes mer maneuverable. The line of thought snapped as it happened. A bike pulled fernant Vim, who fell into it, the bike falls ower, the rider hits the deck, another tries to ram into Vim as he struggles to keep his feet but the back wheel skids alang the curb. One had me by the collar. I break free but pull the arm sharply with is. He tries to hold the bike and pull back, instead falls off backwards. Then we're off ... advantage wors ... no for lang, they drop the bikes in a heap and pump after wi. Vim is cornered against a wall and thumped from all sides. Holding his arms up ower his face, the thick thuds resonate in the cavity of his skull. At the same time, the lads are laying measured kicks into his thighs and belly. Though bent and crouched, Vim keeps standing, buffeted and brayed wall to wall. Me, I'm off like a rocket, drop the rucksack ower a low wall, hope to distract them ... it doesn't, one vornie gives up, but another aboot the same size as me is haring alang aboot a snatch distance ahint. Running, gasping, heaving, eyes blurring ... This will het ti be gud ... het ti be gud ...spin roond and clog the bastard before he kna's it.'

But the momentum of the gallop carries me body backward nuw, and Ah'm gaanin doon like a sack of spuds, the side of me heed stots with the force of a mell-bla off the pavement, spins as a boot lands smack in the side of me face, me hands spread oot flat on the concrete in an effort to lift me heed off the deck. Distant voices, pain sharp and then ackwardly distant in me back and chest, I'm wet with blood oozing from the heed, the tongue which me teeth have gnashed following a kick in the jaw, the blackness surrounds me vision, me vision spins. The Teds jaunt away, pushing each other, reliving the chase. Rain is soaking into me jeans, maybe its blood, can't be sure, gaanin te bowk ... try ti get up ... Christ, Ah want a shite as weel. God, what a mess, get a grip, get a grip, dinnit faint, ye'l shit yasell. A small clump of trees on a circle of village green. Succeeded in dropping me strides, me back spragged to a tree, fainting, stick the heed between the bare wee knees, throwing up, vornie ower balancing, heart bouncing, blood courses, have to rip the bottom off me shirt to wipe me arse. ... God, not enough, the lining from the combat jacket. Done.

'Ma, Ah'm finished.' A chuckle bubbles through the memory of a little la, just ken'd ti sit the edge of the lavie bowl, dangling ower the brim, hinging on but ower wee ti wipe the bum as well, mun shoot the ma ti wipe it foya.

The befuddled Vim retrieved the wet bag. 'We must contact the movement people here.' 'Ye sure they've got any?'

'Oh *ja*, der atoombomb gaigna.' Enquiries brought shrugs, as did requests for crash pads all bar one: a direction to the YMCA. 'The fucking YMCA? Vim, wa anafuckinists!' '*Ja*, but rain, thumped, knackered. For tonight, we say we believe in God.'

'God? Where was that bastard back there? He didn't hev ti mek is fall ower, if he wes there he cud a helped drop the yob.'

'You think God will help an anafuckinist?'

The greet YMCA building stood in silent parkland. We brayed on the door. The MCs must aal be a-bed. Soon a Gestapo uniformed jailer came to the door and looked through the glass

'*Nein*, *nein*, clos-ed, clos-ed.'

'Can we sleep tonight?', I spelt out in slow English, which everyone knows helps foreigners understand.

'We sl-ee-p here, this build-ing, to-night?'

'*Nein, nein,* you must return at 8.30 to sleep.'

'But wi divind want ti sleep at eiyt thorty, wi'll be gettin up then.'

'8.30 tomorrow, sorry.'

'*Kijker, kijker*', Vim in a flash of inspiration pointing to the faded YHA badge on me second-hand rucksack.

'YHA, ja, ja', he beamed, his hat peak raised and he pointed to the floor. This was the YHA building too?

'Ya, YHA!'

'Great can we stay in the Youth Hostel?'

'*Nein,* clos-ed.

'Wi'll just doss on the floor.'

'*ya, mit schlafsacken, ve hail moo, ja Ve lig'ht op der vloer, ja?*' and shouting while pretending to disintegrate into a heap of tiredness: 'I*k val om van slaap*.'

'*Nein,* clos-ed.'

'Stupid bastard!' we yelled in unison.

'*Dit* is typical of the Germans', Vim confided as we sagged away doon the path, each squelch of the soaked saunies leaving wee pools of mud. 'They will always follow orders, even when they are stupid orders. If the building was burning down, he would still not open the doors until 8.30.'

Finally, wet and dejected, we sat on a wooden bench by the Autobahn and cashed up wa stocks of food: one large tin of peas, one small tin of beans. My cadet training ensured even in this revolutionary and beat attitude encounter that I had an aluminum camping plate and a can-opener, plus a spoon. The contents of the tins were tipped onto the plate, and pea-green water mixed with tomato sauce, the rain belting in its own flavour, as we ate turn and turn aboot, a spoonful each. It was a magnificent meal. The prospect of walking further was not on the agenda and, seeking what shelter I could, I got laid oot in the schlafsacken under the bench. It was poor shelter, but sleep forced the lungs into rapid and deep breaths. Vim curled up in his donkey jacket, collar turned against the rain.

Some time later enough time for the bag to be bright green from rain seeping its way through the down feathers into my skin it seemed a lorry with two trailers had pulled up on the bench. But it wasn't quite. The German driver had thought Vim a girl and nearly shat himself when the bespectacled lang-haired Dutchman pounced on the opportunity to request a lift. My emergence from beneath the seat, lang hair bedraggled and young face blinking at the headlights, once again made him see a girl where there was none. It didn't enamor him to take us anywhere.

'Money ... he asks if we have money ... nae ... nae ... *kleiner, kleiner*. How much will we pay?'

'Fuck's sake Vim, for a lift, what sort of country is this?'

'Shut up your fucking hole, I'm freezing.' We gave him £5 each.

That nearly breks me.'

'I have money in Holland.'

'Holland, is that where were gaanan?'

'*ya ...ja* ... a better climate of people, OK?'

The road to hell....We rode not in the cab but in the unheated, unsprung trailer ... bounced to hell, half asleep, half frozen. But then the driver, slapping it up at his unexpected good luck, decided to stay at a roadside cafe between blankets overnight. We sat tight.

The sounds of drunken drivers 'drinking wor shekels, likely.'

'*ya, und* laughing at the stupid beatniks in the trailer.' We laughed too.

Amsterdam was pregnant, though not in labour, the embryo not yet ready to be born. The full flood of the progressive rebellion had not yet reached high swell and lay as yet beneath the unsuspecting surface, its facets multiplying geometrically, the tentacles of tenuous links, like ancient ways, elaborating.

Dam Square: the pioneer's belt out the songs, strumming like a demon sing to fill the air the foothills of the provo Amsterdam elfedon when the anti-freak backlash came, fed by a terrified press and led by disgruntled conscripts pissed off by a generation changing without them. Where had GI blues gone? Hip Elvis in uniform:

We'd heard rumors from the bases, Frankfurt girls have pretty faces.

The devil had now got the best tunes, the freaks, the sexy chicks and all the fun.

As the drunken troops raged towards the Square a Dutch lad *spraken der Nederland's*. I looked puzzled. He handed me an iron bar.

'What the hell's this for?'

'Defend your fucking self, man.'

Such a thought had never occurred to me.... It had not yet occurred to the movement. As the troops reached the Square, a wave of hairies, lads and lasses, pitched in. The cry went up: 'Hold the Square, hold the Square.' For both sides the Square meant freedom: freedom to be the same, or freedom to be different.

As each morn broke, the beats were there, lighting up the first joint, emerging from the schlafsacken, an early morning Om for the Amsterdam elfedon and the R & B harp with the bongo's beat, lang-haired lasses dance and weave their arms like snakes and hips like currents in a challenge which said to the waken city: 'What will you be doing today, and why are you doing it?'

Heady joss-stick odor, a whiff of good stuff permeated the Square and its dwellers.

Joint between little finger and the next, make a funnel of ya fist, draw up and swallie, hadin' it doon and doon till there was nowt ti cum back up.

We strolled Amsterdam's streets, we absorbed, inhaled, reached into it, their cigar smoke, wor pot smoke, an inner peace, buoyancy nie ti busting, joy. Joy. We smiled, smiled till it hurt, we radiated joy.... It had been raining and a huge puddle lay on the roadside. As the juggernauts with little towing train in chain ploughed through it, a wave was cast into the air and the city sun caught, caught each droplet, in an instant mini-rainbows fell across the city in a wave as if in slow motion.

Wa perception was as one: 'Oh, maan!' 'Sheeesh, man!'

Collapsing in a communal heap of hair and raggedness and admiration on the pavement, we prayed before the altar of the puddle, each pore of inner vision opened as a truck ploughed by. We beamed and cheered and sat padmasana in its rainbow spray. Some girl with a scent like an Indian temple draped, lay, leaned against me; we fused in a collage of poised waistcoat, denim shirt with numerous little buttons, silken hair and youth; the passion was all-consuming, we cared not, na knew not, life gaanin by, just a writhing twist of limbs unbuttoning, groping and stroking and suddenly, it was a big dipper and we were coming downhill too far gone to stop. I'd pulled her jeans over her bum and while the zipper on me jeans snagged bites out of my prick, she drew me unmistakably in the direction of a naked and unadorned bare-back! Her knickers kept rising into the way, rubbing round me bollocks, and we lost contact more than once in the hopeless unrhythmic knee-cracking shagging right there on the pavement, the squat of bodies, cheers still for the wave, the bliss of the moment, providing distraction perhaps; something alive pulsed through her, through me, through the others, through the puddle.

From 'Hold the Square', soon the cry would be to Take

the streets.' The million-leafed lotus of the Dutch rebellion, street power, squat the buildings, decorate a million lampposts with hanging flower-baskets, dig up the concrete, plant a park, white bicycles mean free transport, the property is all ours, there are no leaders, we are all leaders, we traded, we swapped, we gave, we begged, we loved and we shagged as well.

'*Because I used to love her, but it's all over now.*'

Der stynky stoners.

Thoughts of hyme, thoughts of Pauline, a yearning in me loins, she never let wi dee it. Ah thowt that was coz I was ower-inexperienced, it wes just the opposite ... though virginity and mer wanting ti keep it was a concept beyond me just then. Ah put it doon ti the hang-up she had aboot me being fifteen and her being eighteen or something daft like that.

But Amsterdam carried on without me, but I visited from time to time as the elfedon absorbed mer and mer of the beautiful city. In later years, as the beautiful people put an indelible stamp on the Dam, John Chesterman cynically wrote in the alternative *Frendz*:

> Amsterdam cares; so much that it is in the process of swallowing the ug-culture, digesting it without any difficulty, and spitting out the bits. Beautiful groovy Amsterdam, where you can smoke on the streets and the heads will tell you how cool Queen Juliana is. But man, when they nationalised her mines in South America, she gave them the shipping line that went with them. Just gave it to them.
>
> For Gays, Amsterdam is the long-time open city. The expensive bars and hotels of the best upholstered ghetto in Europe. The new steambaths, with their psychedelic swimming pool, is the end of

a line of wall-to-wall orgy no-names instant sex houses. So why ask questions, man? Don't rock the boat. The Gay Liberation Front was disbanded months ago.

Fortunately, a few of the hard-core activists are still holding on, and trying to set up an information service (KIS). Their activities are reduced to leafleting the ghetto.

As for frightening the tourists, this is what they've come to see. Holland, See the Canals, See the Windmills, See the Hippies Tour.

In an effort to get this small dealing off the streets, the Melkweg Centre intends to sell straight dope this year, along with the hash-cakes they had available last summer.

The Melkweg. Warehouse of sanity. The Milkyway, with its own drawbridge, off the Leidseplein. Powered by direct current off Jack Henry Moore, who once poured so much energy into London, in the old Arts Lab days. Cuddly as Ginsberg, and very high horsepower. In setting up a video centre there, he has made the Milkyway a crossroad's of radical magic. Video Freex and the Global Village video caravans from the States were both passing through a week or so ago, when GLF/TV from London was there, swapping addresses in electronic Esperanto. Video junkies with their video junk.

Setting out new perspectives on Amsterdam, it's a post-revolutionary situation. It's all over. The problem is how can you shock anyone any more? And planning to do exactly that, the next thing we'll do is to fit out all the odd corners and cupboards with mattresses, put locks on the doors, and let people borrow the keys as long as they like. If they want to get away for a while, they got privacy. Anything they want.

But he'll do it, and probably screw a grant out of the council for a public service.

Rock bottom, Amsterdam, are the 'sleeping boats' converted barges on the Amstel canal. 'Sleeping boat 2.50g.' Rickety structures in danger of immediate collapse, full of damp mattresses from end to end, in a sleeping pattern like the cross-section of a slave-ship. Lit by candles and heated by open stoves. The fire hazard is overcome by the fact that they leak. But they are full of rucksacks, and guitar music, and joints being rolled, and Dylan harmonicas, and Spanish flamenco-rock, and French smack-freaks, and spaced-out West Coast Americans, and luscious sixteen-year-old Germans who have escaped from their mothers.

Ask, and it will be given. You want dope? Have some municipal hash. You want premises for your 'counter-culture'? Sure, have it on the rates. Rock, and what was that? Oh yeah, rock and roll. Think of me as a friend. You can sell anything but politics in Amsterdam.

They are starting to sell back to us what we once made ourselves, and nobody is asking questions any more. When you want to break in, they just open the gates.

Sex was revolution, an act of revolution just in itself, or so we thought. *Oz* believed the advocacy of sexuality, screaming contempt at the so- called 'age of consent' and piss-taking of virginity along with bourgeois morality were causes enough to centre a whole journal round. Sufficient also to reap the state's repressive clamp-down and punishments. The rise of feminist politics, and revolutionaries who saw much of heterosexual revolutionism as continuation of the exploitation of women, indeed, would look back at the 'sexual revolution' and term it exploitative and oppressive, *Oz* would be put on trial today, not by a repressive state fearful at the breakdown of 'morality' but by an army of women activists and self-styled vigilante hit squads who simply would class it as another porn book.

At this time, though, we thought it 'right on' and right into our youth rebellion and sexual freedom. Wallace had set me right a couple of years before as I sat filling out an application form for the Youth Sexual Liberation Movement. 'Sexual freedom isn't something ye join, Davie, it's something ye get on with!'

The beautiful, beautiful people, in magic signs and open hands, and sex is love and love the world, make love not war, make love, not money, make love, be cool, laid back, not heavy, not heavy, touch first with our pure hearts, join with our pure souls, then fuse with our naked bodies.

9
Politics of the Deed

Something between the iron bar in the Dam Square and the fellow wee guys in the black pajamas in Vietnam, forced first in the afterthought, then in the sub-thought; then it rested uneasy in the soul that moral self-righteousness was not enough. Knowing ye were right was not enough, crying moral outrage was not enough, laying your own body on the road in protest was not enough.

Oppression was not an abstraction, it was the force of men. There was no philosophical guidance in the napalm bomb and the burning rattan hut. The state was no mystical entity, it was a collection of armed men, manipulating the organs of power. These armed men were being challenged with selfless, almost miraculous, heroism in Vietnam; our challenge must also challenge the power of the state's repressive forces, and the successive conspiracies of the state against the people.

'What have we here, Constable?'

'A singing spy, m'Lud.'

"You mean he sings whilst spying?'

'No, m'Lud, he sings official secrets on the street.'

"Well, I know a secret, a big official secret
But it's not for the likes o' you and me
We all know the secret, the big official secret,
Well, they call it the RSG.
Where is it hidden, the big official midden?

That is a thing you cannae know.
But we all know the secret, the big official secret,
That's hidden in Warren Row."

Yes, the cat was out of the bag. Deterrent, be buggered.

No, the bomb would never actually be used, they told us. But just in case, they had dug deep fall-out shelters all over Britain. They had reserved places for royalty and the rich and the captains and the kings, but not for the suckers. They had stacked away their water and food and energy because they knew there would be nothing on the surface but starvation and death. And they planned to continue the war from underground till all signs of resistance, foreign and native, were blitzed from the face of the earth. And, just to be sure, fall-out-proof armoured cars, with fall-out-proof soldiers, would be set the task of emerging after the smoke cleared and massacring any survivors. The Spies for Peace were well-placed civil servants who, shocked at what the state was contemplating, let loose a thin stream of the facts and let us do the rest.

Spies for Peace

> The Government has secretly established a network of RSG's covering the whole country. RSG 12 lies far behind the WW2 gun emplacements in the cliffs of Dover. RSG 2 is in a converted fort on the outskirts of York. RSG 4 is in a concrete bunker underneath Government offices in Brooklands Avenue, Cambridge.
>
> RSG
> 1 Catterick
> 2 York
> 3 Nottingham
> 4 Cambridge
> 5 London
> 6 Reading (warren Row)
> RSG Scotland Edinburgh
>
> The HQ called Chaplin is in London. We know the RSG network to be linked to the military HQ in

Aldershot, we know it has exit points in key London streets, and for every mile of official tube lines there are two miles of RSG-connected rail and rapid transit systems.

RSG 7 Salcombe
8 Brecon
9 Kidderminster
10 Preston
11 Dover
RSG Northern Ireland: Armagh.

In later years we tempted fate and printed the map of the secret subway but by then 'the Left' was too Leninist, too responsible, too 'near victory' to touch the information. The first pamphlet gave the telephone numbers of all the RSGs, but it didn't take too long for the top brass in their secret bunkers to get fed up with loonies phoning them up and giving them general abuse. The numbers found their way onto bog walls over the city, re-titled as pros' numbers and dating agencies and offering all sorts of kinky fun. The generals were not amused and had the numbers changed.

Secrets are kept from you because you may be a spy, not for the Russians, but for all people everywhere. Because you may believe you have the right to know what is being done about your future, in your name, at your expense, but without your consent.

The revelation of the RSGs lay in that the ruling class had accepted privately the inevitability of nuclear war and were preparing for it. This sector of the ruling class stands above the army, the police, any of the ministries or the Civil Defence, as it was then. They based themselves in fourteen secret HQs each ruled by a regional commissioner with absolute power over millions of people. In the whole of Britain this body of the ruling class numbered not more than 5,000 people, and these are the cream of the 'Shadow Government' perhaps the 'true' government already; it is the government which will rule during and after the nuclear war; it is Britain's military government.

Their HQs were called RSGs (Regional Seats of Government). The people in the RSGs were top right-wing professors, civil servants, air marshals and top police officers, quietly awaiting the day when the bomb will drop, and they will emerge from the shadows and take direct control.

Elected representatives can represent the ruling class as its direct Tory statesman. They can also represent the ruling class if they are elected by the masses of Labour to look after Labour's interest. But not a single elected representative had a place in the RSGs. Democracy would of course be dispensed with during and after a nuclear war.

Major-General J. F. Metcalfe had a place. Rear-Admiral F. E. Clemitson had a place. Air Commander J. B. Coward had a place, and the Chief Constable of Hampshire, and an army of captains and lieutenants. The bunker's scientific departments are staffed by a host of Oxford dons and others: Professor Black, William Davey, BSc, PhD, FRIG, AMInstitpet,MBIM.The scientific department of RSG 4 was, of course, staffed by a host of Cambridge dons.

The hand duplicator needed little encouragement. It whirred in joy at human touch, its cylinder turning the rolled sponges, squeezing and pressing.

> In the exercise, the war game PARAPLUIE, Southern Region troops were needed to help the police 'keep order' but as radiation levels rose higher, all military personnel were ordered to their secret bunkers for 84 hours. The levels of radiation doing the jobs the troops had been called in for.

> In the exercise, Fallex 62 played under the observation of Sir Charles Cunningham KOB, KBE, CB, CVO, Permanent Under Secretary of State, Home Office, the most powerful individual in the country and the highest-paid civil servant.

This was an exercise, but real reservists were called up all over the country. So the game was acted out to test the system's preparedness.

17 September: Hospitals evacuated.

18 September: Regional Commissioners (dictators) take over absolute control of regions.

19 September: Official evacuation of heavily populated centres starts.

20 September: Ports evacuated.

Official evacuees included half the population of Southampton and Portsmouth. The roads became blocked with evacuees. Meantime householders at the drop of a hat told to stock up with 14 days' supply of food and water (from where?) and stay under cover for seven days.

Large heavily populated areas such as London are classified as Z Zones and are to be abandoned to the effects of the bomb.

The war began on the 21st.

How did the island fare in this imaginary war?

It all started with an H-bomb attack on German NATO bases followed by a similar attack on Turkey, Italy, Britain and the USA. The principal purpose of this exercise wasn't so much the readiness of NATO but the degree of civilian control and emergency plans for dealing with

Civilians. Within a few days 15 million people were dead in Britain! The West German Minister of the Interior said: 'Under present circumstances nobody has a chance.'

This despite the fact that six days had been allowed for preparation before the 'war' started. It is unlikely the Russians would ever have served six days' notice before starting the war.

The medical services broke down completely. Every hospital in the Southern region was destroyed or out of action because of fall-out, deaths of doctors and lack of supplies. All roads were blocked. Gloucester, Oxford and Plymouth were destroyed. London was paralysed: above ground was certain death. A belt of radiation lay across London to Windsor, but the royals were OK: they have their own shelter. Three-quarters of the police in *the Southern region were killed, injured or irradiated.*

Soon the duplicators all over Britain, in back rooms of bookshops and corners of bed-sits, were whirring the deadly information that the state was consciously preparing the mass murder of its own citizens. 'Here we could take you to the Regional Seats of Government', we announced. The RSGs all over Britain: we had the locations. We pinpointed their presence. The handles whirred. In J.C.'s bedroom the stacks of *Spies for Peace* mounted all over the floor, ready for surreptitious dispatch roond toon or on buses, one here, one there.

Let the news spread. Blow the lid off it. Crashed out on the floor, reeking of ink, head propped on a newly printed pile of official secrets-and suddenly a sickening pounding all round. A distant sound of J. in struggle with the downstairs door. Shoulders crashed against the door as J. wedged brushes and garden spades to hold them back. The fuckin' filth, man, the filth. Spread the word, the word.' Diving for the window, struggling with the old sash-cord and bits of decaying woodwork, pulling it open while blue lights clashed with the dawn and big-footed Mr. Plods stomped up and down yelling at each other. Grabbing armfuls of the pamphlet, I started to flee them oot the window with a vision of the oppressed proletariat flooding onto the streets, pushing aside the feeble forces of law and order and grabbing the incendiary literature.

In reality they fell in greet clumps on the wet pavement

and the cops gathered them up in armfuls, shouting Thank you, thank you' as they fell. 'Saves me a walk up them stairs', jested a witty wag. But it was no witty wag in uniform who charged into the bedroom a second later.

Four young thugs in plain smart clothes and short haircuts, one holding J. by the scruff, his face drained of blood, his arm contorted up his back, his bare feet bleeding from the toes.

'Yee, sunshine' stottin' the heed on the wall with every word 'are mine. Yee will nivor see the light of day again, yee puffy little bastard.' My face too is white to the gills as me head is dragged smack into the wall by me hair. I thought we would both be shot right here.

There were no uniformed cops around now, just these Gestapo, real Gestapo.

Separated in cells deep down somewhere in the back of Pilgrim Street police station, alone in a narrow dungeon of a cell, no window, no noise. Nowt. Silence. What comes next? What horrors can your brain invent to keep the feeling of sick in the guts, danger and apprehension?

'Dave,' I ask myself, 'what the hell ye deein' all this for? Always danger, always in bother. These bastards have got your number well and truly nuw. Ah'll be a sack of garbage oot by the bin th' morn, and ney bugger ti knaa any different.'

I was brought up to be charged. J.C., already sittin' in another corner, looked like he'd had a rough neet, couldn't dare manage even a nod. They watched him like a hawk.

They were talking quietly and animatedly about what to charge us with. The Official Secrets Act seemed appropriate but they didn't seem sure. 'Yee' J pushed the pen inter me cheek' can expect Borstal. They'll sort a weak shite like yee oot there, ney bother. And yee, coz you're the oldest, see, will get nowt short of twenty years. I tell yee what, divind believe is. Ah'm a lying fascist cop, man. Isn't that reet, eh'

(Poke.) 'Eh?' (Poke.)

'If ye like', I spat.

'Huh. Well ye'l sharp see, little cunt. Now fuck off, and he sent me sprawling against the floor. Marching me back down narrow little stairs, the cop says: 'He's not kidding', ye knaa, divind believe is if yi like. But if they charge ye under Official Secrets, it's bliddy serious stuff, son. Ah mean, ye weren't nicking milk, were yee?'

We were in fact saved when an MP introduced it in Parliament, protected by 'parliamentary privilege' mentioned the RSGs and a couple of locations. Before they knew what was happening, *Hansard* had printed and distributed it. So the official secrets (or some of them) were now on sale, too late to recall, at Her Majesty's Stationery Offices and branches of Smiths all over Britain. Couldn't very weel dee us nuw, cud thu? J.C. and me went wa own ways after that for a while, certain that we were both about to be blown away by some Special Branch man with a licence to kill.

RSG 6, its posh name 'Post-Nuclear Government Centre, Reading'. Some of its offices were at the then Regional Civil Defence Building at White Knights Park, but the real power lay in the secret garden-sheds in the aptly named village of Warren Row, less than a mile off the A4 main road from Reading to London.

The entrance to RSG 6 was only a few yards from the Red House pub, at the east end of Warren Row. The landlord was a bit dubious about accommodating 1,000 Russian spies come to give away the nation's secrets. He was none too pleased about accommodating busloads of raincoated cops called in to defend the garden-shed and likely, to kill his after-hours trade with his non-radioactive clientele. Luckily capitalism prevailed and a promise of 1,000 cheese sandwiches and Muckle beer and cider broke down the drawbridge and allowed the scruffy Russian spies into his bar lounge, while the cops got served on trays in their buses.

Ah, but the garden-sheds hid a secret. Apart from the couple of wooden sheds and a boiler-house, there was a concrete ramp broad enough and thick enough for heavy vehicles. The ramp runs down into the hillside until it comes to a pair of locked wooden gates. At some distance further is an array of wireless aerials whose cables disappear down a vertical shaft into the hilltop.

Why there? It is near the US strategic air command and the RAF bomber command HQ at High Wycombe, the army tactical command HQ at Aldershot, and the army strategic reserves concrete bunker near Salisbury. It also happens to be just outside the anticipated bomb range of the 60-megaton bomb expected to fall on London.

It was ironic, but that RSG 6 was on the route of the Aldermaston March. Leaflets proclaimed its existence and urged the march to proceed there. The CND organisers, sweet on their respectable image to hasten a Labour victory, were horrified at such a proposal. Breaking the law, damaging the country's security system, wouldn't help our standing with the public. As we neared the break-off point giving access to the shelter, someone had painted OFFICIAL SECRET ... RSG 6 THAT WAY and an arrow pointing the way. A number of willy-wet wardens tried to block out the sign and Peggy Duff shouted 'CND and tea this way', pointing along the established route. She was greeted with the chant which had become synonymous with anarchists on CND marches: 'Stuff Duff! Stuff Duff!

Stuff Duff!', while groups of lang-haired beats and anarchists in full get-up (red-and-black neckerchiefs, black berets and red pompoms) pushed the wardens aside and streamed off through the woods.

Coppers' heads appeared here and there from behind trees and blackberry bushes.

In a clearing surrounded by coils of barbed wire stood a small innocent-looking brick building an entrance in fact, and in front of the barbed wire cops and dogs, and all around people squatting, eating, singing, making speeches while the bees buzzed and the butterflies convinced everyone that this was just a peaceful piece of English countryside. Cops sweated under helmets and tunic, while speakers bawled out: There's no room in there for you lot, you know' pointing at the cops '*your* kids won't be sheltering in here. There's no stockpile of food and water for you. You know where your lot's going to be, don't you? Outside here with the rest of us frying. It's not just our kids that'll roast in the explosion yours will be there too!' The blue ranks shuffle uneasily. Some smirk, not wanting to let the message find its mark. They would be outside with us!

'"What is it for?" you may ask. Well, you won't' pointing at the cops 'but we will. I'll tell you, shall I?' Inspectors whip out their notebooks ready for crucial evidence in case of arrest. This is the standby HQ with an operational staff of several hundred. In the event of war, it will take over the government of the southern region: Oxfordshire, Berkshire, Hampshire, Dorset, the Isle of Wight, the county boroughs of Oxford, Reading, Portsmouth, Southampton and Bournemouth. The anticipated casualty rate in this district: three million dead. Three million dead!

This is a wholly self-contained community, with its own generator, fresh water and sewage disposal. It has its own supplies of fuel, yes, it has its own bar. The whole place can tick over 24 hours a day while the rest of us, THE REST OF US, get blown to hell. There's room down there for four hundred, but that will be a special four hundred toasting, while we are all put to the torch!'

Are they listening now? Can they hear us?

'Inside this place, this centre for military government, every government department is represented, the Central Office of Information will be responsible for censorship and the wartime public announcements, if there's anybody left to make announcements to, perhaps to organise the playing of soothing music to prevent panic while the country is consumed by blast and firestorm! The Ministry of Housing has been given the job of disposal of the dead! HMSO is to be given an office charged with printing notices against rioting as if those who riot during and after a world nuclear war are likely to listen to statements against rioting.'

Subsequent scenarios from Spies for Peace concentrated on new developments of the state's war plans. The detailed underground system was not now to be a place of safety during the war. It was to be the extermination bureau, the centres from which the vehicles would come to put down the population before the war. The shock for the white-collar spies was that all London RSGs were disbanded; the decision was made that London and its entire population would die! All that remained underground would be self-governing extermination squads for the mutant rebels who remained, to contain the spread of their irradiation and rebellion. All centres of war government and military government would be moved out of London. Did we doubt the extermination exits?

'Come with us!' the anarchists screamed on Labour demonstrations at Labour MPs but the secret, if they weren't in on it, was too horrific to take on, it was a challenge from which the state's loyal Opposition couldn't or wouldn't draw the conclusion.

'Come with us the entrances are on Horseferry Road, and Great Peter Street and between nos. 31 and 33 High Holborn. You can see the damned entrances from the platform of Chancery Lane Tube station, and there are two entrances in Furnival Street and near Goodge Street Underground linking to the unlit track Underground system, Faraday Building, the Inns of Court and the Ministry of Defence in Whitehall.'

Other than wor Monk Street demo, (a conventional London street which housed the entrance to a complex of underground installations and bunkers) where the Marxist Left stood in confused delusion of ' anarchist paranoia' and knowledge of the state, nobody has since taken on the monumental crime planned by the state against its own citizens. If you don't talk about it, perhaps it won't happen. But time has marched on. The state has elaborated massive computer networks and check systems. Whole cities will go, but the extermination squads will get to the island's militants first ... knock out the buggers with a tongue and ability to organise. Not just reds, local community leaders, activist women in working-class communities ... the state will reach these in the first throes of a nuclear war, perhaps in the first throes of a real change of system. The infrastructure is in place, has been for decades, and it grows night and day. Of course, many of the holes and tunnels and entrances are for the first stage, EVACUATING the rich and the leading figures of the state, but quite a few glittering well-heeled debs and capitalists will find a bullet at the end of the corridor they have helped to create as the state throws off its dead weight. The bodies in the bin-liners flushed up to the surface of an irradiated Britain will not just be of militants but of the non-essential sectors of the ruling class.

Don't believe it... check the space.

REGIONAL COMMISSIONER. POWERS TO MAKE LAWS. DEFENCE REGULATIONS

84a THE CROWN MAY NOT ISSUE COMMISSIONS IN TIME OF PEACE TO TRY

CIVILIANS BY MARTIAL LAW (PETITION OF RIGHTS 1627) BUT WHEN A STATE OF ACTUAL WAR OR REBELLION AMOUNTING TO WAR EXISTS, THE CROWN AND ITS OFFICERS MAY USE SUCH FORCE AS NECESSARY IN THE CIRCUMSTANCES TO RESTORE ORDER.

WHEN ONCE THIS STATE OF WAR EXISTS, THE CIVIL COURTS HAVE NO AUTHORITY TO CALL IN QUESTION THE ACTIONS OF THE MILITARY AUTHORITIES. THE REGIONAL COMMISSIONER MAY ALSO MAKE ANY DETENTION ORDER AGAINST ANY PERSONS HE CONSIDERS NECESSARY TO CONTROL BECAUSE OF HIS OR HER RECORD OR RECENT CONDUCT IN AN AREA WHERE REG 18b GIVING THIS POWER IS IN FORCE, OR ANY WORDS RECENTLY SPOKEN OR WRITTEN THAT MIGHT ASSIST THE ENEMY.

IF ANY PERSON OR ANIMAL OR THING IS IN ANY AREA CONTRARY TO SUCH AN ORDER, THE AUTHORITY MAKING THE ORDER MAY, WHILE THE ORDER IS IN FORCE, HAVE ANY OR ALL THOSE PERSONS, ANIMALS OR THINGS DESTROYED OR MADE USELESS.

That was the word then. It remains the word now. This publication renders by our recent record a short sharp trip to the death centre before a war or insurrection inevitable, unless of course those who read it now take steps to neutralise that state!

So to whom will the food gaan, to whom will the fresh water gaan? With an endless siege in sight and the planet clouding over, all sources of survival will be grabbed by the state's armed men. We the people will doubtless try to capture a share. Reg. 38a covers this fact:

> ANY PERSON WHO STEALS ANY ARTICLE FROM PREMISES ... BECAUSE OF WAR PREPARATIONS OR ENTERS ANY PREMISES, DAMAGES ANY PROPERTY CAN BE SENTENCED TO DEATH.

Regulation IB makes it punishable by death 'for any person to force his way past a sentry or police cordon posted to protect or prevent access to any premises or place for controlling traffic'.

The regulation on war-zone courts proceeds with proper British style:

> Where a person has been sentenced to death by a war zone court [in which, as said, civil authority and law have no say] and can without due difficulty be taken to a prison equipped for hanging people, THEY WILL BE HANGED. In the absence of these facilities a sentence to death will be carried out BY SHOOTING in the same manner as in the case of a person on whom sentence of death has been passed and under the Army Acts by a Court Martial.

The true horror of the state, despite everything I had read before, believed before, came home with a shock, only briefly reinforced by the absolute certainty that my comrades and I were on the death list. The greenhouse 'atrocities' of me marra's in me near-childhood were indeed small fry compared with this conscious preparation for mass murder of the native population by its 'own' ruling class.

The 'saints' sat *padmasana*. Bare-footed, toes pointed to heaven, hands laid on knees, a rough circle of sorts, lights dimmed. Meditate for peace ... peace ... peace ... and 'my beloved India'.

There were stories of a black-magic coven in Durham we'd picked up the bad vibes for days. We sat to let ripple the thoughts of peace. Om in drawn-out chorus. OOOOOOMMMM and power-wave on wave like a sea rolling forth break into open and irresistible sound: OOOOMMMM OOOOOOMMMM.

The golden occult waves radiate first round our circle ... then wide and vibrating further and further in a golden chain round the hall ... and wide like a pulsating rope round the city ... and the county ...

OOOOMMMM OOOOOOOMM madme padme sadme OOOOOOMMM.... all evil thoughts from all evil sources swept away in the pulsing golden prana of peace ... the voices join in a huge choir of peace and passion. Over the dark fields of Durham the rope of high spirit weaves and is rocked on the circle of black witches squatting in a field, their inverted crosses and sheep's heads impaled on devil-headed daggers, and their darkness rises to break the golden cord ... OOOOMMMM OOOOOOMMMMMM and the power wavers ... thoughts must knit, lose the self in the mutual voices ... in the mutual spirit, in the great spirit of the universe. Searing pain at the centre of my forehead, and my brain blows to explode in a colour of flashes which blind me. The link was broken for me, but the others swaying to meet the challenge carried on, their voices sallying forth ... a thick cloud of incense hanging . . OOOOOMMMMM madme *padmesadme* OOOOMMMMOOOOOO MMMMM *madme padme* oooooommrnmmrn. The thoughts of golden peace flowed and the rising rock of evil gushed forward and back from the coven.

As the moment left and the voice, slowly dies away, eyes open slowly, breathing returns to normal. I was found to have a small red burn circle in my forehead. The coven had focused on a weak thread in the chain of mutual thought and homed in down it. Could bodies, images, and actions follow the thoughts down such an occult tube? Whether or not, the coven was well and truly aware it was being spiritually assaulted and prepared more sinister revenge.

Fiona, the middle-class daughter of a Labour MP, the virginal vedandist and loveliest if haughty sister of our circle, was kidnapped and led away to some dark circle elsewhere. While police talked of 'a student prank', we knew otherwise. The stories had been drifting back. Nude male and female witches at the new witch initiation had been photographed in the grounds of Durham University. A great coven, including Edinburgh and London, was assembling. The vibes were heavy, heavy. A black mass in an ancient corner of the cathedral was planned, we'd picked up the vibe.

Police in wigs and raggy jeans mingled with students in the upper-class Durham bars, while we formed a circle of the occult. We would travel to Durham. We would locate the lovely Fiona before she became a gangbang or a more permanent source of sacrifice or torture.

Fortunately or not, a caucus of the Go-Go crowd overheard the lofty plan. Intelligent, yes, but given to violence. Certain of them gave off an aura of evil almost as strong as the coven. But they resolved to go along, to be the muscle: you be the spirit, the karma, the brain, we'll just be the muscle, they're boond ti hev some. It seemed a good idea. The counter-plan to intercept the great coven as it gathered for the black mass had to be kept secret, no even thought aboot hard in case the listeners ... yee knaa?

It was a word-of-mouth secret, closely kept, perhaps on risk of death...On the night of a full moon, the normally reserved city of Durham, if it had been looking, might have noticed a surprising rise in the mod population. A coterie of gleaming scooters parked here and there.

Working-class bars with unusual huddles of eccentric Victorian collars and capes. If it had been looking, the student bars had an influx of Beatniks strangely quiet, though. And an air of waiting expectancy ... if Durham had been looking.

They moved, dark forms in habits, some in white robes, many in death masks, white skull-faces, they moved. Forty, maybe forty-five, some barefoot, across the shadowy meadow fernant an ancient part of the cathedral. It was a scene straight from the Theatre Royal Pantomime and yet, as the cloud drifted away and the moon let loose its illumination, the dark figures started to rotate, spinning slowly this way and that in a crazy motionless motion, then all halted, inverting their arms at the elbow....

When, from round the hedgerows and the fringes of the meadow, we stood up. Tom-toms throbbed and golden bells sliced the distance between wi.

We advanced. The shapeless forms turned to greet wi. Some laughed out loud and defiant as if we were puny. Others started chanting, pointing and drumming up curses, while we walked slowly towards them.

Our Leader, rising tall, lang-blowing hair, anonymous, who had it seemed just tagged along, now stepped forth, face painted and mascara, chanting forth: 'I AM A REAL BEING ... A REAL BEING ... A REAL BEING ... A BEING PART OF THE UNIVERSE ... UNIVERSE' (the mind's eye spins from the greenness of the planet and out into the black silence, the darkness and stillness of the all-powerful, all-peaceful universe). 'I am a silver fragment of the power of the Universe. I am indestructible ... I have eternal being ... am eternal being ... I cannot be destroyed ... my body is an instrument of passage ... it is matterless ... I am ... Om ... Om ... fearless ... free ... we are the caucus of the friendly universe. In chanted unison: 'The friendly universe, the friendly universe....'

Some had started to turn and run. Others threw oils and dusts in our direction and a skull-face voiced an incantation, deep, loud and foreboding, carried here and there by the wind ... but we neared.

Then a roar hit the night, and across the field surged a mob of city mods and non-philosophical beats. Before they had got within range, the hooded figures were starting to break up and head for gaps in wor ranks.

Then the distance narrowed and a volley of broon-ale bottles hit the huddled magicians an ancient evil force dunched by an ancient force hardly less pagan.

'Get the stupid bastards ... cum here yee huw Lucifer ... Tek that, horny bastard.'

Some vitriol, some acid, some smoke bombs, some blinding dusts were raised, thrown, and flung into the lads' advance. But the volley of broon ale was an easy match for anything the De'el could conjure up, and all roond the figures scattered, or were kicked and rolled around the fields, chased and scattered, until the distant sound of police sirens caused a brief assembly and rapid dispersal. Back to the city. The coven was smashed.

But what of the virginal Fiona? Was she still virginal or had she been poisoned in body and soul by the warm-up ceremony somewhere in the wings of the black mass? Enough that when we arrived back, clarty, excited and reflective, at the ILP hall, we found that the undercover cops had disclosed her whereaboots and staged a low-key raid on a student flat on the Durham campus where she had been held, frightened but apparently unharmed. Little did she suspect that her fate awaited her just ower the dark fields.

Mind, the city mods, tanked up and impervious on broon ale, were mad as hell that someone was aspiring to a heretical fraction of barbarism, and even more maddened when the skull-cap shooted 'Christians' at them as they swept across the field that night cheeky bastard! No, these would never have left Fiona to her fate. Though her fate at their hands was also uncertain. For a long time we spoke little of the incident, and then only as we squatted for another period of meditation, scanning the county with wa minds, with wa vibe detectors alive, checking that the evil presence had gone. If it hadn't, it had at least for now stopped transmission. She continued to insist the police knew it had just been a rag prank gone too far, while Ralph who, we had been sort of certain, was the mysterious 'White Priest' perhaps with a wee bit added theatrics and boldness we didn't quite understand denied not only his participation but ours! He mocked our 'excess of schoolboy imagination'. There was speculation as to whether Ralph had a secret brother, while he claimed my description of the wizard was nicked from the persona of Gandalf, which would have been even more remarkable since I had never heard tell of him or Tolkien at that time or for quite a number of years after.

Having returned to England I was back to square one: ney job, ney money, and the object of me lusting had buggered off ti London, from where she wrote me cooing letters aboot London mod boys and parties she was at though she didn't dee nowt still. Funny lass.

The dole office, musty as ever, drew oot a card: bakery, Hebburn, apprentice needed to become a confectioner. Whey that was aboot my sphere of influence. Ah went an, Ah got it, in a sizeable back-shop bakery on Tennant Street. Me Dad mused: 'What a coincidence, David, yee knaa ya granddad Douglass had a fish shop on that street whey it wes ya greet-granddad's ti begin wi ... but me dad tuek it ower. Still, he lost it. Divina if he didn't gamble a lot, or anyways drink a lot. Anyhuw, he lost the lot and had ti gaan ti the pit, shaft sinking at Follinsby, which wes just opening up then. Whey David, Ah hope yee dey weel at the bakery. Stick it, man, divind be gaanin' off again.'

This apprenticeship had things aboot it that touched me heart. For a start, Ah got ti gaan ti Rutherford Tech, studying bakery technology. It wes grand. Ah could wear a scarf ... looked like a philosophy student ... didn't tell anyone Ah was studying bakery technology. But it wes interesting, the theory side, as well as learning to make cakes and scones and decorate intricate, majestic designs. But the hoors wes lang and, as trade picked up, got langer and langer, and the battle started at the bakery for conditions. Meantime I wes quite the popular lad, returning from the Tech of an evening to enter the hallowed halls of the Bridge Hotel Folk and Ballad Club, the crood all locked in choruses of chanties or pit sang, my carrier bag full of fresh-med pasties, pies or scones. Bakery work felt like honest work. But then it became drudgery.

I wes ower-free with me politics: organise! form a branch of the bakers' union, meet the manager, demand set hoors, overtime payments, demand.

'Shut ya hole, silly wee shite, ye've anly been here five minutes!' But the grumbles continued. The head confectioner jacked he could get a job anywhere. The senior baker laid the manager oot on the floor and jacked. We went to the manager and demanded. 'Yes, yes, time will be monitored. Yes, yes, ye will get away in time.

No, you won't hev to work weekends.' But bit by bit the promises fell and mer and mer left. Jacking was the way non-unionised workers dealt with situations like this, leaving increasing amoonts of work, and ney time for me ti gaan to Tech, the bastards.

Rising at 3.30 a.m. to pedal away in the middle of the neet doon ti Hebburn, past the forst-shift pit lads tramping ti the pit sunk be me granda, ti the street where he mislaid a whole shop, silly bugger.

In the winter, the snow swept waist deep, and doon from the Ellen Wilkinson coz I was back at hyme nuw I mun carry me bike ower me head and wade like a bloody fur-trapper through the drifts ti get ti work. A permanent tiredness sat under me eyes and me skin. Sleep and the thought of sleep eclipsed notions of Nirvana. Peace for the whole of humankind was canny, but rising class anger class against class, the need for class identity and class action returned to me mind with a consciousness reinforced by that damned alarm clock every morning. That alarm clock which nuw prevented me presence at the Down Beat, which restricted the all-neet party, which sent me away ti me bed at 11 p.m. like a naughty lad, but still not in time to capture the beloved sleep.

Sleep was a phantom, a distant, unachievable goal.

Landing at the side entrance, I was the first, the opener-upper. I dreaded it, for, having opened the door, I would push me bike into the blackness of the bakery floor. Leaving the bike lamp oot, I pushed me bike through the black, black of the room. And all around the walls, all over the ceilings, the cockroaches sat, fat, black or copper, and clicked at the intruder. On the far wall, me destination, was the light switch. I would put me head under me combat jacket, feel for the switch and 'snick'. Then all at once the space was thick with flying bodies and swarming, scuttling fat creatures, their feelers twitching, dashed in all directions for cracks and holes in the walls. I hated them, the only creature I truly despised. The bakery was inundated with them. The rest of the street was being demolished, and the black swarming army was reinforcing the hordes of bakery roaches. A trip with me new girl friend to an insect museum for her homework project revealed nowt like my bakery bugs. The creature marked cockroach in there was a wee third of the size and was ginger. Most of wors were black. These things the Gadgy telt is couldn't fly. Wors could, in a fashion: they flitted, or propelled thasells.

The bakery manager was a fat, aging cockney, droopy-eyed like a beagle. A disciplinarian ex-army cook, he wore a sergeant's stripes on his once white, now yellowing, tunic and barked the whole day, for pies, for bread. At bait stand all of ten minutes he supped a big mug of tea and dipped bread in it, deeply day-dreaming. I complained bitterly aboot the cockroaches. 'What's wrong with them?' he asked in his cockney accent, They're a beautifully clean creature.'

'Ah hate the bastard's evil bloody things.' 'No, they're like a nice shiny pair of black shoes!' One day, me and two other apprentices were sitting upstairs. You could take a pie or bread bun or cake for your bait. Roger sat on a pile of old baking-tins and wagged his feet, eating a bread bun. We sat in front of him. He had just taken a bite of his bread bun and was munching merrily. The lad sitting next ti'vis suddenly grabbed me arm. My stomach turned. We both looked in revulsion, Clearly visible in the uneaten half of Roger's bun was a portion of cockroach.

He followed wa eyes, turning up the bun, slowly stopping chewing. Urggh, it made him sick and sick to his soul. I couldn't stop thinking aboot it for months ... years ... ever.

They had ti gaan! We resolved they had ti gaan. Health inspectors were frequent, and we tipped them off. We worked on innocently as the two-besuited men with clipboards marched roon the bakery. Roaches must be cunning bastards: not a sight nor sound nor sniff of a cockroach ever made an appearance while the health inspectors were there.

'Aye, you're alreet', one of them telt the dough-faced cockney. 'Ye dee well not ti hev cockroaches or mice when they're pulling the rest of the street doon.

Ney cockroaches! There wes ney mice coz the bliddy cockroaches had frightened them away. Even a rat couldn't live with them things. On a Sunday morn I would come in to light the fires under the ovens. Down in the crumbling basement a furnace of sticks and coke sat under the ovens, waiting for ignition, which came in the form of a huge gas poker aboot three and a half feet lang. The wall was cracked, and ancient red bricks provided an impregnable sanctuary for the insect army. I stepped doon the stairs. The switching antennae searched. The heads wagged forward from a million cracks. Me skin crept. I turned the gas on and lit the flames, which ran in a lick alang the full length of the poker. The heat increased and brought them out to bask and watch me. A million eyes sat behind a million set of twitching antennae. 'YE BLIDDY HORRIBLE BASTARDS', and in an instant I was spraying the walls with the gushing flames from the gas poker. Carcasses ignited, glowed. Flames surrounded their forms. I swept the walls. The flames carried on. Aged red brick took light and burned. The burning creatures vanished. The walls aroond is burned. I was trapped, then in a final gasp of suffocation, a pall of light smoke marked the end of the brief fire. I breathed a sigh of relief: silly bastard, nearly killed mesell. I stuck the gas poker into the coke and watched the flame attack the mineral.

As I stood up a million antennae twitched back oot the holes.

Beneath the ovens in use was a bank of unused ovens, hot, undisturbed and occasionally swept by waater as we swilled the floor each evening.

This was the breeding-ground. This was the source of the insect army this was my target.

Everyone in the bakery clubbed together and bought a greet tin of insecticide. It came with a pump device designed to produce a deadly spray. We hid the concoction in the flour store, until the manager left early one day. Then we rushed to the store, dragging the greet tin oot and fitting the pump like a mortar team in the middle of a battle. We flung the bottom oven doors wide. They turned and stared. I pumped and pumped. The pressure rose. The mist sprayed forward, engulfed the oven, engulfed the teeming foe. There was a sudden rush of air and a massive explosion blasted oot from the old oven. Me jacket caught fire, me hair caught alight, the pile of trays with a thousand pies ready for baking took to the air and splattered all ower. One of the apprentices was black with smoke. Smoke marks were everywhere. The poison mist was highly flammable, wasn't it? The oven was tinder-hot. I had nearly blown the whole shop up, but the oven was cleared black bright, but cleared.

The next day we swilled the floors, opened the doors of the old Oven and a million cockroaches turned to greet the light, and stared.

The first attempt to expand the existing University Anarchist Group into a Newcastle Anarchist Federation ended in us the workers walking out, and the psycho Wallace hoying a broon ale bottle at the 'snotty bastards'. The aborted meeting at the Adelphi divided into snotty bastards and the Tyneside Anarchist Federation. The city abounded with ANARCHY and REVOLUTION, SMASH THE STATE, and WORKERS' CONTROL. In midnight raids, darting from shadow to shadow, we hit city centres with the whitewash night after night back-street walls were for the YCL. We sought to advertise our existence and create an agenda of debate among the toon folk.

Back at the ILP hall, the anarchists now dominated all

other events, and the ILP had stopped meeting. The all-night parties dominated the Shields Road and the 'rinky dink' again, again the 'rinky dink' pace stepped the shadows of moving bodies criss-crossing the hall floor, the cops on the street corners grumbling up at the reflection of decadence.

At other times you could crash out alone before the spluttering gas fire, on the battered old couch and belong to a place, be part of an aura, a centre. It was a lifeline. It was a place always open, a place to take a bird on a dinner time for shag, a quiet corner for a bottle party and mass grope-in on the floor.

Coming back with Mick and Dave, full of black-and-tans and cider and looking for a Sunday afternoon kip, we found the back door locked.

Locked? Shinning up the drainpipe and swinging along to the window-sill, a keek through the window exposed a squatting, sweating Jackson, head erect, eyes closed. We knocked on the window.

'Fuck off, Ah'm meditating!'

'Open the bliddy door.'

'Fuck off, Ah'm trying to establish a climate of tranquility!'

In wilder moments we searched for a flammable substance with which to test wa bomb-making capacity, discovered that surgical spirit a gift from the ever-helpful Mrs. Bell for wounded feet in lang marches did not ignite but spluttered miserably. 'Reet, whe's gaanin'?' The silent column rose, sneaking through the back allies of Heaton. A giant cider-bottle petrol bomb is carried through the evening streets.... Viva La Quince Brigada hoombaara huumbarraa hooombarra.... The target, the police box on Shields Road. A few late-night punters travel the pavements. The anarchist squad picks its moment: a car coming up the

Tyneside Anarchist Federation (1965)

road, a bus and two cars gaanin' to Newcastle. After the bus, reet, after the bus. Right ... go ... wait ... light it ... nor keep gaanin' ... light it at the other side ... somebody coming that way ... thi's a boatload of yobs coming out that pub ... bugger it ... light it now ... right, whoosh ... a geet flame leaps from the rag fuse ... that shouldn't happen ... dropped the bomb on the road. It rolled alight, then Keith leapt forward, picked it up. Petrol dripped on his sleeve and caught light. 'Ah'm on fire, ye bugger.' All this in the middle of the road. Two of us together picked the flaming bottle up with a yell of determination, launched it at the box, and turned to flee. The traffic was building up again now, nearly upon us. The crowd stood and gaped. The bomb landed short but shattered. A sheet of flame shot up the front of the box.[13] We tuek off in mad panic, splitting up. Ah kept running and caught a bus coming back the same way past the scene of the crime, as it were by which time the box was burning like a Guy Fawkes bonfire and the kids were oot tha beds and dancing aroond. The pubs had emptied and geet cheers went up from the crood every time a new shower of sparks hit the night sky. Two bobbies stood homeless and somewhat hopeless-looking, giggling at the spectacle like the rest of the crowd. Probably hated that little box anyway.

We later regrouped spontaneously, separately, in Les's front room, the old man being away. Flopped on the floor, supping the pre-arranged bevy from the ice bucket, a rain barrel in the back yard, but freezing. Laughed, retelt the story, worried for them not here, explained their absence. Knocks on the back door ... taps on the front ... lads wi tha lasses back from the Doonbeat ... or parties blossoming aal ower the flat accommodation in the city and occasional homestead on the estate. 'How ... the toon's gaanin mad! Somebody's bombed the police box on Shields Road ... aal the cops have got stuck into the pub crood and the Byker folk have driven the bastards reet off the block!

Yee's been sittin here boozing while the revolution develops. . .?

Typical!' We laughed hysterically.

The last knock, the last BIG knock, on the front door woke us out of a stupor. What if they come? Here?

Nowt on us, eh? 'Weeeell', drawled Les; opening the cupboard door for the umpteenth time, pulling oot the home-made booze, 'it isn't aal home-made booze.' A second cider bottle, swilling with the explosive liquid, dangled in front of the swollen throng. Money-where-ya-mooth-is time.

'Dump it, quick. Na, hide it and wi'll hit them again in a month or so.'

'Na', said I, in sullen commitment. NUW! It must be NUW while th' still canie work it oot. A near target. Get it done. Boom!'

'OH, hey, this is gettin' stupid. This isn't the revolution. We aren't the vanguard ."Fuck vanguards! We are who we are. We do what we want to do no preordained path. NUW! tha slaughter-hoose on Byker Bridge!'

A general memory of revulsion that yard under the bridge where heavin' kie were pulled, to be slammed to death. And the blood-soaked yard, and the smell of death wafting up to the bridge. It would be the slaughter-hoose. And so it was. Ney pratting aboot this time. We were in deadly earnest of being caught, in deadly earnest of the task. The bridge was staked out like a regular commando raid. Torches guarded either end of the bridge. Despite the earlier blitz of cops and revelers, the traffic was scarce. Two of wi walked, the big cider bottle in a poly bag, handle each twe lads wi a carry-oot. Four sat each side the bridge. The raid would gaan on. If the cops came early, the bridge teams would brick them. They didn't come. But we vornie did.

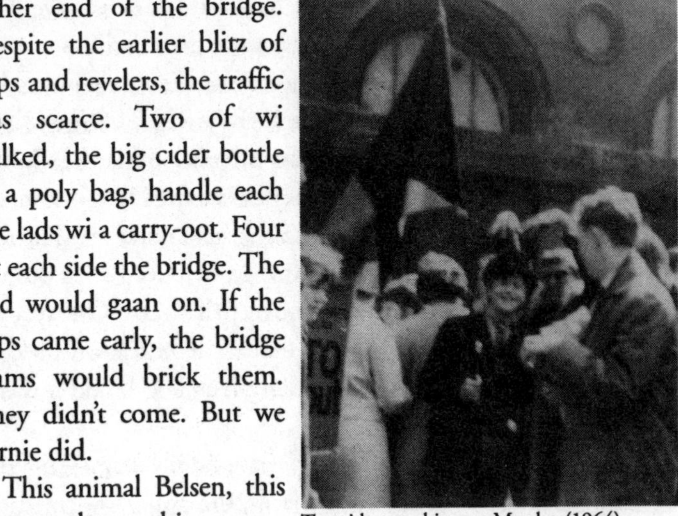

Tyneside anarchists — Mayday (1964)

This animal Belsen, this torture-place, this never-ending place of human barbarity. As we lit the fuse, a feeling of all-consuming commitment soaked me head ti toe. Let the bastards come. This has to be done. Bonny did burn the fuse, and it left a soft blue trail as it fell. We didn't run, but watched as it hit the roof of the biggest internment shed empty, of course. It was not a place of detention, otherwise we'd have liberated them, ainly a place of death and torture.

The bomb was meant to explode on the roof. It didn't, but disappeared through the old slates on the roof to an unknown fate. As we retreated ower the bridge we assured each other it was aleet. As we reached the Heaton side an explosion hit the air, and a small glow of red, projecting as if in a beam from the wee hole in the roof, seemed ti light the Newcastle side. Ten minutes later the sheds were consumed in flames of petrol and animal fat and all kinds of explosive mineral rendered from lang-gone deed beasts. Poor struggling beasts. Let the bastard burn!

This time was for real. Panting nuw, we sat in Les's front room, smoked, tried to doss, let the realisation that we had acted subdue our fear.

Dope was neutered, except in the most depressive 'OK man, Ah've had enough, come for me nuw' fashion.

The squad disperses in all directions. Geordies! Mental.... Feet tek wings and fear is the flight itself. The squad-cars teemed through the evening city streets, raided the Go-Go and the other culture spots. They closed the Doonbeat never to open again a den of anarchy, drugs and illicit sex. The folk bars had unusual visitors as swaying, evil-eyed cops pushed into bars full of bearded border balladeers. Oh aye, an agenda was being agenda'd as the whole knock-on tuek off on its own. The cops hated all lang-haired kids and it wasn't just the young uns.

While we lay low in wa respective family homes, or tuek off with friends to far-flung places, the police swarmed the Bigg Market pubs looking for the outragers.

A youth from the periphery of the movement, not heavily into politics, was seized while boozing in the George, ostensibly for underage drinking, and because he was overheard laughing about the police box. His protests met with a violent thump to the ear which smashed him against the wall. The pub, packed with YCLers and old CP members, and just Sunday-neet boozers, erupted, and a rush was made to rescue the lad. Before the cops could draw their truncheons, punches were being traded. The hapless lad was dragged doon the George steps by the hair, the other two cops kicking and punching at the crowd.

As he was dragged across the Bigg Market, the free-verse poets, the holy rollers, the crowd of debaters and piss-takers, yelled in indignation and set off to the struggling lad's rescue. By now a meat wagon had rolled up and four cops with dogs were trying to chase the crowd, which was swelling as the news got roond the Bigg Market pubs that they had beaten up a poor lad from the George, as one corner of the crowd pressed forward, the cops drew their truncheons, but the lad was dragged into the Transit. Attempts to grab the back doors and pull them open led to three of the boozers being knocked doon with a cop fallen on top. He was assailed by boots from all directions as the van inched away, the sides being banged and thumped and the windscreen covered in spittle. As the van sped up the road the crowd chanted TORN OWER THE BOX ... TORN OWER THE BOX ... TORN OWER THE BOX and broon-ale bottles started to fly. Reinforcements of meat wagons came screaming into the Bigg Market and a column of police in a line started clearing the street from the Percy Street end and sweeping everyone down towards the Bridge.

Retaliation was widespread and immediate. The hall was raided. Parties were forcibly broken up. Couples engaged in various forms of undressed intercourse were dragged off to the cop shop and passed over to parents. Underage drinkers were nicked, whitewashers ambushed as they set off on missions. People landing at the hall at the deed of neet for the usual crash-pad facility were held on suspicion. Underage sexers and drinkers were issued with care notices and whisked away. The pubs we frequented were raided, young drinkers evicted picked up as they went off hyme. Then double barrels. The licence for the hall came up for renewal, the police put on every ounce of pressure they could, and the ILP Hall was no more. Poor Doug Kepper must surely have rued the day he ever met wor lot. And us lot, hymeless, partyless, Crash-padless where to gaan nuw on a rainy afternoon with the women when the city had little grass to lie on?

Blow for blow. Blow for blow. Nuw it was wor turn!

The bottom of Shields Road, a gang. Across the road by St. Colombo's, a gang. And doon the alleys. Then we all start to walk doon the road toward Byker Police Station. Two dozen of wi converged on the small entrance. The desk sergeant looked up.

'Can I help y ?''Aye, tek this' and a volley of half-bricks demolished the front of the police station. The cop fled in a shimmering of shattering glass and wooden frames.

Anarchy! Anarchy!

Standing in a bog in Worswick Street, funny to be popped this time of day (3.45 p.m.), watching people squinting at the sun, low in the sky. Feet all sore from walking out the thoughts in me mind. Slowly wondering with my mind drifting over green and swaying bridge (Tynewise).

Dusty dog a-lying, and my thoughts are just like his as I pass with breath a-smelling. He strains to look and see, but he's just too tired a dog to bark or roll and look at me.

On the bus, girls dressed to display bodies well, and filled short-sleeved blouses and legs blow cooling at the sun.

Funny laughing at two young boys who strut on the bus with low bottles slung from pockets of their drapes. But they're just too young to realise that life ain't impressed by hard lads or schoolboys or Dreams or you and me.

In the centre of the city was Eldon Square, in the centre of which sat a square War Memorial flanked by two broad steps. The square itself was enclosed by short grass and borders of flowers. It was a place like the Dam Square where we the idle generation came to sit, play music, discuss the state of the world, or just lie in the sun. Impromptu speeches and poetry readings had begun happening from the steps. As the repression against wor generation went up a notch, city notables started to complain aboot the horde of disrespectful unwashed beatniks camped oot in the square. Then some faceless watch committee, gloating already over having closed the ILP Hall and taken the licence off the Doonbeat, decided they would keep the kids from the Square.

One Saturday afternoon, a pleasant sunshiny day, a group of beats laid oot, booze-sodden, sleeping it off in the park. We, the 'movement people', sat in an enormous circle having a communal picnic of raw cabbage, pea-pods, carrots and fruit. Suddenly there was a rush, a feel of heavy movement, a sudden fear in ya belly, and black-coated cops were leaping over the short walls and running at us from all directions.

Before we could dey much but shout and complain, they were pushing us, frog-marching wi and generally herding wi from the Square. The lads laid oot after the bevy slept on regardless, till PC Plod decided to wake them up by kicking one of the lads hard on the soles of his feet. It was a mistake. In a flash the kid was on his feet, nutted the cop and thumped another standing next to him. His marra's next got in as a rush of cops headed for them. Feet and fists flew and we made for to join In but half-heartedly, for philosophy had robbed wi of wa working-class spontaneity so prevalent in the 'C' Class. Seeing wa movement a knot of cops started pushing wi hard. Arra fell ower and one of them grabbed me by the lapels and sent is reeling into a wall. The hard lads were by now on the grass underneath a pile of black gabardine and a welter of thumps.

City shoppers gaped. One old pillock clapped the cops and shouted 'Clean the scum up, clean the scum up', while two similarly aged women shoppers shouted at him 'Get yem, yee daft owd get, the kids wes deyin ney harm', and others muttered darkly that it was 'a bloomin' disgrace'.

So the Square became a frequent centre of confrontation. Every weekend saw a cordon of cops, excluding anyone who looked like us. Meat-wagons blocked the back streets in readiness for a concerted effort to breach the Square, but we never did mek it. Pickard strode into the Square and began

Tom Pickard and Alan Ginsberg

reading his free verse, only to be dragged from the steps and arrested.

The Socialist Labour League organised a march against police repression, and the Committee joined it. But they were marching off to an indoctrination class at the University. We tried to get the march to turn off at the Haymarket and storm the Square, an idea which struck a chord with the young uns on the march, but the SLL stewards violently dissuaded the small number of Committee members from taking over the route.

The leader of the SLL youth was a city-hard lad called Diamond Jack. He had a diamond tattooed in the centre of his forehead, wore steel toe- capped boots and was all dressed in denim. He was programmed to wipe out the influence of the anarchists among Geordie kids. By Wiping Out The Influence of Anarchism the League elders may or may not have meant an ideological war. That's not what Diamond Jack took it to mean. He meant Wipe Out The Anarchists.

At the University we had intended to gaan ti the meeting an' argue for a charge on the Square then and there, but after everyone else had gone in aboot six of wi had been held ootside. We sharp discovered why as bloody Diamond Jack and a thuggery of marras charged oot of the ancient building. Wa dear comrades nicked off but me and Wallace got grabbed. Jack, with me heed under his arm in a grip like death, punched and punched at me upturned face until the blood fell from me mooth and nose in great globules.

'Anarchist pig', he chanted as if to keep the momentum of his thumps.

Elsewhere Dave was being kicked aroond the paving

stones but had managed to roll in a ball. My body wanted to fall to the floor also in the hope that Jack would feel satisfied ... but he dragged me lifeless body like a big dog with a rag doll, thumping in regular beats, eventually dropping me on top of Wallace in what he obviously thought would he an artistic arrangement.

'And dint yee challenge the pro-let-ar-ian leadership again, ger it?'

My face a mass of blood which seemed to be running from places I didn't have holes in ... distantly hearing the self-justification: 'Revolutionary Duty.' 'Had ti be done. "Misleading the workin'-class youth.' 'Ah hate them little bastards.'

Jack was a thick thug but honest.

Things were not always favourable to them.

Cathy wasn't simply archetypal of Tyneside Committee folk, she was a larger-than-life personification of it, a founder member, with the rhythm and blood of her progressive generation coursing through her.

Tall and blonde, sexually uninhibited, randy you might say, switching sexual options as the mood took her, as attractive as she was Geordie and she was Geordie. Born and bred in the roughest area of pit toon shipyard Wallsend, she carried a punch like a mule and had a nut technique better than Massambula.

We were on a demonstration coinciding with the Labour Party Conference at Scarborough. We were there aboot the bomb. Earlier the SLL and their Young Socialists had marched for the revolution and against expulsion, etc. They sat on the beach-front wall as we marched by with the Tyneside Anarchist Federation banner. 'Bourgeois pacifists ... bourgeois pacifists', they chanted. 'What's he say?' asked Cath.

'He says you're a stuck-up softy', I replied, and with that she dived oot from the march and smacked two of them right off the wall, heels ower heed into the sand. The chanting stopped, and later the *Newsletter*, after condemning everyone on the march, contritely added: 'The only working-class contingent on the march was a group of Geordie anarchists.'

Cathy was a front-ranker. She believed in the politics of the deed on all subjects. At Monk Street, when we found oot the Central RSG for London, we crammed doon the tight lane and faced rank upon rank of cops, the chief of whom was telling us, There is nothing here', to which Cath shoots: 'What yee lot aal deeying here for?' and, as the ranks start to push and edge toward one another, Cath, pointing at the young cop opposite, shoots 'Yee yer mine, yee bastard', a promise quickly fulfilled as the sudden confrontation breaks. Cath delivers her flying heed-butt, which floors the cop in one.

While others misunderstood wa Geordie Cong chant as piss-taking, Cath had added her own chorus: 'Geordie Cong, Geordie Cong, bring ya hardest bastards on!'

Nadhu Chaterjee was my spiritual guru when I first discovered a book which opened up the treasure trove of jewels and wonderment: *The Guru By His Disciple*. Magical, mysterious to be taken literally or metaphorically or both I never did fully reason it out he was the most important of my long-distance gurus, though we were never to meet in the flesh or maybe I did.

Soon after, there was a visit to the river by a Canadian submarine, and a bunch of the lads and lasses had sauntered along to subvert the crew.

In fact the lasses were more than welcome on board, especially with their avowal of sexual freedom, their pubescent genes leaping out from every pore. The sailors didn't mind being subverted at all, although they didn't seem to wor ear to be accepting much of the arguments. As time went on and some of the cross crack became more abrasive, Arra lit a handful of bangers and tossed them doon the conning-tower. Then the shit hit the fan and the attitudes changed. The lasses were furious with us. It was, said Lynne, 'tantamount to bombing the sub'.

'So?'

'We're supposed to be against the bomb, against violence, aren't we? Or is that some other organisation?'

The heated debate was gravitating, as it always did, to an outpouring of proletarian abuse against the grammar-school girls, now retitled 'petty-bourgeois schoolgirls'.

Yee stupid little middle-class bitch, the bomb isn't an evil in itself it's the state's war machine we're against.'

'Oh, with our own war machine I suppose?'

Just about then the River Police in their silly little chuggy boat pop-popped along toward us, headlamp shining from the bow. Loudspeaker:

You young people, wait there. Stay where you are.'

Piss off, Pig!

Arra launched another couple of bangers at the boat, and a second later someone hit the search lamp with a brick. It shattered and a crunching sound as if the boat had hit the anchor chain on the submarine was heard.

We all took off, the lasses shouting at us: 'Ignorant bastards, you're no better than stupid yobs.'

'Ow bastards', we mocked, 'jolly gumdrops.'

The Tyneside Committee of 100 was something of an oddity. While the Committee nationally and the anti-bomb movement in general were largely composed of the petty bourgeoisie, and the whole effort was pervaded with the image of studentish, tweedy brogue middle-class conscience, and NICENESS, the Geordies were nowt like. The grammar-school girls were in fact mostly from clerical and skilled working-class families and the others thoroughly proletarian in composition: unemployed working-class kids, labourers, a couple of bakers, miners, seamen, shop lasses, builders, railmen, and a few clerks.

The whole thing was edging to the edge, with differences of outlook, of motive. Wor bent towards violence was clashing severely with the outlook of universal love and humanitarianism. Just nuw being homeless as a team wasn't helping. We were a community organisation based in a constituency. We had to have a centre, a constant life, an alternative to home and control.

In other parts of the country, the Committee strained to find anything like a hundred activists. We had to set up sub-committees, such was the enthusiasm: a Tyneside branch, a Wallsend Committee, a Heaton Committee, and a Wardley/Felling Committee, the latter, finding venues so difficult, staged moonlight meetings or torchlight meetings in the crescent of Wardley pit tip or in the fields of the White Mare Pool. Something the Miners' Union itself had also done in its early years.

Clandestine activity was a joke. A flyposting attack attracted 35 folk, sauntering along playing Luxembourg and skip-jiving from target to target. But the Committee achieved something not since achieved: it was a product of the working-class youth of the city; at least in Geordieland, it was wedded to the youth culture; it was their organisation, even those who didn't attend its camps or binges, and there was few of those. The Committee and the Committee people were part of 'the scene', and 'the scene' was itsell heavily influenced by them.

While demos were announced from the stage of the Go-Go, Mike Jeffreys, manager of the Doonbeat, spoke at the

Committee meetings. Wor rock stars spoke for us, we felt, not for tin-pan alley, what shekels they had wasn't the bother, if they stuck to tha roots and the direction of the generation.

When news came through that wor comrade Stuart Christie had been kidnapped and whisked away to a Spanish jail, an impromptu gathering in Eldon Square on a rainy Saturday afternoon and a determined push onto the road to march to the Spanish Embassy culminated in a march of above a thousand as friends, comrades, shoppers and 'Saturday afternoon beats' fell in behind the march. 'Free Stuart Christie' become a slogan the city kids understood within forty-eight hours. And within forty-eight hours the Spanish Embassy on the Quayside sat toothless as all the windows went through, and we hadn't done it. Though in fact we did consider bombing it, but an ordinary family lived on the floor above so we decided against it. The slogans appearing roond the toon were not Committee-organised. The seed had found a new home of its own.

10
This Was Wor Land

Unkind souls called him Thick Sandy. Mesell he caused me days of pondering on his seemingly inexplicable utterances. Surely he was some form of super-intellectual. After all, Jackson talked nonsense and stunned all to silence, calling it artistic existentialism.

Sandy was a living personification of a cut-oot IWW worker rotten with muscles, with a heed like a bullet. A determined fighter. As we traveled northward on the steamed-up bus Sandy began with a verbal flourish to impress the throng:

'Ah draw a man in a telephone box, see' he draws on the steamed-up window 'ye've got ti guess what it is.'

What was the hidden meaning in such speech? Again, 'What's half metal and jumps up and doon?' A happy sandwich. It was a sick joke when told right, but the way Sandy told it....

A happy sandwich?

Sandy's apparent inability to deliver the punch-lines of jokes correctly left the story hanging like a mantra.

They had laid out the sleeping bags, both still zipped up, the lass still open to persuasion or convincing. As other couples breathlessly struggled to climax, or giggled in the tight confines of the tents, Sandy's efforts could be heard

'Where's ya hand?' (The City's way of saying 'Gi's ya hand.')

'Where's ya hand?'

Sarcastically: 'In me pocket.'

'Where's ya hand?'

'In me pocket.'

'Oh man, where's ya hand?' And from six hysterical tents:

'It's in a' bliddy pocket!'

"Oh shurp man, ya crampin' me style.'

Later: 'Sandy, NO.'

'Ohwheyhawayman.'

'NO, Sandy!"

Oh ha-weh man.'

'NO!'

'Ah've gorra Tampax....'

'Durex!' we all shout.

'Aye, a Durex', he thanks us.

'Whey he's not using either on me', she yells.

That date flattened. His patter to impress nivor flagged.

Four or five Go-Go mod lasses, their short hair flopped in a wave over one eye, their flat-heeled shoes in constant mimic of the mod dance, involving a contorted heel-swing and simultaneous body move.

'Whey', Sandy begins, 'Ah wes lifting this crate of bananas an Ah see this geet hairy leg come oot amang a bunch....' The girls stop jiggin aboot. 'Ah started ti put the crate doon ... sla, ye knaa ... but this geet taranchela started ti push its sell oot o' the bunch before Ah could put it doon ... it wes crawling on me arm....'

'Eee,' the lasses shrieked, 'what did ye dee?'

Sandy raised hissell up, pulled up his jeans roon his waist and carried on:

'Ah waited till it got all the way ti the inside of me elbow ... then Ah went...'

He suddenly moved a muscle on his upper arm.

'Squashed it!'

'OOH, bugger off Sandy!'

True, man .... What's wrang wi ye?'

But once onti what he considered a good chat-up line, he didn't let it rest.

We were traveling back from Bellingham. Sandy

occupied the back seat of the bus. Not far doon the road a bonny lass in a straw hat boarded the bus. Seeing ney other seats, she proceeded to sit fernant the strange existentialist, who realised this was his cue for some witty repartee.

'By,' he ventured, 'Ah like ya hat.'

The girl smiled politely.

('Wuw, Ah've dun it', thought Sandy.)

"Aye ...Ah like that hat.'

Thank you', said the girl.

(Got ti keep this flow of conversation gaanin'.)

'Ee ... It's a grand hat.'

(Ney response this time)

'By .. that's a grand hat.'

'Ah say—' He leaned ower to her. She took off the hat.

'Pity ... Ah liked that hat.'

In the once highly bourgeois suburb of Jesmond, the bed-sits had fallen to students, lonely single folk, and whilst a few haughty bourgeois held onto the whole hoose it was by ney means exclusively theirs ney mer. Especially not nuw.

It was a sunny Sunday afternoon as Ah strolled the Jesmond streets and into the sedate square of big hooses: Grosvenor Place. From an upstairs window hung a greet reed and black flag. We had fund a home. Keith, Les, Cath, Marie, others from time to time, some all the time. This was the new pad. From here, the Committee of 100 reconvened. Its support was getting so big nuw, with young people aye and some not se young filling every corner of the big front room and swelling the wee kitchen. We resolved to set up a sub-committee for Heaton, one for Felling and Wardley, one for the City, and send representatives back to the central meetings. All who could get back or squash in were welcome to stop for a binge. There was a new influx of lasses some Gateshead grammar-school lasses, a coterie of working-class mod lasses some quiet-spoken middle-class lads, a few intellectuals, us bakers, bus-drivers' sons, miners' lads, shop lads and lasses, building labourers, railway workers, but ney students!

The Animals:

"Baby let me take you home
Baby let me take you home...
Ah'll love you all my life
even then Ah'll treat you right
Baby let me dance with you
Baby let me dance with you
Ah'll do anything in this godalmighty world
if you'll just let me dance with you.

The shadows run across the square. The music pulses.

C'mon, c'mon Baby C'mon, c'mon Baby
Alright ... alright."

Floor vibrates ... the whole room in motion ... Burton's Geordie twang joined in a chorus of voices:

"WEY WHEN A SAW YI BABY
AH COULDN'T IGNORE YI
AND AH WANTED YI FOR MESELF
WHEN YI SAID YEA
AH JUST COULDN'T CARE ABOUT ANYTHING ELSE IN THIS WORLD ALONE".

Beneath the big table me an' Angie, stripped off by now, rolling on top of one another an trying to eat lumps out of each others' necks. Other couples similarly inhabiting corners of the flat, yelling in outrage every time some silly bastard put the leets on.

Dancing stopped aboot 4 a.m. though the music pulsed on non-stop. Dossing off to the John Lee Hooker doodoodoodooo doooo doooo bass pulse and waking to it, half-sleeping through it, waking, finding the naked body next to mine, necking with dry mouths and bleary eyes, and more relaxed erection.

Later in the day two students, hearing of the tales of wild debauchery and asking how to join the Committee, were ushered into the big room still strewn with empty bottles, half-consumed cans, and couples rolled up in each other and sleeping bags.

'Bloody hell', says one, seeing two lang-haired blondes, their naked backs and thin arms embracing. 'Bloody hell there's two of them in here together.'

"Fuck off" I responded 'One of them's me, yee blind bastard', gettin' rather pissed off with everyone always thinking I was a girl. It was in the early mornings following the parties when the Committee dispersed through the town, buckets of whitewash or paste ready to rewrite the next day's discussions to and from work.

The dirty angel in the Haymarket, a war memorial with a number of splendidly flat sides, was ideal for the Committee symbol, the 'Ban the Bomb sign' and the 100 and the words TYNESIDE underneath, on the front WHY WARS? A couple of the City churches also had splendidly large walls in full frontal view of the city folk. Wor sloganising them with whitewash was nothing personal: just a handy wall. Why should churches be exempted from peace slogans, after all they had caused enough wars?

The fat was well and truly in the fire though, and City Tories as well as respectable Labour and the official CND, as they were described in the local Chronic, all heartily condemned the whitewash raid. Police, it was said, were searching for the vandals.

The party was well in session. The floor bounced to stomping and in the bedrooms a folk caucus was striking up. On the stairs, all over the building couples sat or lay on landings, their hands a stroking, fondling rhythm of movement, overrunning the obstacles of clothing. On the steps outside the building people stood around on the road and a group of partiers had pushed a double bed from somewhere and chained it to a parking meter. A couple were already under the sheets, cheered on from people in the other flats. But not everyone was cheering. While we stamped it out in the folk room, spending our money on Sally Brown, and the Animals were being not misunderstood in the big room, and the bedsprings bounced in the roadside, the meat wagons were already rolling. They sped into the square from both sides of the block.

FILTH! The Filth's here! Everyone made a charge to get out. Why, I've never really reasoned. We all thought they'd come for different reasons. I thought they'd come for the Committee and was heroically destroying minutes and what evidence I could of whitewashing and worse. Others thought it was for drinking, shagging, who knows? In fact they'd come because of the noise but it didn't take lang for them to add up who we were once they got in. Later I realised they had no right to come in, but when a dozen big sods are rolling up the stairs toward you with hate in their eyes, the niceties of civil rights don't always occur to you.

The couple in the bed, quite impervious to the raid, were seized. The lad protested that he'd put the money in the meter. Others had charged past them. There had been some scuffles on the stairs, but it was too late for me. They were coming up the stairs. I thought to retreat upwards, knocking on doors of higher flats, but neybody come.

Then I squeezed into the upper toilet, closed the door and waited in silence.

I heard the hoof prints coming closer, seen the great dark shadow outside the frosted glass, squashed myself behind the door as the handle started to move. The door opened slightly, a face peered in, then the door closed again, only to be flung open hard, crashing into my head. The cop flung his full weight against the door and repeatedly banged it into my body. I fell forward in a crouch. He dropped with both his knees in my back and whacked my head into the floor. When he dragged me out of the netty I was bleeding from the mouth and forehead and couldn't straighten up. Two or three other lads were being held downstairs. They had me against the wall when they noticed me Committee badge.

These are the bastards', one said, banging me with each word. 'It's these who've done the vandalism.' As they pulled me down the stairs, a couple of them were having a whisper I think about the state of my clock. As we reached the meat wagons one of them suddenly pulled me back by the collar and held it tight so I was choking.

'Listen, cunt,' he said 'we've got you now. We can pull yee when we want, so watch every fucking step.' He rounded it off with a clip over the head; and let me fall backwards into the pavement. Then they got in the Transits and zoomed off, sticking two fingers up at the group of youths who were running up when they seen the latest assault on me. One of them, Cockney Bob, a beat who carried a rolled umbrella to signify his region of origin, waved his umbrella and shouted in cockney: 'OI! I seen that, you bastards.'

The Tyneside Committee was more than a political organisation, more than something you joined. It was something you became. It was more than even a mass movement of Geordie youth cultures. It was a youth culture in itself: a mobile commune of beats, freaks, mods, poets, and workers, philosophers and teds, orators and jivers, magicians and pot-heads. And the City was a total constituency of the community.

We soon lost the Grosvenor Square flat. Paying the rent varied from day to day, ner mind week to week. Usually we depended on bringing the bottles back from the parties to mek up the differences. The pressure was on from the cops now with almost nightly raids. And they lay in ambush for the flocks of young en route laden doon with booze and occasional pot. Grosvenor Place was becoming a place to avoid.

The cops weren't the anly adversaries either. The Trots (the Socialist Labour League) had been recruiting 'the youth', as the Marxists always called us. But they didn't mean us. It was 'proletarian youth' they wanted. Vegetarians, free love, beat poets didn't qualify. 'Proletarian youth' was translated in the Healyite mind as 'thug', and they recruited a couple of crackers, one of them being Diamond Jack.

'HUW, KID', the voice from the doorway would shout. But before you could tek ti ya heels a hand had shot GOT and grabbed yi by the lapel. Yee an anarchist?' 'Well.... I mean ... sort of.'

'THUD', as a diamond forehead with the force of a brick crashed into your ideologically unsound cranium.

We had most of us nay, all of us been full of the conviction of pacifism when we first joined the Committee of 100 up in the ILP hall, refused to retaliate to cop or city thug or last bus workie-ticket.

'Ah winnet hit yee back.' We thought we were demonstrating another way of living. Many things were breaking most of us from the conviction of non-retaliation: the nature of the beast we opposed; the devastation it was wreaking all over the world; the stubborn, almost impossible, heroism of the Vietnamese peasants against a mega-rich, all powerful state. It led to the break-up of the second Committee in the Grosvenor Square flat as voices were raised in protest at 'members of this organisation who are involved in arson attacks upon the police and property no matter how despised'.

'Listen, the National Committee passed a resolution for non-violent pushing. The logic of which was if a big demonstration were pushing against the cops and you were in the way ... to push back would be violence against our side. By non-violently going along with the push, we would direct that force against the enemy side without using violence ourselves.'

'Yes,' argued Lynne. Then you lot passed a resolution in favour of non-violent punching.'

'Aye whey, if the liberals doon sooth can have non-violent pushing we can have non-violent punching up here. What d'ye think the cops use like?' 'Yes.'

'Now have we got non-bomb bombs or are they non-violent bombs?'

"Listen, that's nowt ti dee with this meeting, that was done by individuals.'

Those individuals, friends, are associated with nay, are leaders of this organisation ... either this organisation stands for non-violence ... or either you lot... or us shouldn't be in it.'

We accepted a monthly suspension of meetings to reconsider the position and reflect on whether the Committee of 100 could be a vehicle for revolutionary Marxists and anarchists.

Meantime the secretary of the National Committee was writing to the Tyneside secretary (22 June 1965):

> I do not think you are suited to the job of secretary of a Committee of 100 group. You are inclined to go looking for trouble and an organisation that believes in organised civil disobedience has to be careful not to allow that sort

> of thing. Your behaviour down here was disgraceful. I was deeply shocked that you should have smashed the windows of the Conservative Party Headquarters. This is just proving to our enemies that we are exactly what they have always said we are and it solves no problems.

The weekends were full of parties: the Paletta, buzzing with addresses two or three check them oot or just stand in the Haymarket on a Friday neet or Saturday neet and wait for the word. It started as a set of twenty or thirty or so, meeting up to find out where the scene was at, to set off in convoy for some far-flung pad where a stranger was aboot to meet some long-lost friends. The party scene became the City kids' scene and upwards of seven hundred would mill and dance and sing and booze all roond the Haymarket, word coming through like orders for a troop advance: Grosvenor Place party Jesmond, a column of a hundred moving off, a mobile carnival, a celebration of life, love on the hoof. The others held on, for something else might come through: beach party Whitley Bay ... the scooters rev up and away ... student party at Gosforth ... that's the one, 'Ha'way', and the 'Whole Cherokee Nation' was on the move again. Course neybody ever invited anyone to a party ... yee just went ... and then it was someone else's turn. Parties belonged to everyone. The cops, under pressure from respectable law-and-order freaks, had started to write to the press about the 'disgraceful scenes in the Haymarket' and 'hordes of beatniks and scooter gangs descending on quiet suburbs and taking over the streets with loud music and dancing' (occasional public nakedness even, as the dope or booze freed the inhibitions and all humanity was letting it all hang out, man, we always got Americanised when we were stoned).

A concerted effort by the cops one Saturday night led to trouble all over the City as teams of cops moved in blocking the scooter teams, driving in front of buses and turfing everyone off them, rounding up convoys of young pedestrians, chasing off to the four corners of suburbia, looking for the outrageous party to stop, and the chief cop went on local TV chuntering aboot 'anarchist mobs who respect nobody's property'.

I actually got me first TV appearance dressed in me mod gear, talking about the wild parties, the stern-faced interviewer asking, 'And do you think that's funny?' and my reply: 'Ah think it's bliddy hilarious!'

It wasn't just within the Committee that different tensions were taking the strain. The National Committee and some of the regions were far from happy about the reports coming through on the Tyneside Committee. Nobody will find anything in the National Internal Bulletins, but behind the scenes, we weren't nice people to know. Doug Kepper, the erstwhile keeper of the golden ILP temple on Shields Road, having become the national secretary of the Committee, wrote to the Tyneside secretary (May 1964) sympathizing with the group's plight vis-à-vis police repression but highly critical of much else:

> I am sorry to hear about what happened between you and Paul McPeake and the police ... you seem to have been particularly singled out by the police and whilst I disagree with a great deal of what you's do, especially the way you's go about it, I don't like the idea of you's being victimised. If necessary, I would be prepared to defend you to the utmost of my ability. I think you are wrong to take the attitude that the police want to stop your wild anarchist parties. I think you should stop these parties of your own free will. If you believe in a world free from H Bombs, Polaris submarines and other weapons of war, you must surely believe in a world free from fear itself. In carrying out these wild orgies, you are creating a climate

of fear among your neighbours. Surely, this is not a good thing?

To the Centre, we were the very base of degeneracy. Despite wa record for *Resistance* sales, we got the impression they didn't like their paper being associated with us.

'It's not enough to fight for a world without the bomb. One has to try and raise moral standards in order to have a better world as well .... As for the excuses you make about your wild parties ... to my way of thinking, you have a perverted idea about what anarchism is' (Doug Kepper, 5 June 1964).

Kepper wasn't the only critic. Another close comrade wrote:

Thomfield Road Shepherds Bush

Dear Dave,

I used to know this lad who lived in Newcastle, who once made my eyes moist when he spoke of love and who was filled with enthusiasm for flowers. He's dead now the world killed him. He made himself a martyr for the working class who rejected him. He himself was classless, the Bourgeois would have nothing to do with him and spat on him, the working class disowned him and they knew him not. He crucified himself a million times on a bottle of beer. Like a lot of single-minded people he became slightly paranoid and vindictive and consequently all his idealism vanished and he did the inevitable he compromised his beliefs and adopted his opponents' tactics of violence to accomplish what he wanted to do, forgetting his former maxim that violence is the last resort of the impoverished mind and that things accomplished by violence will not last. Need I say who this person is?

Yours, Brian

Meantime the Haymarket, the Bigg Market, the Bridge,

were all under wor sway, this was wor land together with the Go-Go and increasingly the Quayside. We, the movement people, the youth culture people, the poets, the harp players, the Doonbeat stompers, the revolutionaries, start to inhabit another area of the toon. Start to hang oot there, start to hold meetings there, to mark off the territory with whitewash slogans and posters. The Haymarket was a favourite, prior to troop movements to parties, poetry readings from the steps, young workers liked the poems ... little knots engaged in sea-chantey singing ... a bigger knot listens to Mick Moreese play the R&B harp and a dozen improvise a blues song.

Ah'm standing here this evening
In this market made for Hay
I'm looking for a party
and a chick to walk my way....

On sunny afternoons, scooters glinting in a line ... young bodies doss all ower the steps and pavement ... it was the scene of wor 24-hour and 48-hour fasts for world peace and against world hunger. We struck a chord with many older folk coming from the pictures or waiting for buses: 'EEH, hinny will ye nor be cad aal neet sittin there?' In the Christmas period, we draped a huge blue banner with a dove and the CND symbol and words PEACE ON EARTH on the memorial, but the cops pulled it doon. In the sunshine, bodies draped on each other.... The *Sunday Sun*, a local *News of the World*, said it was 'Public heavy petting', indeed ran a shock-horror front-page story that the Tyneside CND (they didn't know any different) was a VICE RING and a front for capturing young girls into sex. This had led to expose stories on the Doonbeat and contributed to its closure and raids on The Bridge, and poor old Jackson got credited with being the Vice-Ring King, something we all found hilarious until his bearded form was a full front page of wicked sex perversion and he started to get beaten up by irate parents discovering the loss of virginity and the presence of a CND badge. Bloody obvious: Jackson and weirdo's had given them one and taken the other! The *Sunday Sun* had exposed it all as a front. But the kids still sat, sang Dylan, burned incense, jangled little Hindu bells.

The constituency of 'the movement', its fragments, its fellow travelers, its friends of friends, had been steadily growing. When a party was announced, house, garden and a goodly part of the neighbourhood began to be overtaken by the crowd. Whilever we'd had the hall we hadn't noticed this image of waselves as a standing demonstration, a mobile open-air concert, but that's what we had become.

Arrowsmith, the six-foot anarchist, seized the opportunity of his folks being away to hold his seventeenth birthday party at home. Expectations of a night of unrestrained stomping, shagging and boozing, and perhaps a little dope, were carried on the four winds of the city, since Dave was at the epicenter of the currents flowing out through the youth.

Having nicked a cake base, I had excelled with me City and Guilds confectionery skills to decorate a cake with the CND symbol, Anarchy, and what were supposed to be red and black flags. I couldn't get the icing black, but everyone knew what it was supposed to be.

As it turned out, the party was to become an apex of personal conflicts. Maureen, the most beautiful girl I had ever seen, the latest girl of my passions, with whom I had already struggled in a sleeping bag among the sand dunes, was in fact someone else's girl-friend. A goodly soul he was a petty-bourgeois intellectual with a terrific panache for rock-climbing, had been away up the wall of some crag face, when we had got to grips. This would be the first time we would see each other since it happened. I hadn't shagged her mind, it had been an incongruous struggle, me in my sleeping bag her in hers, trying to get it down, to get her jeans down, to get me sleeping bag unzipped, and she wouldn't be naked it was too cold, so we both squeezed into mine, but it was wet on the bottom so she wanted to keep her feet up a bit, and there wasn't enough room for me to get on top of her, and I was pleased to stay on the basics, basics with her, a heart-stopping, well-spoken, devastatingly beautiful girl, basics were just fine. I was king of Northumberland all that week-end. Still, all would come together at Dave's gaff; it would be High Noon; she would be calling the shots on who would walk away.

The back room of the Bridge heaved, with folk already tanked up. The birthday cake paraded aroond the room. Arrowsmith, arms in the air, a bottle of Broon in each hand, leads aboot twenty off in a Geordie war dance. In a corner my latest pash is in serious and worried conversation with the regular lad. Looks of disgust and betrayal in my direction, though he was no bosom buddy to me. Shit! It's up to her get pissed. Score wi someone else.

'Don't want anyone else!'

'What's this? No one else?'

'Stop thinking, stupid bastard. Get pissed.'

That's what I said the first time.'

Suddenly we're leaving. The pub is emptying, pouring into the street. Hundreds of bodies besiege the buses or set off walking ower the High Level.

By the time we entered, the hoose was full to capacity. All the windows were open, Bo Diddly provided the backup but the crowd as one sang 'Hey Bo Diddly ... hub bump bum; OH Bo Diddly Dudumdum.' As I struggled through the door, cake aloft ... a cheer was raised then some silly bastard leaning ower from the banister of the stairs took a bite oot of it as Ah went by. This was the start. Half a dozen others did the same and the banister collapsed. Loads of bodies heaved ower the side of the stairs and fell among them in the corridors. In a split second, Dave had dived body-lang into the throng and come up with the cake. He had time for a bite before bodies dived in all directions to bite the cake my bonny cake! Dave took off through the crood heading for the kitchen but a sortie from the living room brought him to the floor, and furious bites were laying into the cake. The living-room team were making for home when three crazies intervened through the front windows without opening them. A great surge of bodies fell against the kitchen wall. It collapsed or a portion of it big enough for two dozen bodies to roll through into the kitchen and tip up the tables with the punch and bottles of beer.

Hysterical, uncontrollable laughter. We were wild ... wild ... wild... A cake-fight ensued, which was backed up by bread, fizzed-up beer, bags of flour. The music boomed oot. Teams of mods camped on the front walls, necking with their short-haired companions. Couples lay in the front garden, young bodies boldly displayed in tumbled old dog shite and grass stains, impervious to the earthquake taking place fifty feet away.

The stair carpet had been pulled tight from top to bottom of the stairs and people were using it like an elongated slidy. Someone had got a bike up the stairs and set off to ride doon the slide/carpet, skidded sideways and careered off into the hall, bringing down the remaining wall ornaments and smashing the hall tables. The bedrooms resembled Sodom and Gomorrah, the beds bouncing to multiple occupancy and engagement, even the floors. I'd had enough, was pissed off. Maureen, the object of the heats, was heavily engaged in choosing me or the climber. The latter had already swapped hurt insults but declined the usually obligatory 'My honour has been insulted, dog; we must fight' syndrome. I hadn't been bothered mesell: Ah was gaana beam him, expect a thud back then presume we'd have been pulled apart. Now I was pissed and miserable. In the living-room lads and lasses trampolined on the settees and competed to hit the ceiling. Every cupboard in the hoose had been looted and the drinks cabinet exhausted. So was I. I staggered from the hoose accompanied by Jackson, who was being Ginsburg, or maybe the other way roond. Either way, one of them stopped me putting a clothes-shop window through in protest at the way the model stared oot at is.

Dave went on the run. The shrieks of his outraged parents could be heard in Seahouses. The hoose was, needless to say, demolished. His folks set off to track him doon and for days he sought shelter here and there, hiding oot in the Paleta.

Leaving the mayhem leaving the Jackson/Ginsburg and the buggered-off shop model I wrote, because now thoughts always needed writing down:

NO MORE

NO MORE BLUES TONY, PLEASE.

I've stayed awake all night reading Logue. I've ran shaking through thehouse.

I owe 30/- for windows from last time I was depressed.

Outside the wind howls hard on wood doors; how nice it would be, if we

were laying warm together, listening to it.

Rain is savage now in my loneliness.

I remember you know, I used to like dark endless nights.

Not now, Tony.

You don't care. None of you do. You're on his side. Go fuck yoursell!!

The final spell of the bakery was broken. I had dropped

mesell in the shite one too many times, the walls stood caked with cake mix, the result of the wrong speed on the mixing bowl. The cockney sergeant bawled: You little idiot, too busy talking up trouble than working, you'll pay for this lot, pay for this lot!'

'No I won't give us me cards.' I was the fourth in as many weeks to have a bellyful of the dictatorship and wage oppression. The idea had been growing. There was always the pit.

'David lad, Ah was rather yee carried on your apprenticeship, yee enjoy the baking; not the pit, David lad, it's ney gud for ye, not for anyone.'

'Ah've had it, Dad. The pit's a place with a strang union, with a real proletarian tradition, I can develop me ideas, within a strang union.'

'David, it's not ya ideas ye'l need ti develop lad; it'll break ya back and the men will break ya heart.'

'Ah's gaanin!'

On the trolley-bus up ti Shields Road, the drop-out message of Keith plummeted hyme: 'It nor a job for life, man, it's a job for death. You'll be buried alive, man. Ya brain will be crushed even if ya heed isn't, man. Regulations, man. Rules. Regular work. What aboot ya life? Ya real life? What aboot the "spirit of the age", Dave?'

'Ah'll still be there, Keith, with the proletarian vanguard.'

'Bollocks or di yee mean with a hoosy card in the club?'

"Anyway, Ah can always fuck off if Ah want tee....' (Did I believe it? Yes, I suppose I did.)

'Once yee tie that chain roond ya own leg, David, it'll grow bigger year by year. Yee knaa mer aboot the mines than Ah dee, ye've always telt is it's a trap that cannot be escaped from once ye've gone.'

So the course was set. The interview over, I was a mining

apprentice and immediately covered mesell in the garb of pit lore, talked like an Amble veteran, even wore a cap for a time. But the first years were years of duality. I wrote free-verse love poems round me helmet. The beat attitudes, the poetry, the shag-happy parties and protest continued. But over the years the pit would worm its way, limit the horizons, deaden the field, but not yet. Now was still in Oz. We had not yet moved back into black and white, and the volume was up loud.

At the end of November 1964 Wallace wrote to me from the Committee HQ in Goodwin Street, where he was dossing with Doug. "I see from *Freedom* that you are now the Convener of the Tyneside Anarchist Federation, I am sending you all the addresses I have (most of which you gave me) and also copies of letters I received from Leslie Francis and Bob Penaluna...I think it would be a good idea for you to get somebody from London such as Tom Brown, to go up and speak at a semi-public meeting...The Tyneside Anarchist Banner is at Ralph Robertson's brother's place...I'll be going to Tyneside at Xmas so I'll see you then.."

At the Youth CND meeting I had strolled along to up Westgate Hill with nowt much in mind, I found Maureen, radiant and happy with her best mate Viv. She was smoking. Kevin, the other bloke, didn't let her smoke! It meant they were through! Does this mean, like, we—?

'I can't see why not', she responded, with her art of making difficult things seem quite obvious. She consumed my whole being. She was like many of the lasses in YCND, slightly middle class, at high school, intelligent, randy and uninhibited. It was the start of the deepest love of my life.

It was Dylan had med wi receptive to poetry, the beat scene and local Geordie beat poets kept the feet on the deck and med contact with the working-class generation. Jackson had after all started his teens as a stocky hard lad on the Shields waterfront....

One colossal work of art imposed on the city a rendition of Ginsburg's *AMERICA* in whitewashed lines, running from the start near the Half Moon on the Gateshead side, doon Bottle Bank, ower the Swing Bridge, up the steps of Castle Garth, then back like a typewriter, the second line starting again at the Half Moon. Crowds of folk en route to the Quayside market reading the poem 1 5in. high for half a mile in one direction, then, impressed, intrigued, crossing back ower to start again and again, till the poem concludes in massive letters on the Gateshead side: AMERICA GO FUCK YOURSELF WITH YOUR ATOM BOMB.

The poem was the talk of Newcastle and Gateshead. People flocked from outlying villages and suburbs to come and read it. A mass of Geordies were suddenly intimately aware of Alan Ginsburg's *AMERICA*. The agenda was being agenda'd. In the stairwells and passages of the old Roman Wall, at the head of Castle Garth steps, other poets now wrote in whitewash. Every local scribe now added his or her piece to the wall, and I added in bold whitewash a poem to Maureen.

And folks stopped off to read the poems en route to market or pub.

In the old days of back-to-back Geordieland, when the whole population worked in shipyard and mines, and whole communities lived in each other's pockets, whole villages would up and off to the coast or hoppins. As wor culture swelled from weird minority to hegemony over all other forms and a whole generation came over to peace and revolution, free love and psychedelia, so we became a single tribe again. When the Bridge crood or the Go-Go crood or the old Committee crood decided to leave the city and go camping, like the parties, the word spread, and all the others would descend on the place likewise. Up ti Amble, Alnmouth or, best of all, Seahooses, camping among the dunes or just dossed oot on the beach. Gigantic bonfires of washed-up wood and tyres. Torn and torn aroond singing the sangs:

"The Diamond is a ship, me boys,
For the Davis straits she's boond
And her keel it is all garnished with bonny lasses roond."

Faces blackened with wood smoke, cheeks red wi the Broon.

Langhaired freaks, girls from the middle classes, working-class mods saw ney paradox.

"And it's cheer up me lads
Let ya heart never fail
For the bonny ship the Diamond
Goes a-hunting for the whale,"

Rhythm and Blues alreet, to dance ti, the blues ti screw ti, folk music for singing and drinking ti....

"Alang the Quay at Peterheed
The Greenland lads come hyme
With a ship that's full of oil, me boys...."

The Roman Wall near Housteads (Hoosesteeds) was a regular spot, beneath the greet crags dotted with climbers, often times black with mosquitoes when everyone walked roond wi broon-paper bags ower the heeds with tiny eye-slits, ti foil the barbed insect. The bus from Newcastle groaned under rucksacks and tents, vornie every seat rocking with voices in full swing.

Free beer for all the workers
Free beer for all the workers
Free beer for all the workers when the anarchist revolution comes.
We'll make Princess Margaret do a strip-tease in the Strand
We'll make Princess Margaret do a strip-tease in the Strand

When the anarchist revolution comes....

And Tom the belligerent Marxist drowning out 'free beer' with

Chaos, rape and bloody murder

Chaos, rape and bloody murder

When the anarchist revolution comes....

The tents spread oot alang the crag floor. Some with regular lasses got away into the trees so's not to be unwillingly roped into some buffoonery while otherwise trying to get to grips with more serious intercourse. We had disembarked at Barden Mill and started the steep climb up to Once Brewed and Housteads Head. Such sights as lang-haired, bell-bottomed or mop-cut, high-collared or mini-skirted or thigh-exposing, cut-doon, frayed jeans, or guitar-slung, airgun-slung, stranger than at any time since the Romans tramped the route. An aud Northumbrian in high Geordie Northumbrian burr, parodying John Wayne exclaims: 'Aye, lukes like the whoole Cherokee nation's on the move.'

As darkness started to fall, Sandy of Greenmarket fame, not blessed with wit, fumbled with his rucksack. His bird, pulled unsuspectingly from a not-much-time-to-chat Go-Go night, looked on suspiciously.

'Are yee sure ye've gorra tent?'

'Aye man, it's in here.'

'Arnly yee keep lookin in your pockets.'

'Well it might be there it is.' He pulled out a folded piece of plastic sheet and give it to the lass.

This is as good as out, man.' Tying a lang piece of string between two trees he slung the plastic sheet ower and staked it oot wi wallers.

In the back room of the Twice Brewed we sang. Us and the climbers boozed and ate gigantic sandwiches a yard thick.

ALL ON THE TWENTY-THIRD OF JUNE AS WE SET OUT BY THE LIGHT OF MOON WE'D GO A CAMPING UP BY TWICE BREWED.
HAVE A JAR OR TWO AND GET QUITE SLEWED.
LADLI FALL THE DAY
LADLI FALL THE DIDDLUM DAIDLUM
SKIDLEDITHEDAIDILUM
SKIDDDITHEDAIDILDILUMDIDAY
WHEN WE ARRIVE AT THE CAMPING-PLACE
TO FIND WE'D CAMPED BY
A GREAT CLIFF FACE
AND AS FROM THE PUB WE
ALL DID DRIFT
POOR AUD LESLIE HOWARD
FELL OFF THE CLIFF
SCREAMING FALLTHEDAY
SCREAMING FALLTHEDAYTHEDAIDILUM
SKIDILDYTHIDAIDILUM
SKAIDILDYDIDAILDILUM
SKAIDILDYDIDAILDAIDILUMDUMDAY!
THE SOUNDS OF MORNING THEN WERE SOUNDS NOT STRANGE
AYE WITH ACHING BODIES AND POUNDING BRAINS COME GATHER ROOND ALL YE BRIGHT GREEN MEN WHEN BY HALF PAST TWELVE WE'LL BE PISSED AGAIN AND SINGING: FALL THE DAY...

Maureen was just coming up to leaving school. But, for now, I got to meet her and see her as a very sexy schoolgirl. She wore the traditional bib-and-brace pinafore with the short pleated skirt, a white shirt and tie. St. Trinian's older girls always did something for me. Walking along with her in her uniform was very difficult most of the time, not least coz I could never keep me hands off her. It was a bit odd, most of our YCND crowd and some of the anarchist girls, even more of the pacifists, who we knew from meetings and roond the toon, doon the pub or raving the night away, all streaming away from school at dinner-times or yem-times, in their uniforms. Mind, Maureen's school tie was her first real gift to me, and I was that proud I wore it. She used to say, 'Don't you think people will think it's odd, a bloke wearing Rutherford Girls' High School tie?' Well, I don't know so much, we all wore red-and-black neckerchiefs, to symbolise were anarchist tribe. It confused the women in the Scout outfitters no end, loads of beatnik, lang-haired, bearded, or short-skirted, or bell-bottomed, leather-clad girls coming in to buy West Beddlington Brigade, or some other place's boy scout neckerchief. Maureen had actually thought Tony Jackson *was* a Boy Scout leader, albeit of unconventional garb, when she seen him in his holey jumper and his neckerchief. Anyway, after finishing school and while waiting for the results of her GCEs and her application to Newcastle School of Art and Design, she was off to Germany "on holiday to stay with old friends of the family. Mr. Hill, a veteran of the Gordon's and World War II, had nonetheless made close personal friends with a German family to whom they had all become very close. I hope it would not become too close as she bade me fairweel.

The postmark read 30 August 1965. My letter to Maureen full of woe, apart from the words of *Spanish Boots of Spanish Leather*.

6 Laski Gdns
Wardley
Gateshead 10
Co. Durham

I'm writing this from Seahouses sitting on a park-type bench, looking out to sea, there's a stiff wind blowing, its hard to write and boy have I got problems, down there I can count 7 colours in the sea, across there islands, there's a big one quite clear and a smaller one just peeping its head out of the water. There's nobody here, just the odd couples lost in each other's happiness. This is one of the worst camps I've ever been on Maureen, I'm in a hell of a mess...

Viv (left) and Maureen (1965)

It seems me and Kilburn decided YCND was going onto the rocks because of Viv, Maureen's tall, beautiful, intellectual friend, in Tom's ruthless Marxist analysis.

Me and Tom duly resigned over what we politically termed 'destructive personal frictions between ourselves and the group, which were counter-productive', said in a very stiff-upper-lip fashion, and then walking dramatically out, to re-pin our colours to South Shields CND's mast, a dubious privilege for them, ney doot.

The next letter arrived addressed to Miss Sweetness Maureen Hill, Wattenscheid, Lohacherstr Germany, 2nd September 65, along with a collection of Perishers cut-outs, which were our favourites, especially the agitating communist beetle in a bowler hat.

It's good to see you're getting a few quotations, both of those you sent were by Anarchists, they must be, Communists don't talk of Freedom, love, and hearts (I think they were by Anarchists, well they should be).

When she came back I wanted to eat her, but I couldn't get

her on her own properly, not yet. Still, we made it up with Viv, we were quite close actually given that she was Maureen's best friend and I was like a rival on that old relationship, in fact everyone thought they were sisters, and they were pleased to let it be so. So soon she came to be my girl's sister and a close mate to me for the rest of my life.

Between March and December 1965, US troops deployed to Vietnam rises from three thousand five hundred to two hundred thousand.

II
In the Cauldron of Hell

Dame Margaret's Home, just opposite the Glebe Colliery, where me Uncle Ned worked, a Stately Home once the property of some coalowner, now a training centre for pit trainees. Mining apprentices. This was not the school yard, but it was no academic institution either. Lads lined the yard walls and stared at each other those from the respective Wear side villages in clumps. A village bond identified them to each other. Wardley had four of us but we didn't know it. The intrusion of new estates and isolation of the old pit community meant at this stage we didn't ken each other though wa Da's had had a lifetime together in Wardley's depths for generations. So, alone, I found a bit wall to lean against, try and look hard though the city clothes, me quasi-mod jacket, me high collar, the tie-stud, the ankle-swingers and Cuban heels identified me at once as a 'toonie', roughly equivalent to 'soft shite'. The village suddenly took on the axis of the 'C' stream, whilst the 'toon', with its strange notions and philosophies, its pacifism, its crazy folk with their crazy talk, approximated the 'A' stream of earlier years, approximated even the grammar school. They stood, Neolithic and terrifying in Teddy-boy drapes, with the still-oiled hair in the Elvis sweep, black crepe shoes with brass buckles, dayglow socks, big studded belts. Eyes squinting on their own, without pretence. The denim-clad, lang-haired youths with the visual aura of the beat generation were a mirage, for they stood not in a huddle of philosophical discussion, but aimed vicious kicks at each other, pushed each other, had mock fist-fights but no so mock: the thumps and clips didn't echo round the yard. They had picked up what the beat generation looked like but not what it thought. The villages would be the last to fall, but when they did, to the dope-filled party and wild sex smash, the spirit of political class resistance clung on and prospered lang after the bell-bottomed generation had given way to the Mohican in the toon. But for now this was the violent school-ground.

I aimed at taken a lang cool draw from the fag and pull it slowly from me gob in a hard film star like action. Fucking thing stuck on me bottom lip and me fingers slid alang its length and stuck firmly on the red end, which came off on the naked flesh of the fingers then the game was up as Ah yelled in pain 'Bliddy hell, bliddy hell' and shuck me two burning fingers round while the empty torn remnant of a fag stayed in me gob.

'Whey's that stupid little shite?' caused all to peer contemptuously in my direction. It took time, by Christ it took time, to be accepted time and courage, as the physical challenges couldn't always be ignored, certainly couldn't be philosophised away.

As the inexorable force of social gravity and class history maybe dragged subliminally at me coat-tails, and I was drawn back through time toward the grey mud and black mist of pit work, the rest of the city generation lived on, loved on and the maelstrom of other city youth, Liverpool, Edinburgh, Glasgow, London and Hull, streamed in and out of each others' lives, a giant chain letter passed one from another, till it almost seemed you could demount a bus on the waterfront at Hull or on the Mersey, and walk into as many kindred souls and 'movement' people, the kids who knew where it was at, and what it is was about, knew each other in every city where it was happening. We were the ley lines, the nodes of the vibes for the revolution.

This gaanin' doon the pit, not an event, more like a process which started when ye'r born, before that even, a thin chain tying you through time and space to a place, a form of activity, born with the dialect.

Slowly it had edged its way forward. An idea of it had been there Lang, Lang before the social nudging had took you to the colliery Personnel Office. Subliminally you had heard the da and ma in conversation, day by day arrival from the pit, explaining how happened an injury, hearing the black-bodied da, awaiting his bath, talking to another black-striped man ower the hedge. The picture of underground had been emerging piece by piece and yee yasell becoming mer and mer of the picture with each frame.

The fate had been sealed lang ago it seemed, the medical over, Ah had joined the queue at the colliery office.

'David Douglass?'

'Aye.'

'John Douglass thee father?'

'Whey aye.'

'I hope yer as good a worker and time-keeper, mind.'

'Ah'll try.'

But even at this stage, in the bricks and mortar of the colliery site, with the steam rising in greet gusts from the nuw-completed baths, the shaft pulleys smudging through the steam, it was still distant. It started to get nearer, with the gurgling feeling in me guts, pit helmet, brass check and the locker, smell of coal-soaked clothes, damp pit-water smell, the feel of hard grime.

The classroom setting was a pause between the impending drop then that day came: The morn this team will ride the pit Washington F and visit some of the backbye galleries.'

All night, Ah had tossed and turned and pondered and the eyes were ablaze with movement and anxiety, what was it really like down there down there?

The lads, troop-like, hobnailed boots, in bunches, stand by the shaft waiting for the cage, pushing ti the back to avoid the fall, hapless lads, faces ashen, or pulling faces of doom, as the cage drops out of eye level and away, and rope runs on, on, on. Every time the lined old instructor looked away there was a dive to the rear of the queue and pushing of slow lads to the gate, just to put it off for a minute. Was there a way oot ? Not nuw. Too late, on board the rusting, wet cage, mesh gates dropped and, like a trapped animal, helpless and bound, the cage started to fall away. Everyone rides with tha leets oot, just- as weel, wi couldn't see each other but hearts beat fit to burst. Dropping yard on yard, rough outlines of wood lagging, huge beams, dripping water, daylight dimming and dimming until dayleet and all that's peaceful up there is just a tiny speck of silver.

And my girl writes:

Words come quickly when I write
As tears come quickly when I think
As time goes quickly when I love.

They're inevitable, uncontrollable,
As the ceaseless circle of the earth
Which always crushes someone on its path.

Oh God, don't let it crush you or else
it must crush me too for to be left in
an unfathomable space like now would be unendurable.

Words would go slowly
I would not write
Tears would not come by will or force

Time would die.

Doon the lang closed galleries of the F pit, the lads sat in near groups waiting the return of the instructors, knackered from late-neet boozing, aal of wi; knackered from early-morning rising, knackered from learning the art of 'hingin on' the rope haulage. I was tentatively putting forward arguments for a young workers' association, a team of young miners to put forward the case of the trainees to the union. I had not often argued politically, though from time to time the challenge of some comment on the bomb or the beatniks had drawn me like a fish on a hook to put the matter straight and at such times perhaps had shown too much knowledge, too much strangeness to be an ordinary one o' the leds.

On this occasion a voice come: "Yee knaa that lad meks is' fucking mad', and a body rose from a group and took steps toward me. The ones to whom I had been talking sort of rolled to the side and sat grinning, as if to better show they were no allegiance of mine. 'Why dint yee shut ya fuckin hole, yee daft little shite?' 'How's that, like?' I said, getting up but expecting in a flat second to get smashed doon again. Another body coming in my direction voiced: 'Because ya'r a communist bastard and yee talk a load of communist shite', his boots advancing quickly toward me. Then another voice: 'Ah divind think he does, Ah think he talks sense.' The heeds turn, it was Spicey, a Ted with a young boy's face, which he was committed to having 'hardened up', as he called it, by getting it hit. Love and Hate tattooed his knuckles and Flash, a quiet constant mass of muscle and violence, was always just one step ahind him. Spicey steps toward the fat pit lad who had marched over in my direction. Spicey's body shot forward like a coiled spring and in a second grabbed the lad by the lapels of his NCB overalls with a violence that took him back off his feet, but dragged back again in an instant. Flash, exuding a grin, which accompanied each and every occasion of violence, suddenly smashed his head into the lad standing beside him, he fell to the dust-covered floor, blood oozing from his lip.

'What ye dey that for?' he asked from the deck.

'Fuck all', Flash said, with his big face and eyes like a tiger, he beamed at me. I smiled back, though I felt sorry for the kid on the deck who had done nowt. Still, can't pick ya mates in this situation. As we walked oot the mine that afternoon, I asked Spicy: 'De'yee agree with what a'h was saying like?'

'Dey Ah fuck', says Spicey.

'Well what yee jump in for?'

'Divind like ti see anyone get picked on. They used ti dey that ti me until Ah hardened mesell up. Me and Flash have fights twice a week now.'

'Every week?'

'Whey aye, every week, just ti keep hardened up, put some hard on ya face, like, yee knaa? Impress the bords.'

My head shook in non-understanding; Flash's grin and his grunt of a laugh made me laugh too. His simple pleasure in life was hitting people in various forms and he was quite happy not to be able to rationalise that to a daft toonie. It tickled me, indeed Flash and me laughed every time we seen each other, for ney apparent reason whatever, there was an empathy of humour which was invisible and non-audible. We were an odd trio ... but, by God, I needed them.

After the first few days, the class turned out as normal for a dinner-break in the Glebe canteen, they all turned left at the gate while I turned right. Spicey claimed I was a weird bastard where did I go? Easy, down to the Black Horse for three pints and two big salad sandwiches. Flash and Spicy were immediate converts and day by day as the smirking deviationists coined right, wor number grew. After the bait we threw open the discussion: UFOs, CND, village sex life as opposed to city sex life. The subjects were chosen by the lads in turn. The debating boozing gang was going great guns when some scab informed on wi, and we were hauled before the head of training. There wasn't a lot of defence but I was unanimously elected to conduct it. Problems with being under-age, with technically still being at work while drinking, didn't sound like casual charges, but my spirited defence of 'boys will be boys', 'pig ignorance of the rules', the spirit of adventure, etc. plus our humble apologies, got us off without charge. We had to move to the White Swan after that.

My weirdness more or less became accepted over the successive weeks, underground training, and work with the gallawa's, work at colliery sites in pissing rain and wind on surface salvage, and shared agonies of enforced athletics on surface training days, cross-country runs on winter pit tips and moonlike landscape, welded joint resilience.

As Flash and Spicey emerged on the Newcastle scene, barriers of middle-class tolerance were tested in full. Weird gear was acceptable if it was sort of intellectual-looking, beatnik-looking. Spicey, however, cut a dash in his longer-than-drape drape with golden satin lining, the fifteen buttons, drainpipes and velvet collar, his lang blond hair hung in a wave over his pretty face which he hated so much. Flash wore black: a black drape with reed lining, white socks under the drains. Their girl-friends still wore semi-back-combed hair and hair lacquers, wore lipstick you could tell was lipstick. The intellectuals were afraid of them, the city kids med them say everything twice to be certain they understood. The girls' Wearside accents and girlish skirts and bodices carried a sexuality reminiscent of the classroom memories. But they came, to meetings at first, then rolling aboot and bopping at parties, until the crack doon the pit fair hung with news of the gaanins on ... and the host of pit lads and rock-and-roll lasses grew. Finally they came on demonstrations roond the toon first, then on the lang bus trips to London and elsewhere. Easter CND March '66. They were raw working-class enthusiasm, the obvious penetration of working-class youth into political forms not used to them. Tyneside Youth Against The Bomb banner, carried alang by two pit-lad Teds, with Love and Hate, or Death, on their knuckles. They became a hybrid, beat-Ted, bopping and listening to free verse, still getting in anti-social, internecine village wars while protesting against world wars. They hung in with the force for peace and socialism but still kicked fuck oot of anyone who looked at them the wrang way.

Graduating from the training centre, I got to start at Wardley proper. I wasn't to be given the drudgery of the haulage system, but put in an almost unique position. Geordie Summerson, colliery linesman, needed a young assistant, me Da put the word in for me, and I got it.

The job was a kind of lay surveyor, keeping the face lines running parallel to the gates and the gates running straight, measuring up the gates, putting the level marks on, doing the measure marks. Key instruments: a pot of whitewash, an oil-lamp, and a lang lump of string.

Dead centre in the gate, you'd have banged a base mark plug, made a hole with a hammer and chisel in the rock, banged a lump of wood into it, drew a white circle round it, into the centre of which you hammered your staple from which your plumb bob can hang, marking the dead centre of the gate. You'd come back in two weeks' time, and the gate has advanced, maybe 20 metres. So you hang your thick rope with a lump of stone on the end on your last base mark, take your oil-lamp out to the one before that and hang it likewise from the base mark, then walk back in to the last arch set, where you take your string and plumb bob, and hang it from the centre of the arch, moving it along the arch, in the dark with your cap-lamp off, until your string intercepts the rope in the middle and both strings line up right through the eye of the flame on the lamp. At that point is dead centre, and you mark that in a line along the arch centre.

Now the magic bit: you string the lang rope from this mark down the gate to the last base mark and tie it through, so the string runs in a dead straight line from point to point, hanging the lamp on the rope, put out your cap-lamp once more. A shadow in a straight line runs down the gate, dead centre. You take your little pot and paint the shadow with gleaming whitewash. This will show the caunchmen, advancing the road, where dead centre is to set their next arch and keep the road where it's supposed to be. Extending the line under the caunch to the coal on the face, then again in the Mullergate, next you repeat the whole process down the face, only this time because of the danger and getting in the way of crawling bodies and cutter blades, and shot blasts you chalk the string, so when you tie it off from one end of the bank to the other, tightly, you flick the string and a thin, just visible, line in chalk runs dead parallel down the face. Next you crawl along backwards, kicking out with your heels and rowing backwards with your elbows, doon the face, face to the heaving roof, painting a broad white line over the string mark.

This will mark a dead-straight line for the timmer to be set in, then the conveyor track to be advanced under. The whole thing, crawling from face to face, over newly fired shots and coal gummins, walking down miles of roadway and headings, wriggling through cramped little staple pits and ower narrow little caunches, dookin' from shot blasts, running under waterfalls, and angry boring rigs on their air legs running with water, was knackering. But, like climbing a crag, it was exciting, it was exhilarating. Plus I got to do the eight o'clock shift, a rare privilege in a coal mine, and when I came oot from the lines I got bathed and went to work in the survey office, doing copying, and shading, and getting out the old plans, and making copies of extracts.

The pit was sending me to Sunderland Tech, too, where I was taking qualifications for the official colliery linesman's certificate. We got to do surveys, do levels, peer through the engineers' levels at the inverted numbers on the staff, do measures using the real chain. The math's was difficult for me, but I was getting there. I felt I was getting good at something exciting and clever and, boy, did it have street cred. I was a pit man, whey aye on the face, I would respond as if I was Wardley's big hewer.

Here I would learn contortions I never could have visualised, someone called it crawling on your ears getting under the low work onto the face, head squashed flat to the side, one arm forward, shoulder square to the floor and flat, slide forward, lay chest flat and flatten your other shoulder. Move your arm forward, your battery is flat underneath you, or else you've taken it off and slung it under. First your arse pushing down, wriggle, kick with your toes, but then keep both feet flat, not turned up, wriggle, struggle, creep, kick out over the coal gumming, arse and back on the roof, belly and face lying directly atop the newly fired coal. You will learn to do this as well as take one pot of whitewash, one yardstick and one oil-lamp down the face with you, advancing each an arm's length forward, before pulling yourself forward, foot by foot. You will learn strange body movements, like pissing while lying flat, or, worse, rolling into the goaf, squashed flat to the roof and stone floor to shit while lying flat. You will learn to eat your bait by taking a bite, then turning your head in order to chew it without hitting your chin on the sharp coal gummins. Someone said: 'When I stand up I feel like I should go to sleep.'

From Geordie I would learn the coal lore. Chiding me when I mentioned that coal came from trees.

Trees?' he responded. 'Look', he says, rubbing the dust from the shinning coal-face, 'look, this coal is end-on, the cleat is running all in the same direction. I can take you to any face we go on, it will run the same way wherever we gaan. Did all your trees fall in the same direction then? Someit else, I can tek ye to the seam above this one, ten million years later than this one, and the cleat will be running all the same way as this seam, did all them trees fall the same way as weel ? And mer', I could tek ye ti any country in the world, doon any coalmine, and all the seams, at every level in every mine all ower the world, be running in the same direction. Did all the trees a'll ower the world and millions o' years apart each time, aal fa'll in the same direction, lad?'

I had ney answer, but he hadn't finished.

They say it takes sixty feet of tree to make one inch of coal, sixty feet! In the United States and in parts of Russia, lad, and in Australia, they have seams three hundred foot thick. Let's see he gets out his pencil and survey book 'that's 300 times twelve equals whey, Dave, that's a three-thousand six-hundred-foot tree, man, and there's hundreds of miles of them.' I stared.

He laughed: 'Bliddy trees!'

'What aboot fossils?' I pronounced, realising that I didn't have a shred of evidence or even much logic now to defend the well-known fact that coal came from trees, except, well they do, they just do, and that wouldn't do at all.

'Fossils, lad, are found under the coal, or over the coal, never in the coal. Look.' He raked down a piece from the freshly fired seam. On the top of a greet lump of coal lay the imprint of a distinct leaf , 'Look.' He slid the furry web off the top of the coal where it fell into powder. That is a layer of siltstone pressed on top of coal. That is where your fossil is, that's the nearest it gets, it is never in the body of the coal such as it will be in the body of hardened claystone.'

Geordie was one of the old-timers. Like me Da, he had been one of Harvey's men in the 1920s and 1930s when they were lads. They followed the brilliantly passionate 'Bolshevik Geordie revolutionary, Geordie Harvey', a member of the Industrial Workers of the World, an industrial unionist, a Marxist from the anarchist camp, he had kept some of the flourish of Harvey's merciless debating style when I ventured, 'So what, where do you think?'

'Nivor mind that' changing tack, 'nivor mind what do I say, what do you say about your trees, they're your trees, lad?'

'Well, it's just what I learned, I suppose I never questioned it.'

'Well, question it, and question everything, and if it sounds daft, let them tell you why it isn't.'

As we walked back to the pit bottom through the gale blowing down the main intake, through the clarty roads and ruts left by the big underground diesel tractors, he announced: 'It's an ore, like iron, or any other mineral.'

I had become quite proficient in first aid, and was the colliery junior leader, winning canny prizes in competitions. I mention that for the phone call I received in the Bridge. It was Spicey.

'Ho, ma', haven't seen yee in ages, what's gaanin on?'

'Aye. whey me and Flash hev been in a canny few barnies thou knaa's.'

'Sorry to hear it.'

'Are yee daft? Wi'v had some crackin' battles, like a John Wayne film.

Anyway, Flash got knifed.'

'Knifed?'

'Aye, the silly bastard,' he laughed, 'gor it reet in the belly yee knaa.'

'Bliddy hell, is he in hospital?'

'Aye, whey, nor, he wes, but Ah'v broke him oot, Ah sneaked up the fire escape and sprung him.'

'Bliddy hell, Spicey, ye'l kill him.'

'Aye, whey, that's what Ah want to phone aboot, ainly he's meking all these funny gurgly noises, yee knaa not oot his gob like sort of inside him.'

'Bliddy hell, Spicey, that means he's breathing through secretions of blood, he's bleeding, yee daft bastard.'

'Whey, Ah can't see any.'

'Nor, it's bleeding inside him, where are yee?'

'We're in this pub, listen' pub noises and laughing; and a weak, stammering 'Huw Dey Dyvie?' from Flash.

'Spicey, he's not drinkin' is he?'

'Whey aye, what's thee think Ah broke him oot for? He's had aboot five bottles o' broon now, or had on, he's fallin' ower making them daft noises again.' 'Spicey, stop laughing, yee stupid bastard, he's bleeding like a stuck pig inside him, aal that broon had pulled the plug, it must be pissing out him. Send for an ambulance and then fuck off.'

I was later to hear that Spicey sent for the ambulance, propped his marra up sitting there in his jarma jacket with his drape roond his shoulders, white as a ghost, bought him a whisky and went. He was unconscious when the ambulance arrived, dehydrated and stiff, but alive, with that thick grin jutting from his face.

The pit was beginning to change my direction back towards Marxism, but the rhythm of beat poetry was, if owt, growing. Pickard, a working-class Geordie poet not given to Americanisms, whose plain honesty was at once observable, captured the abandoned Mordon Tower on the city walls for the beat generation.

Writing poems
keeping rabbits
each day the shite
to be cleared
fresh straw to be laid.

If not the Mordon Tower, if all parties had expired for it was true we often searched the city suburbs and neybody was having a party and we, like a dejected tribe, wet and bedraggled, shuffled from place to place till the last buses were also extinguished, then to try and doss in the Central (but the cops weren't allowing that now) or kip under some bridge or another. For these reasons, we adopted the abandoned GRAND Music Hall; just over Byker Bridge. We had secret entry points and left a store of candles stuck in bottles, made beds from cardboard and straw, and could always fall back for a late, late Music Hall. The folks at deed of night swore they could hear the ghosts of the aud artists still playing in the Grand.

We thought the Stones' Paint It Black was about us, we thought it fitted the world of the pit and sang it all the time.

A little while earlier, I had made the most remarkable discovery. I had discovered the clitoris, I had never ever come across it before. I believed, like most of the lads, that girls got hot and excited because your dick was stuck up them, or your fingers made them feel it would soon be stuck up them. When I discovered it, I thought it was unique to Maureen. I called it her 'nerve'.

The intensity of love brought an evil jealous sensation, a mixture of fear of losing, of trespass, of property violation, hooked into inferiority complexes deeper than an ocean; wrote to my lass:

'Dazed, but it's half nine and you're still talking ... to that guy [John]. Art, you bugger, I was lost lang ago and I'm confused. No not just this 'art' (I've been to an anarchist meeting) and I's sick coz that not what I believe. "Pit men are strong, you know?" Looking at those fellows from an artist's point of view, workers' culture can be "interesting", looked at from a distance, of course. I wanted to wallow in the pitness, in the basics of survival. Art, because I knew fuck all about it, was an affront to me, like the schooldays, the poxy pink forms again, something I hadn't had the chance to see.

(Thinks) Shit! you ought to see me dressing for the pit, its magnificent, vomiting like fuck before I get into the cage; me marra Spicey just sixteen and 2,000 foot down.

(BBC COMMENTARY) 'So this is life in the pits, young lads happily thinking of their girl-friends, old men giving kindly advice.'

'Get the bliddy hell oot, lad, before you're knackered.'

Singing the coal-dust melodies through secretions of black phlegm.

'But I ain't chatting anyone up....' No, but he is ... the old cultured bit, even I've used that line, by Christ!!! C'm here ye.

Listen, I love you (yeah, she listened, now that's enough for tonight, so long). Hey ... you're happy with that?

All day ... all night ... (this ain't no poem ... this is my ... this is what I believe.) I love you till, till you ... God, I don't know ... What is all this I've wrote? It's not what I mean, really, forget the rest.

Yes, marriage was betrayal of a long-held rejecting of the state's interference in people's private lives, but the system all the time pushes in that direction, just for easiness, and for mutual possession.

Your cheeks when you're whistling, or the little rise on your belly before it slides down past your tight hipsters.

Silhouette of your breasts, gentle uphill rise belly, slow sweeping like, down to your womb neck.

Very slight dimple on your chin, two either side of your mouth.

Your lips ... your lips,

Bottom one petted, sore with long sucking,

Prominent, top one playing hide and seek with your teeth which are cool and moist and when you wear your tartan jumper smock!

7 p.m., just four hours, then we wave goodbye.

To separate beds, why not together?

Softly breathing beside me, sleeping sometimes but warmly, so it don't mean That's enough' but rather 'Stay Dave ... stay.'

What a young neck you have.

A little later than the discovery of the clitoris, came another almost as earth-shattering, I was standing suppin' broon at the lounge-bar in the Bridge and holding forth on a range of subjects, technical, political, historical and mostly made up on the spot, when a young voice I recognised cried out: 'Ye're a hypocrite, mind.' Oo, that stung: a hypocrite! It was Malcolm, Maureen's young brother, taking the piss actually, but he advanced the position further:

'Ye're supposed to be a vegetarian, aren't ye?' Supposed to be? 'Whey huw come ya suppin' broon?' What was the youth jammering on aboot?

'What has the noble broon dog got ti dey wi non-consumption of animals? "Elementary, my dear Douglass, it is made from fish!' This must be some unfunny jest, so I wrote to Scottish and Newcastle, and true enough, the broon ale, indeed all their ales, are processed using fish swim

The elope-ees following the posting of the Banns, Edinburgh (1965)

bladders. Not sup broon!? Ye might just as weel of said I couldn't have sex and still be a vegetarian, but there it was, haven't supped the broon since.

Body and soul, I began to feel like part of a movement, the movement. Ah began ti see mesell as a proletarian edge of a beat generation. Jackson was big on the fringe at Edinburgh and mesell and Maureen frequented the fringe, me deyin the horny-handed son of toil poet bit but chuffed ti wee bits when I appeared in the fringe poetry mag New Gambit alang with real poets like Adrian Henry, Adrian Mitchell and Tom Pickard. Wallace and Jackson were in as well o' course, but that didn't count. Mind, mine was a weird sound-type poem about Maureen's dimples and how they got me horny, but most people thought it was an Inner vision of something. So we hit on a new plan. We'd elope and get married in Edinburgh. Didn't tell neybody in case they stopped wi. Waited till all the gang went off camping to Jedburgh, and told the folks that we were going too, even bought some Jedburgh postcards in the Toon and wrote

Just married (1965)

them as if we were camping, sneaky. First, we had to spend the two weeks in residence, to become sort of naturalised Scots. We spent the time easy on the beat scene, doon at Bobby's Bar, on the Mound, staying with a couple in the tenements behind Arthur's Chair.

Then we came home while the banns were posted and prayed neybody would spot it and tell her folks. I let it slip doon the pit to me marra Geordie Summerson, and I think he give me Da the wink as to what was gaanin on. But me Da knew once I made me mind up Ah'd gaan reet on and dey it, so he just let things bide to see what would happen.

15th Aug 1966 in the district of St Giles in the City of Edinburgh.

The cream of the Cherokee nation journeyed north for the wedding, Tiny and their lass, Tom and his partner, Viv, of course, Jackson and the whole beat crowd from Edinburgh, some passing Indian Scottish children, the folk we stayed with. We cut quite a dash. There was hell on. We didn't really know where we would stay when we returned and made a joyous entrance to the informal reception with the rest of team back at Paddy's. Jim Pearse, the intellectual IS man, took pity on us and said we could rent a room off them at Jesmond, so that's what we did. Then we set off to face the music and the folks. When we arrived at me Da's place he was abed, having been on night shift. Me Mam warmly embraced Maureen as the 'lovely, lovely slip of a girl' and shouted up the stairs, 'Jack! Your son is married!'

'Oh aye? well, congratulations, La,' he shouted down, 'Are ye all reet for money and what not?'

'Aye, Da, we're great.'

'Well, good luck son, Maureen, see ye at work.' That was that, I think he had prepared himself for the event, still thought he might of got oot of his bed.

Dread filled us as we neared Maureen's place, but they were out, and that made it worse. Maureen just left a note saying we had got married, were happy and not to worry, we had things to sort out and we'd be round later. It was a devastating discovery, triggering anger and sorrow. They felt robbed, robbed of their daughter, and robbed of the chance to see her married. Their sadness put a damper on our joy, and we regretted that it had to happen like that, but we had done it. We were married.

Why had we done it that way ? We were at 18 old enough to get married, in theory, but Maureen's Mam and Dad had warned they would make her a 'ward of court' and since she was still living with them, get an injunction to stop me seeing her. On reflection now I don't know how much bluff that was, but there was no way we were ever going to get their consent. So we just up't and did it. Maybe we should have argued it out with them more, maybe we should have been more determined to win them over, instead we just did our own thing man as we believed everybody should.

The kindness of the Pearses didn't make up for the clash of

class cultures. Middle-class mannerisms and notions can be deeply infuriating, Sandra's view on child care being basically to let the kid do what it wants, go in the fridge and smash eggs on the floor, bombard the rooms with flour. 'If we spent lots of money on toys it would cost more, and this is more creative', Mum would say. From their viewpoint I was everything repulsive about working-class blokes: I got drunk, I was nasty to Maureen when I got jealous, and said stupid things about art and culture. We could never agree about diet, about how much food 'was necessary' and what requirements were, and argued about the difference between what one's body technically 'required' nutritionally, and what ours mine and Maureen's anyway wanted.

I had told Geordie the plan, of moving to the Doncaster coalfield. He shook his head from side to side slowly, as aud Geordie pitmen are inclined to do when troubled.

Tha knaa, lad, they're not like us doon there, they hev a saying: "Hear all, see all, say nowt, eat all, sup all, pay nowt, and if you're gonna dey owt for nowt, allis dey it for theesen".' Coming across the hewers having tha baits in the tailgate, next day he told them of my Plan. 'I worked doon bye, in Doncaster, at Askern, what? Marras? there's two of them there, one says: "Fuck all them, there's just me and thee and fuck thee, that's me!"' They all started to relate stories of meanness, selfishness, lack of comradeship, till I fair wondered what I was letting mesell in for.

'An' when the belts stand, they all shout "Get to know". Aye, and we'd better "Get to know".' Off they went being Yorkshiremen shouting in mock Yorkshire accents: 'Get to know youth !"

William Short, better known as Lofty, was a huge coal hewer from the shallow Northumbrian drifts, occasionally switching to railway guarding as the mood took him. His

Northumbrian pitmatic, drawled as wondrous tales, humorous or in deedly dreed, true or utter bullshite, cast a spell ower the young comrades sitting in rapt awe at the crack.

He was the only dissident member of the SLL I had ever met, picking up his armful of *Newsletters*, the sale of which was an act of faith and devotion as strang as Sunday communion. What the hell, I wondered, was he gaana dey wi them as we heeded oot ower the Swing Bridge forra neet on the pop at Gatesheed? The question was soon answered as he hoyed the bundles of revolutionary gospel ower the bridge and into the Tyne with a roar of irreverent laughter. I wondered how many other bundles of the revolutionary words of wisdom the quotas of loyalty from the steely Healyite cadre ended their days in the drink, dumped without ceremony.

A quick moment's reflection on the actual nature of that crowd led me to conclude that Lofty's sacrilege was perhaps exceptional.

Lofty struggled with the weighty texts of Marxism-Leninism-Trotskyism, poring ower the pages with his sleeves rolled up, in the wee smallie hoors between shifts. He had ney problem with the hard Bolshevik countenance. He despised frivolity and gentleness, and from time to time, when he fancied himself as the steel cadre, would brook ney comedy or tenderness either. 'Bourgeois sentiment' was a favourite put-down. When me and Maureen hit the Edinburgh street in a carnival of the weird, following wa elopement and wedding, Lofty and their lass Pauline posed with countenances so stern they would have done credit to the graduation photos of the KGB.

At times Lofty was capable of unrestrained violence. Craig was an emaciated threadbare hippy without the bonny clothes, a walking charity shop who considered the

Army and Navy Stores to be the height of boutique shopping. He was gentle, quiet, kind. His Gateshead flat housed him and ten dogs of various shapes and sizes, all of them as threadbare and emaciated as he was. His poor Mam, equally threadbare and pleasantly eccentric, was dying somewhere doon sooth. Craig was utterly naive. To Lofty, no great lover of dogs or hippies, he left care of both flat and dogs. Greet mistake! A couple o' days later I ran into Lofty, gob half full of stottie-cake bait, pint in hand. How, I asked, was he faring with the dogs? Swilling doon the remainder of the huge butty, he responded flatly: 'Disposed of.'

I stared in a mix of fury and non-comprehension, though certain this was ney gam'.

The stupid bastard was starving because of the bliddy dogs. He couldn't feed hesell or them. It was a revolutionary duty, Douglass!'

'Whey what then?', I started, hoping to save the lad's feelings if nowt else, 'ye gaana tell him they ran away or what?'

'On the contrary, Douglass, I shall explain how I shot each one in the heed with a 12-bore, in order that his grief will prevent a repetition of his stupidity.'

Jimmy Fitzpatrick of a large family of red-haired leftists, was famous in my mind for the near death-defying feat of painting a huge anti-Vietnam-war slogan on the riverside of the High-Level bridge. Visible for miles, it had involved balancing on a narrow crumbling parapet directly over the fatal drop straight into the river. U.S. AGGRESSORS OUT OF VIETNAM, it yelled at the bus passengers and drivers crossing the Tyne Bridge opposite.

Forebye, Jimmy heading off yem for his much looked-forward-to Sunday dinner, following wa mass leafleting of the Gateshead flats and estates against rent rises, was to discover Lofty tagging alang, 'just till opening time'. Jim's sister had laid oot the Sunday dinner, Yorkshires, roasted tatties, bright- coloured veggies and roast beef.

Not having expected an additional diner, she had nonetheless laid out a smallie plate for Lofty. When Jimmy returned from his bathroom freshening up, he stood thunderstruck as Lofty, already at the table, was half-way through Jimmy's scran.

'Ye greedy bastard', growled Jim and, pushing the small plate towards Lofty, sarcastically suggested: 'Here, ye mun as weel eat that anarl!' Which Lofty, without a hint of guilt, obligingly did with a gob- filled, muffled Ta'.

Pauline, during the later occupation of the LSE prior to the mass Vietnam demo in London, gave the self-declared revolutionary vanguard a lesson in class relationships they are unlikely to have forgotten. A student had accused her of being ignorant of Marxism, a fatal mistake. A working-class lass bred and born, factory worker, shop steward, passionate Geordie revolutionary socialist and wife of the big sociopathic coal-hewer, she was ignorant of little and had commanded respect from far better men than these. The words had scarcely left his lips when Pauline, in a spring, shot forward, felling the shocked student with a flat hand-blow to where his chest should be, followed like lightning with a leaping double knee-blow which stayed stuck in his chest as he collapsed backwards, Pauline on top of him, drawing a big dagger from behind her back in mid-flight and landing with the steel blade right against his juddering throat, screamed, 'Ye petty-bourgeois shite, Ah'll kill ye', while the student army of Trotskyist Maoist revolution stood in shocked silent inaction and confusion.

March 7. 1966 Clywedog dam, supplying Welsh water to Birmingham, attacked with bombs from the Free Wales Army, does £48,000 damage.

Eeh the Welsh Free Army. At once exciting and to our minds not the slightest doubt that this was a noble and justified cause. They dressed in redundant German bottle green army uniforms. They had organized themselves into 'flying columns' went on parade with Alsatian dogs . Marched like an organized force. They had emerged into the now largely demilitarized Easter Uprising commemoration, in Dublin marching in uniform and in step under their own Free Wales dragons and colours. At a time when the Old IRA was becoming 'the old rusty guns' this was very impressive. Cajo Evans, who had founded the unit must have had bollocks like a bull, since we are reliably told by Ian Bone, as the column stomped past Dublin GPO the scene of the insurgent's last stand, Evans pulled out a shotgun and blasted the air in salute and defiance. Cajo's first lieutenant was Denis Coslett, a miner with one eye, the other lost during shot blasting in the pit. He covered the blind eye with a black eye patch, David Frost christened him Dai Dayan, after the one eyed Zionist tank commander.[14]

Kilburn too had a strang band of bitter Calvinism, which rendered him at times mirthless and dour, mocking levity and happiness. 'While millions die and languish in poverty' was a sure way to put the dampers on festive occasions like Christmas or New Year. Because he was the person everyone either respected or wanted as a best friend and wished to be approved of by, it could rapidly render us all guilty and hypocritical, throwing us back to introspective feelings of time-wasting frivolity, ensuring that the paper party-hat was discarded. Tom, was capable of a steely countenance and deep-voiced seriousness which he assumed to be correct social protocol for the Bolshevik, an illusion shattered as Murphy, wor big black cat squatted on his lap, paddy-pawed his jumper and suckled his beard. Tom had a wealth of

Gateshead Jewishness which rendered him, like many of that community, a walking encyclopedia with virtually universal knowledge of any damned thing you cared to mention, coupled with a irrepressible faster-than-lightning wit and humour so typical of the Geordie-Jewish community. He was an excellent singer with a bottomless wealth of songs, as well as being a brilliant precision-engineering tool-maker and craftsman. Tom was the archetypal Proletarian Vanguard. A faultless chapter -and-verse-Marxist-Leninist who insisted on rendering everything to a dialectical materialist analysis, he was the scourge of utopianism, anarchism, religion and mysticism. With an undying hatred of pop music, rock bands and juke boxes, he was not a man to invite to a hippy rock festival.

Maureen was soon down at the Art College in Hull for her interview, while I sat in the station buffet, drinking bottles of beer and wondering what the hell this place was like. Then it was my turn at Hatfield Colliery. God, a huge sprawling place, loads of people milling about, coal Lorries trundling about everywhere. I knew from the first interview things were going to be different here, very different.

This was no cosy family mine, this was INDUSTRY, there was no glamour here. Also no automatic house, you had to go on the damned waiting list. And mining apprentice? You'd start on haulage with the other lads, and wait your turn for coal-face training.

Returning to Jesmond, things were not going to plan. Right, we'd live between Hatfield and Hull and both commute in different directions. The map showed us the ancient port of Goole as our location. Meantime I had bought a scooter, a 175 Lambretta, from Les, with a view to traveling to the pit each day. Next I'd trek back to Hull and stay at Johnny Mac's and look for a flat in Goole, take our bare shekels, and give meself a few days to come up with the goods. It was not to be, I wrote to Maureen dejectedly.

Postmark 27 August 1966
127 Albert Ave. Hull

Oh God, this is harder than I thought. Right now sitting in a pub on me own, this is my first pint, time about half past one.

I've spent all morning trying to find somewhere and I'm still in Hull, because there are only two agencies in Goole and both are shut all day Saturday. The bus runs every one-and-a-half hours to Goole. I've no idea what the fare is, but it's 1 s. 3d to phone from Hull.

Here's 18 numbers I've tried.

And many many more, they're all shut, they will be Sunday and Monday (bank holiday) as well. Christ, that'll leave two days.

Anyway, Mac met me all right. I prayed all the way down. I feel down, Maureen, way low, things ain't going well at all.

An I hate these tongue-tied bastards, I'd better not write anymore except my love will have to wait but it's here inside me as I sit on this slippery pub seat and walk this God-forsaken city. It'll all work out. I really wish you'd come down with me, you'd think of something.

I've just been out in a last attempt and phoned 'The Party'. There was only a little six-year-old boy in. I told him I'll phone again tonight, coz if the worst comes to the worse maybe there'll be a party member in Goole who'll put us up.

I've bought the paper but nil nowt in it. My God, I feel conspicuous in this pub and stupid and feel like crying in desperation. Christ, let it work. Don't worry pet, it's got to. I'll ask Mac for a loan.

I'll keep writing or start talking to myself, Mau. I'm

missing you.

I've noticed some of the women in this pub and they wear their wedding rings like yellow teddy bears, it's sickening.

Postmark 28 Aug. 1966 (no stamp, postage to pay)

127 Albert Ave. Hull

Dear Maureen,

Sunday. Mac's gone drinking, I'm sitting on the bed, no music nor nothing, on me own again. £2 left for food, bus fares, phone calls and an odd pint (I mean that I'm dying for one now. I wish I could go out tonight but I can't). This must last another four days.

God, I wish I'd come up on Monday night. What the hell was I thinking of? We should have known everywhere would be shut Friday when I got here, and over the week-end and bank holiday Monday.

I could go to Goole on Monday to look round but I think Tuesday's the best, because I can't afford both.

It's deathly quiet here, awfully lonely Maureen, dear Maureen, I miss you, right from when the train left the station. Oh, roll on Wednesday night. Maureen, I hope I can get somewhere, it's tearing me to bits just thinking about it, not being able to do anything. I've got half a tab left!

Honestly, Mau, I'm gonna make it last.

I reckon fares from Goole to Hull every day are gonna be quite expensive. Never mind, getting somewhere is the main thing.

I've been to the phone and back and halfway down again but finally decided against phoning the CP. It's an awful cheek, an what about all our stuff and the scooter anyway?

Well, I hope you're being very good. Please, please keep yourself for me, it's hell here. I know it sounds like

I'm exaggerating but not really.

Postmark 29 August 1966
127 Albert Ave. Hull

Monday. Had to post a letter yesterday without a stamp, because I didn't have any money on me.

Mac's out at work, I'm on me own again, I've tried to phone but being bank holiday there's no one in anywhere.

Went out late last night and had a pint. I'll be getting up early tomorrow to go to Goole and see what I can find. Please God in heaven, I must find somewhere.

Anyway, how are you?

I hope you're feeling well and have had no nasty pains. I'm dying to see you, pet, really.

I don't think there'll be any papers today, but I think I'll go into Hull and get a stamp for this (if the post office is open). Still, I need to find out the times of the buses tomorrow, anyway. (These Embassy are all I've bought down here. One of them you bought me in Newcastle, so I'm not doing badly, am I?)

Well, I've done all that and I'm at a stamp machine. With any luck I should get somewhere tomorrow and maybe be home tomorrow night.

All my fondest love.

Dave

But God, if he was there, had other plans .We would not find a lodge in Goole, and instead would rent a room at Albert Avenue, in Hull, and I would ride on the Lambretta to Hatfield. The first dummy run took me two-and-half-hours to find it, cruising along in me pit helmet, with me hoggers balanced on the running board. Getting me key to the lockers and sorting me pit gear out, the training officer asked: 'Why the knee-pads?'

'Well, I'm a face linesman', I replied proudly.

'Not here, you're not, you'll not need them.'

No eight o'clock start on this game, you had to be down the mine by six a.m., at the pit by five-thirty a.m. to get into your duds and collect your lamp and ride. There was no magic any more. I would no longer collect my oil lamp. There would be no need for such on the pit bottom. I had to get up at three a.m. in the drizzling rain of the Hull streets, as the North Sea blew in its blasts, I would start the scooter, cutting ney dash in this God-forsaken place, at this God-forsaken hour. Wet through, soaked to the bone, frozen stiff, my hands could scarcely hold the tea in the canteen as I tried to burn some sensation back into me mitts and face.

Rushing through to get changed, through armies of men, nude and shouting, mekin' crack, but not in my twang. Despite the warning I still wore my knee-pads on me belt, wanted them all to know I wasn't just a haulage hand. I knew about coal, about coalfaces, but who wanted to know that?

Kit Robson, the ancient Geordie pit bottom overman, lining the lads up on the bottom at the start of the shift, points them off in one direction or another. Here in the No. 1 pit, the main air-intake, the icicles hang from the shaft wall, a freezing gust blowing without reprieve, two decks top and bottom, full tubs running on, empty tubs running off, both sides left and right of the shaft, eight lines in all.

The tubs arrive in a constant stream, in couplets of two. As the cage comes down the barrier is raised. The full-side lads push the empties off, while the empty-side lads pull them clear. A few months into the job and it nearly killed me.

I had been deployed to the top deck empty-side, the worst job in the pit bottom and, if the crack could be believed, one of the worst at the pit.

In the freezing, mind-numbing combination of sweat running down your body inside your clothes and icy cold blowing your face and hands off, the earliness of the hour made you stagger, while your bones and muscles ached. Trying to get the set of two mobile again after coupling, and without thought, I splayed my back to the tubs and put both feet on the full tubs in the cage to flex my knees, straighten legs, and push the bastards away. The only thing was, the cage had been rapped off and was ready to whisk up the shaft any second. My feet would have shot up with it, dragging my body upside-down up the shaft as far as the landing-board, whereupon I was for beheading and my back breaking. I took my feet off the full tub as the empties started to move and change round, so my arse faced the shaft and my legs strained to keep the tubs in motion. In a flash the cage and tubs were hurtling up the shaft, and I looked over my shoulder, trembling as I realised what I had just done.

Ah, but the delights of the top deck were yet to come. This was my first shift. I would get only the second worst job in the bottom.

'You, Geordie.' He points to me.

'Straight.' What? The bloody straight.

As the empties roll off the cage, the first two lads couple one to the other, then again one to the other on the twin narrow tracks, so they stand in four sets of four. Then they heave and push the tubs into motion, fly-coupling the two twos together. I, on the straight, would keep them all in motion, pushing them on, while diving between the sets of four to make eight, then stop them in a vice-like object called the juts, by which time the cage is down and the tubs are rolling again, until I have a set of eighteen which I push away and send off round the turn on their journey to be filled at the loading-chutes. The work is endless. From beginning of the shift until the last minute the cage flies up and down, bouncing off the sump timbers as it lands, onsetter's bell ringing incessantly, dust swelling in a mist at the full side, a thick fog of cold air hovering like a cloud on the empty side. You run all day, but the cold eats right into your bones. There is no colour here, there is ney canny crack.

Riding back to Hull in bright sunshine, it could almost have been a nightmare, but for dropping eyes and aching bones. To roll into the clean sheets, and our flat, which Maureen had tried so hard to make nice and personal, and just sleep, dribbling in unconscious stupor. By Friday, in the early morn, as I rose and kissed Maureen, I felt like my Dad, creeping about in the twilight hours, but aware of a rising dread, and hatred of that damned straight. From the top deck would come a set of empties in a team of sixteen, timed to miss my set rolling out from the bottom deck. The only way to get a minute's rest was to time for a collision, as both sets met on the junction. The 'doggies' pit bottom charge-hands would scream and shout abuse at us, but fuck them, let them sort it. This was punishment. This was punishment without end in sight. I was stuck here, it seemed.

At the weekend we hit the pubs with Johnny Mac and crew. Senses rose as the live band banged out blues and got the whole pub chanting: Tigers!

Tigers! bomp bomp bomp bomp bomp bomp bomp..bomp bomp.' Like, 'Let's go!', only they shouted TIGERS, Hull football team, or something like that. Then they'd get into the swing:

Dinah, Dinah, show us ya leg,
Show us ya leg
Dinah, Dinah, show'us ya leg
A yard above your knee!

The rich girl rides a limousine
The poor girl rides a truck
But the only ride that Dinah gets
Is when she has a fuck !

Oh, Dinah, Dinah, etc.

The rich girl wears a brassiere
The poor girl uses string
But Dinah uses nothing at all
She lets the buggers swing

Oh, Dinah, Dinah, etc.

The rich girl uses Vaseline
The poor girl uses lard
But Dinah uses axle-grease
Because she likes it hard

Oh, Dinah, Dinah, etc.

The rich girl wears a ring of gold
The poor girl one of brass
But the only ring that Dinah's got
Is the one that's on her arse!

Dinah, Dinah, show us ya leg,
Show us ya leg
Dinah, Dinah, show'us ya leg
A yard above your knee!

The following week, I waited two hours in the canteen, dozing on the canteen table, waiting for the training officer to arrive. When he did, he got both barrels.

'What about this Mining Apprenticeship? I'm supposed to go on to different jobs every three months.'

'That doesn't apply here. You're on haulage until your name comes up on the face list.'

After a month of this never-ending back-breaking bone-chilling torment, I'd had enough. The lads were always grumbling, always throwing off work to escape the job in the hope some poor bugger like me would arrive while they were off, and they'd get roped into it, instead of them.

They had a whole elaborate pattern of injuring themselves to get off the job. Like hanging up a big arch girder-plate on a rope, swinging it away then walking straight into it! I even tried that, twice, but each time ducked and let the big metal plate swing past me head. Another was to sprag (as these Yorkshire folk called it) the plate upright with a stick, lay your hand underneath it, then whisk the stick away with your other hand, letting the plate fall onto your fingers. Tried that too, but each time pulled me hand away as the plate fell. The alternative was to find ways of smashing the job, breaking the top-deck creeper by wedging great wooden boards into it, while running a set of empties onto it, then hiding the broken board.

One lad, crazed with the job on the empty-side pulling off, asked me to whack his arm with a locker when he wasn't looking, so we could say he caught it between two tubs.

'Are you sure?' I asked. This was a big lad.

'Fucking whack me with it or Ah'll happen whack thee with it before shift's out!' he said, with promise. I waited until the thick of the fury with the tubs bouncing off the cage, the dust rising in great clouds, the others from the last draw still rolling, and he pushed with his head stuck against the back of the tub, his arms fully outstretched, his back in a straight line, his legs flexing and pushing to get the set away, when whack! I aimed a hefty blow at his forearm with the thick wooden drag.

Tha fucking little Geordie cunt!' he yelled 'Ah'll fucking kill yi.' As I set off running, he chased me, screaming about his arm, at the same time throwing lockers and fish-plates and any bits of ramble he could find. Wooden lockers bounced off me helmet and hit me square in the back, but I kept running. Later I peeped out from behind the turn and heard the bell for Riders. They were talking him up the pit. I hoped I had done reet. Three weeks later, I saw him in the canteen bright and breezy, a plaster on his arm. He caught my eye and jumped up. I made a move to dive away, two steps too late. He grabbed me with his good arm.

Thee,' he says, 'I owe thee.'

'What?'

'Here, get theesen a pint', and stuck £2 in me hand.

Two bliddy poonds?'

'Hey up man, Ah've gorra Common Law in, Ah'm gonna be quids in, and off that pigging job, and Ah'll mek this bugger last a month or two on t' Club!'

Well, fine, but a more permanent solution was needed, and I started to work on a Young Workers' Committee, which at once drew almost 100 per cent support from the pit-bottom lads. We needed change! Our first meeting, in the George Hotel, Stainforth, saw all the lads off all the shifts, and an agreement to demand a rota system, so all the jobs would change and nobody would be stuck on the straight or the top-deck empties for more than a shift. We could all stand it for one day every month or so.

The *Mineworker* article (second edition) of the period tells the story:

> The recent spate of accident posters proclaim 35 out of every 100 accidents are on haulage, our black spot. No attempt however to reason out why this should be is

made, if I might hazard a guess based upon the conditions at Hatfield Main Colliery, Yorkshire, and if it is correct then the rise in accidents on haulage isn't really surprising.

One of the main things that struck me as an immigrant from Tyneside to the supposed modern pits of Yorkshire, was the antiquated haulage system, the majority of young workers being employed on this, having little or no chance of changing their type of job, even though their Mining Apprenticeship agreement states that they will have a different job every 3 months, culminating in face training. Most are doomed from the time they enter the pit, to remain on the pit bottom until the list for coal face training gives them a chance to go, which is at the best of times (if you're old enough to put your name down, which many young workers aren't) will be a year and a half.

The modernisation of the faces, the installation of faster machines and means of getting more coal in a shorter time, has built up over the years, putting more and more strain on the haulage workers their conditions can only get worse as coal output goes up. Certainly at Hatfield many workers, old workers especially, will tell you that the pit bottom has altered only fractionally over 30 years and only small improvements with great reluctance have been made. Hatfield No. 1 pit bottom was never made to handle the coal it does today, the inevitable speed-up to try and get the tubs away makes the use of coupling blocks and safety devices impossible.

On at least three occasions when the haulage workers decided to use the coupling blocks the pit was stopped within fifteen minutes.

Out-dated track systems, and juts, speed-ups, redundancy of safety regulations who would be surprised if it was fifty out of every hundred accidents on haulage, certainly not the haulage workers.

The haulage workers at Hatfield felt that the problems were peculiar to them. They had no trust in the union officials and considered many of the majority to be gaffers' men and the others to be only interested in the colliers' disputes.

Trying to get anything done for the haulage workers from the union was certainly an uphill grind, nearly always met with the rebuff 'Well, the pit has got to work, therefore you lads must bide your time till things change.' [1970 was one of the dates for pit-bottom reorganisation.]

Almost the majority of workers were young lads between the ages of 16 and 18. They'd all signed up with the union, but that was it, no attempt was made to recruit or interest the lads in the union not even a friendly chat from the secretary about what the union is, or a copy of the rule book. Most had the impression that the branch was there as last resort when everything else had failed.

The course of action was obvious. A Haulage Workers' Committee, made and composed of haulage workers for their problems to be met in a way they decide also an education class to teach the principles of socialism and militancy.

The first meeting was called with 40 or 50 lads (almost the entire pit bottom) present. The policy was decided upon and to stand on a correct solidarity footing a young engineer from Tyneside spoke on the problems of their industry and the history of the Engineers' Apprentice movement.

We were surprised to find that not only young haulage workers but apprenticed fitters had also come to the meeting and provided a wider base for the committee .One of the main sores the lads were smarting about was the unequal distribution of jobs. Some jobs were markedly harder than others and it was those who were most outspoken and prepared to take a lead, those who were repeatedly put on top and bottom deck, while other lads got easier jobs every day. The obvious victimisation had to stop. In the following week a system of job rotation was decided on. The majority of young workers signed an agreement which read:

We agree that a system of job rotation on No. 1 pit bottom should be effected and that the rota should take the following form:

1) Top Deck Empty Side Coupling;
2) Bottom Deck Empty side (Straight);
1) The Top Deck, by far the most difficult pit bottom job;
2) Bottom Deck, an easy second to the top, not as hard, but harder than any other.

That these two jobs, being the most difficult, should not be given to any haulage worker as a regular job. That (e.g. person 'A') goes on the top deck on, say Monday. After doing his turn he will not go back on that job until everyone else has also been on it. He may be placed on the bottom deck on the Tuesday, if the Deputy so wishes, but he will not expect to have either of those jobs again until all the other workers have also done top and bottom deck. He may after his turn be placed on any job except those mentioned.

In the case of absenteeism, if e.g. someone is off when it is his turn to go on the top or bottom deck, then the person immediately next in line goes to the job. When the someone returns he will then get his turn.

When this Committee first started a great interest (even support) was shown by the Communist Party. However, as soon as it became obvious that we wouldn't be tied to their party or help in their elections, all support was withdrawn. Their guns were then turned against us, as they used their influence in the branch to attack the Committee, whispering here and there that 'a Trot' had been sent in to destroy and undermine the influence of the CP. Many times at branch meetings the officials openly accused me, saying I had been sent (where from, Cuba?) to smash the union and pit. No defence was offered or expected from the so-called 'Left' of the meeting. Strange, union, management and Communist Party huddled together in fear of the workers' committee.

Next came the SLL, a group who claimed to be Trotskyists but had no connection with Trotskyism, either in what they said or in form, having a similar relationship to Trotsky that the Communist Party have to Lenin PRACTICALLY NOWT AT ALL.

They came and patted me on the back.

'That's the stuff, they said. 'We'll support the committee.' Great, thought I, and brought some of the lads along to a week-end school they were having. There Cliff Slaughter, one of the big lights in the SLL, attacked me and the workers' committee in front of the whole meeting of

65 or 70 people: 'Join the SLL, not these useless committees.'

Under constant barrage from all quarters, the Committee fell apart, but how naive they were in thinking that the militancy and comradeship of the young workers would be broken because the Committee was. The lads pushed on with their claim for a rota system. Victimisation of myself and other workers was met with work to rules: The Block ! Stop the Pit!

Until finally the system was introduced and the lads more or less ran the pit bottom themselves. There is no shirking, everyone knows whose turn it is. Not content with this, when a lad gets the top deck his mates swap him for an hour each, so possibly he gets the bad job only for 2 hours a day and shares a vast variety of others, which greatly eases his situation.

However, although the system has continued for some time now, it is still not the official method of work. A copy of the rota system with the signatures of the lads was given to the Union Secretary for him to have it made official, there has been a month of forgetting and losing it, and still it has not been done. The fear is that keeping with the present repression by Coal Board the management may try and smash the rota. One thing is for sure, any attempt to do this will be met by firm militant action, both within and outside the Branch.

Combat Haulage speed-ups with work to rules and the coupling block.

Build the Haulage Committee to pressure the Branch and cut official red tape".

This Cliff Slaughter, projecting his no-nonsense, Bolshevik steeliness at the long table of the Youth Hostel of their Cadre School at Ilkley, surrounded by my young marra's from the pit, and new recruits to the self-declared revolutionary leadership, responded with disdain to Maureen's and my request for just vegetables, because we were vegetarians, with the observation: 'Personally I see no difference between a cow and a cabbage!'

'Really?' I replied. 'Dialectics isn't your strong point, is it, comrade? You wouldn't be too hot with the shopping either, come to think of it.' Which drew a laugh from those who knew what I was talking about, and a look from his fellow intellectual leaders as if I had just committed sacrilege.

'Petty-bourgeois dross, which has no place in the proletarian movement', he responded angrily, and we left, after what we were certain was indeed a plate of vegetables and not a herd of cattle.

In years to come this base of pit lads, with their girl-friends and wives, would become the bedrock of everything we did in the Doncaster coalfield. They became our personal friends, they partied at our house and intersected with the old traditional Geordie freaks, they were the folk who started to frequent our folk-music socials at the George Hotel, Stainforth. In the words of the Big Hewer: 'From this day on, these men will be your brothers!' and so it was from boyhood or adolescence to manhood. The bulk of this team, formed on the freezing pit bottom, in the teeth of local bureaucracy and prejudice, would stick with me in all the epoch-making battles which lay before the pit communities in times to come.

By now I'd given up traveling on the scooter and had taken on regular nights, so I could travel on the train. It was far from satisfactory. For a start, the train got me there an hour and a half before the start of me shift, which was long enough to begin with. Then, going back home, I had to wait nearly an hour after getting bathed and reaching the station. It was hell. Maureen would just be getting out of bed as I was getting into it, unless I got her to bide a while, but that wasn't too common, with me eyelids scraping the floor. This was drudgery. There was no thrill in this game. The world had gone decidedly into black and white.

Still, soon we were offered a house of our own, in Dunscroft, and it was take-it-or-leave-it time. So one

Saturday we donned a couple of pit helmets, Maureen's tied on with a scarf, and set off on the scooter to view the hoose. Course, I was still a learner, and like a clod had left the 'L's on. We were excitedly driving along in the sunshine, rabbiting on, when I suddenly became aware of a police car, cruising in dead slow about two 'feet behind me. God, hand signals, all the right shit, ney gud, he pulls me over.

'Who's the owner of the vehicle?'

'Ah well, I am, legally, but I'm going to give it to her, and I'm giving her lessons, which is why we've got Ls on.' Not too convinced, he gives us a producer to present my FULL licence down at Hull police station. We set off again, arriving past Hatfield church, and down the two-mile-long avenue of miners' streets, Broadway, Abbeyfield Road. As we turned into the street, the little lads kicked a football up and down, and four little girls about eight chanted 'Bow to the King', doing the actions, little ribboned heads bowing with folded arms, 'And curtsy to the Queen', drawing out their dresses and bobbing down in a curtsy, 'And show your knickers to the football team!' they said, pulling up their dresses to their chins and displaying their knickers. I nearly fell off the scooter, and got a clip off Maureen.

Meantime we tried to kid the cops on, turned up at Hull police station with me provisional licence and walked in.

The cop who stopped me thought I didn't have a licence and asked me to produce it here, so here it is.'

'Yes, that seems OK', they were starting to say, when he picks up a scribbled note. 'What about your pillion passenger?'

'Oh, well, she has a full licence, she was giving me some tips.'

'Well, you'd better give her one, and tell her to present her full licence, or you're getting done!' It was no good, I had to own up, so I was charged.

The house, this would be our house, Maureen would use all her artistic skills, and I would turn it into a revolutionary centre. It would becomes a standing stone, as revolutionaries and comrades trekked south to London, or back north to Newcastle and Scotland. Now we could make a start. Mind, it meant now Maureen had to get up at five-thirty every morning to head off to the Art College, not returning till seven-thirty p.m., cold, tired and knackered. It was hardly conducive to creative thoughts and art, but she stuck it out, finally getting the degree, hard won, hard fought for in the teeth of difficulties and real hardships. She had taught me about art meantime, I no longer feared it, I now understood it, knew its allies and those from the other side. Oh, the charge: we sold the bike to Johnny Mac, who told the cops I had high-tailed back to Newcastle, he didn't know where. Hee hee.

The Committee of 100 had broken in argument and the contra-pulls of pacifism and revolutionary action. The YCND, on whom we sometimes dropped, was constrained by regulations, rules and constitution, weighted down by overseeing from the big grown-up proper adult CND. It was to meet the need for a dynamic organisation for peace and revolution, not organisationally tied to national bodies and able to respond to what it wanted when it wanted that TYNESIDE YOUTH AGAINST THE BOMB was founded. It was all-embracing, covering all the old gang. Anarchists and ex-YCLers and Young Socialists, few of wor members were currently in organisations other than united fronts. We had long since tired of The One True Party' type of jargon and 'Only Roaders' who began every sentence with The Only Way Forward...'

TYATB occupied most of the Bridge Hotel night after night, its members pontificating on all subjects ... knew better than anyone else ... nobody was ever quite radical enough ... quite right enough ... They got the nickname Geordie Cong as a play on Viet Cong and a little parody I wrote.

You'll have heard of the Workers'Army, of the Great Napoleon too
Of how the town militia beat the Turks at Waterloo
But here's a page of glory that as yet remains unsung,
And that's the war-like story of the bold old Geordie Cong.

DOWN FROM THE BRIDGE HOTEL ALL SWAGGERING IN SONG
FIFTY LOYAL SUPPORTERS OF THE BOLD OLD GEORDIE CONG.
WHEN GAANIN' INTI ACTION CAME A SHOUT FROM OUT THE REAR:
'BEFORE WE FIGHT THE BOSSES, LADS, LET'S HAVE A PINT IN HERE.'

Now there's many a workers' barricade erected in the street
Many a policeman's been found dead as he patrolled his beat
But here's a tactic Geordies use that's of a strange new brand
A mass sit-down in a public house with a pint in every hand.

DOWN FROM THE BRIDGE HOTEL ALL SWAGGERING IN SONG
FIFTY LOYAL SUPPORTERS OF THE BOLD OLD GEORDIE CONG.
WHEN GAANIN' INTI ACTION CAME A

SHOUT FROM OUT THE REAR: '
BEFORE WE FIGHT THE BOSSES, LADS, LET'S HAVE A PINT IN HERE.'

So come and fill ya glasses lads, this is the final round
The gallant corpse is real enough and, strange though it might sound,
Wor fighters off in Vietnam and Ireland do quite well
And very soon they'll be as good as the lads in the Bridge Hotel.
THEN DOWN FROM THE BRIDGE HOTEL ALL SWAGGERING IN SONG
FIFTY LOYAL SUPPORTERS OF THE BOLD OLD GEORDIE CONG.
WHEN GAANIN' INTI ACTION CAME A SHOUT FROM OUT THE REAR:
'BEFORE WE FIGHT THE BOSSES, LADS, LET'S HAVE A PINT IN HERE.'

Tyneside Youth Against The Bomb tried to hold the constituency of working-class city young 'uns. Individuals not organisations tended to be invited to talk about their personal perspectives. Subs were fixed at a shilling per member. An 'Action Committee' was set up which met to plan activity, public and illegal. We launched a fine fund for the impending and inevitable arrests.

The minutes for 25 January 1966 record that the meeting was as usual held in the Bridge Hotel, and the room cost 10 shillings. The group continued until it evolved into something else, merging with Young Socialists, Syndicalist Workers' Federation, Young Communist League into a common front: Tyneside Vietnam Action Committee. All funds were handed over to them in August.

Something of a cataclysm hit me with the first ever visit by our guru, our poet, our leader Bob Dylan to the toon, a toon whese kiddhas had basked and soaked in the raw blues and taken his songs as gospels. I may have start a world wide mutiny against him. Well not really, I was simply one of the first to make a public protest against him. A protest against Bob Dylan? Is nothing sacred ? Apparently not. Me and Maureen were chuffed to wee bits to actually get tickets, albeit in the balcony. The rest of the gang were scattered around the theatre. This was almost personal. He had emerged in the first half to a somewhat lacklustre performance of his acoustic set, and many of the words we taken as anthems. In the second half he emerged, with an electric band, dressed in red shiny suites, he in a shiny combination, and electric guitar in hand. He launches into some mindless rock and roll numbers of his own creation, devoid of political content, devoid of the movement, devoid of all the things we thought he shared with us. It was like a hard slap in the face, my blood boiled, I felt utterly but wretchedly betrayed. Angry and then deeply sad, as the wall of electric shite wailed forth. Maureen urged 'c'mon' lets go. We stood up, but instead of walking away I walked to the front of the balcony, just as he finished a set I yelled "Read ya poems Bob, the Shadow's were here last week!" As bouncers came running forwards to grab me, but I was going, he looked up to the balcony, smirked ,shrugged and struck up again. Ejected and dejected, I hated myself for not having thought harder about what to shout, about not having shouted more. But it struck a cord, by the end of the evening the boos following each song grew louder, and the kids outside poured forth their scorn to the TV camera's and as he left the stage door. The protest followed him to his next gig in Sheffield, until by the time he reached the New Port Folk Festival, Pete Seeger went and got an got an axe to hack the electric cable in two and shut off the row and the vacuous verbiage of personalised drivel.

As Bob said later in a song "Don't follow leaders, watch the parking meters !" Ian Vardy of the original Prelude line up, actually taped the concert, and though blurry, you can clearly hear my scream of protest, which is followed by a ripple of laughter and a scattering of claps by those who had heard what I said. Bob wasn't in fact part of our movement, he had never taken the idea of actually belonging to something, and doing anything political seriously. By 1967 he was saying words to the effect that he had 'done' the political thing, he had been 'old' now he wanted to be young, which he associated with non-political, drug punch drunk, egocentric and playing thoughtless rock and roll tunes on electric instruments. Whey aye, we moved on too, we got to like some of his long meandering pros, initially some of his comic lines, but soon they would go to the 'done that' pile with the young protest songs and deeply moving polemic.

Easter March (1966): Trafalgar Square

The group, now though formless, remained as a retinue, a milieu.

Soon Geordies would trek down regularly and stay the weekend, or the ones still not working would take up residence. We carried out whitewash raids on unsuspecting colliery village walls, denouncing the war in Vietnam and the atom bomb. We had already established the Young Haulage Workers' Committee, and were soon working on developing a revolutionary miners' paper, *The Mineworker*, and setting up a national committee under the title and aim of Mineworkers' Internationale, but we still went hyme nearly every week-end, hitching the roads back up, to be with the old crowd, to be part of the movement. But the movement was soon to be everywhere. We returned every holiday, nearly every rest day, as well as those I had off for the queen, as the old Yorkshire pitmen called their 'laiken days'. We still tied our red and black neckerchiefs to the guy ropes of our tent whenever we camped amid the dunes at Seahouses, just in case any dispossessed ghosts of our lang-lost tribe were wandering through the dunes and would spot a comrades' camp.

Mind, Maureen for a year or two, suffered intense jealousies, especially from me, interrogating, the poor bugger on her whereaboots and conversations must have med it hell for her. I had rules about the length of her skirt, questioned her about who she sat with and what he said. It was more crucifying than the haulage. But when ya sure ... jealousy and possessiveness gaan aal thegether, which makes for a much more liberated sex life. It's like having ya cake an' eating it, someone once said. No, it's not, it's like havin ya cake an eating someone else's. No its not, coz someone's eaten yours. Sh'rup, stupid bastards, it's not like cakes at all.

But for now we were a mass of strangeness, we dressed different, we acted different, we talked different, lads doon the pit thought I came from another planet and had crash-landed here. Kids would shout 'Gypsy' at us on the street, because of our strange attire, and there was no 'scene, man', not yet awhile. We were indisputably toonies, despite coming from Wardley colliery, wor village was cosmopolitan, was in any case within walking distance of Gateshead and Newcastle, village people we could be in Greenwich, N.Y., but in Dunscroft? We were fish's weel oot o' wa'ater.

Cursory flights of memory back to the late 1960s flash

Newcastle (1967): mum, me, Maureeen, Cats and Trotsky's *Russian Revolution*

bright with memories of rebellion, music, sex and sensation, but deeper reflection shows, for me and Maureen anyway, another, quieter side. Every year Ralph would buy us a big ILP desk diary, with some socialist pacifist quotation on every month, and notes of great events for labour and rebellion across the world almost every day. The entries show, first, the overwhelmingly happy and loving couple we were, amid an exhaustion of mental and physical toil, my labours on the shaft bottom haulage, her 12-hour day, up at the crack of dawn and away on the long journey to Hull and then back again. Long exhausting hours ate into our youth, dampened her creativity, made art a drudgery, a task, while the pit now equaled punishing unromantic work in a village with none of the colour and life of the toon.

2 January 1967. My birthday. I'm 19 years old! (Christ) Get some nice presents and cards, nice dinner off Maureen, Malcolm (Mau's brother) and Maur took our books back to the library. I'm glad you had a nice day, pet.

Saturday, 11 January. Went to town with Maur, got a TV (black and white) and stair carpet, God knows where the

cash'll come from. TV man cometh with wor TV. Stayed in with bottles and watched a Western.
March 12. Cross gates in the Elan Valley- 40 sticks of gelignite discovered wired to the pipeline carrying water from Wales to Birmingham, the work of the Free Wales Army.
1 April. Tiny's wedding today. Went to church. Took photos.
28 April. Tiny and Pauline come, put Put-U-Up up! Nice chat.
Saturday 6 May. Tom and Ev arrive this morn, glad to see them. Ev and Maur go to town shopping. Me and Tom chat then make path, Len and Marion come for tea, we all go down to Abbey for drink. Me get drunk, faint. Mau go bed ill. Nice night. Give Mau 10 shillings coz I drunk and love her very much.
July 1967. The First Of May Group founded on the programmed of armed international revolutionary solidarity. They were not intending to actually hurt anybody, but still violently attack the state and its projects. They machine-gunned the US Embassy, leaving a note demanding Stop The Criminal Murders of the US Army ! Solidarity with all people battling Yankee fascism all over the world ! Racialism no! Freedom for American negros !

Stuart Christie, in his autobiography (*Granny Made Me An Anarchist*) tells us :-

> 'This group initially called itself the First Of May, then by a variety of tongue-in-cheek names inspired by current outlaw-friendly films such as *Butch Cassidy and the Sundance Kid*, and *The Wild Bunch*, finally settling on the Angry Brigade. The choice of name was an ironic reference to the middle-class 'Brolly Brigade' who had been winning the hearts and minds of middle England by attacking striking

railway workers with their umbrellas.'

Tuesday 15 August. Wedding anniversary. Took day off.

21 August 1967. Three rebels in a car rake the consular section of the US Embassy with machine gunfire. Scattered leaflets call for solidarity with the Vietnamese. The action claimed by the First of May group, five of whose comrades have been jailed in Spain for trying to kidnap the chief of an American air base in Spain.

But for now back at Hatfield, a notice on the NUM notice-board caught me eye. It advertised the union's three-year day-release course at Sheffield University, studying industrial relations, economics, and politics. Beginning in October 1967. Just the job, a day off work to study, for three years, at University! I was thrilled to get it. The huge recommended reading-list and advised book-list showed this was not to be some soft option. The day a week needed supplementing with eight hours a week at home. It was great. Maureen's armoury of art-history books and books of famous painters was spreading along the alcoves next to the fireside range. Now my formal politics books would join the Marxists and the anarchists, bourgeois economic theory would join the labour theory of value, a mass picket of books on unions and industrial relations would outnumber them all. Many nights we would sit, in absolute quiet, me smoking me pipe, which I started to do when it was the 'mod' thing for teenage boys to do, the two of us reading, or else debating with each other something we had just read. That way we didn't get too isolated from each other's homework. We would always read each other's essays and make corrections. The house was becoming a library, but had a long way to go yet.

30 September. The pipeline from Lake Vyrnwy to Liverpool damaged by explosion at Llanrhaiadr ym Mochnant, £28,000 damage. Free Wales Army.

2 November. (Maureen) My birthday [she draws 20 candles in a line!] 20. Got nice presents, dress and money for shoes, lots of lovely cards and vodka and After-Eight mints from Dave. Very nice day indeed.
17 November. Bomb in Temple of Peace, Cardiff, £30,000 damage to entrance hall. Free Wales Army.
21 November 1967. Met Maureen off train when I came home from me day-release course, fog very very thick, when oot the Haar comes a beaming face, Ralph has come down shining in aura and black PVC, where did he come from? He wintered with us, our revolutionary centre had the duality of a temple also.
25 November 1967. Tom and me and Ralph went to the Democratic Club and had a few while the lasses went to Doncaster. Later, after dinner, me and Tom went back bought ten bottles broon for home and had a couple each. Came back and got some more booze for the lasses. We all had a great rant bringing previews of Christmas booze-ups singing till 1 o'clock. Tom found the lighter he lost last year, in the chair !

Coal-face training took place at Rossington Colliery, a pit with a bend in the shaft, such that when the cage got to that point in the shaft it hit a set of rollers to guide it round the bend. It was quite noticeable when dropping doon belaw, where your every muscle is tense and the slightest bit of oddity impacts rapidly in your brain as Danger! Danger was a new discovery. Coal-face training took place on 84s, a unit so 'exhilarating' your heart was permanently in your mouth. The unit was supported on link-bars and props. As the face moved forward, your job was to take your 71b. hammer and aim at the link-pin, which kept the bar sticking out horizontal to the roof, holding the roof up.

You needed to do two things: hit it first time, a good smack so the pin dislodged; and, in the same movement, bugger off, for as the bar came down so did a whole area of abandoned roof. The 84s flushed very heavy. It was worse if, for some reason known only to the earth, the roof decided not to come down in sections but bide its time, until maybe only one prop and one bar were left standing in the worked-out section, holding up the roof for 250 meters long, and 100 deep into the goaf. Nerves of steel were required to inch towards the bar, aim, then smack and run for it, as in a split second the whole worked-out section came down in a great crash of stone and rock, sending an explosion of dust thicker than a sandstorm, and often skittling out props and bars all over the face, causing new falls among the men in the working areas.

Link-bars were strange creatures. You fit the bar that you've taken out of the worked-out section and, balancing over the blades of the face-chain, fit it up to the newly exposed area of roof and bray home the wedge with your hammer. Apart from the danger felling the bar, there was the danger in retrieving the prop, which was more often than not buried up to its cap in big stones. Trying to pull these out was donkey work, made worse by the creaking roof ready to come in. Even with the use of a Sylvester and chain, a kind of ratchet pull-lift, the earth would cling tight to the barrel if you'd wrapped the chain round the top of the prop. And if you kept pulling and the earth kept hold, the telescoped part of the prop could start giving and drawing itself out of the barrel. If it came out, it did so under extreme pressure and would fly 100 yards, and if it hit you it could kill you stone dead. In the stables,[15] you bored shot holes, had the shots fired, then laid into the mountainous pile of coal, struggling to establish a floor to work off, to get to the rock floor, so that you could make the shovel run level and bite more easily into the coal.

In theory you were supposed to reset all the timber which

had flown out after the blast, and set new timber under the newly exposed ground. In reality the temptation was to leave the timber out till you'd shoveled away all the coal, so you had room to fling it unhindered onto the chain running behind you. Sometimes you had no choice. The prop and bar would be under the pile of coal, which stopped you setting it right away and at the same time kept getting in the way of shovel and your efforts to find a floor, so you'd try and heave the damn thing up through the gummins and set it where it stood. The heat was so intense, everyone worked naked, except for boots, helmet battery and knee-pads. You felt a bit vulnerable at first, but as you got stuck in and the first sweat broke from your body and the dust began to cover you, you couldn't really notice, except at bait stand, when it was odd to see naked black men, sitting on their hunkers, the genitals hanging down, eating their bait, and talking aboot politics.

As usual, not everyone appreciated my politics, or me in general. A couple of the really big lads doing their training, who were from Hatfield, seemed to feel it was duty to dissociate themselves from me by attacking me every day how puny I was, how stupid I was, how I couldn't do nowt right. One of them, whom we should call Dudworth (because he's still huge, and still a bastard, and still around) used to illustrate the point by amusing himself on the bus going home, by grabbing me head in a vice-like arm-lock, then, when me face went blue, setting fire to my hair! I wouldn't back down to him though and tried to match him blow for blow. On the way out of the pit, riding on the belt, he crept up behind me, then jumped on my back as I lay on the belt outstretched. His mate then tipped his nearly full wa'ater bottle, or Dudley as they called them in Doncaster, onto the belt, which ran along and, since I was unable to get up, soaked me from head to toe. The following day, I shot out first, and doon away on the belt. Dudworth and mate thought I'd buggered off out of their road, but I hadn't. I got off the belt next to the fire-hydrant, put me lamp off and waited till them two came bobbing along on the belt shouting and bawling. They shouted a lot more when I quickly opened up the fire-hydrant and a full charge of water knocked Dudworth straight off the belt and swamped his mate. I turned it off quickly while the confusion still reigned. Dudworth was nearly out cold, having collided with a belt strut on his way to the floor. Still with me lamp out I dived on the belt and rode out in the dark, quickly joining everyone else in the pit bottom waiting to ride. The crowd roared with laughter as the two bedraggled thugs, soaked and dust-covered, bloody and furious, limped into the pit bottom. I was sitting by a tub, obviously not at the end of the line.

'Was that thee, tha little cunt?' Dudworth yelled, pointing at me.

'Me?' I responded innocently. 'Not unless I can time-travel, I was first in the bottom.' That seemed to make sense, given my early departure. 'I wish it bloody had been though', I added,

'Aye, and tha'd be a deed man by now, youth.'

No, it didn't finish, they caught me going down the tail gate, which is what I did to avoid them. They tied me hands behind me back with tie-bands, which electricians use to hang up cables, and then picked me up between them and threw me into an empty tub. I landed hard and thought I'd bust a bone in the base of me spine. Me lamp went out, I was dazed and felt sick. I was totally disorientated and in the dark couldn't quite manage to stand up or move from the side of the tub. When I did, it was in time to be rescued by the stall deputy, who also disliked me intensely. 'If Ah catch tha messing aboot again, Ah'll report thee, and tha'll be off back to fucking Hatfield.' Me messing aboot?''Well, thee cause everything thee gets, wi' daft ideas, an't talking.' Next day, after the web of ripping was fired, I was working in the gate. Dudworth and his mate worked in the pack-hole, building a drystone wall and shoveling it full with loose stones, until it formed a solid pack to the roof. At this stage, though they were trapped in all directions by stone, only one hole remained nearly directly over them and me, and a barrel of oil was standing over that. I unplugged the oil and it gushed down the hole, covering both of them, like a pair of sardines.

I was in the gate, with a jigger, what we call up north a windy pick, working on a lump of rock which refused to break, when Dudworth worked his way free of the stone. Catching me by the throat as I turned round, he wanged me up against the arch girder and off the ground, squeezing my throat. In agony and pure rage, I swung the jigger up to his throat and squeezed the trigger. The blade actually made contact with his skin but only glancingly as he dropped me and fell back, nearly falling over, I lunged at him, determined to stab him with the blade, and he knew it. He picked up a pick shaft and swung it as if to hit me if I carried through the attack. I was panting, so was he.

Tha's fuckin' mad, thee!'

'Fuckin' reet, I responded, picking the jigger up by the barrel like a spear, and going to throw it right at him. 'Get off my fuckin' back, ye big ugly bastard!'

He backed off, crawling back down the hole, and began shoveling for all he was worth. It was the last incident with him, but the first of many from now on. Me Da's words, 'The men will break your heart, son', seemed to resonate. It would take years upon years to win the respect of these men, but once it is achieved you can take it to the bank, for it's worth more than gold.

The intense jealousies rooted in sexual and personal insecurities were soon swept away in the tide of all-embracing love and sexual freedom. Love was universal, we could love everything in general and another in particular and especially solely, but sex was a physical sensation just for the hell, sex meant nothing unless you wanted it to. Otherwise it was just for fun and everyone shared it, like an umbrella in the rain.

12
Talking About My generation

The Who nuevo heavy spokes poets

Why don't you all... f-f-fade away?

The crowded room now bounced in empathetic collectivist rhythm. Don't try an' dig what we all say...

To those on the outside, the bourgeois commentators, the vicars, the moralists.

As Dylan had said, 'Old Lady Judges watch couples in pairs, limited in sex they dare, to push fake morals insults and slurs, while money doesn't talk it swears obscenity all is phony!'

Not trying to cause a big sensation.

TALKING ABOUT MY GENERATION

The strands of wor early movement together again at Christmas time at Les's place, things had moved on. The weirdo's were the norm. Love wasn't soft, a world-wide generation had been subverted and 'everybody was talking aboot revolution, revolution, revolution'.

We all want the war to end right? OK?

Not just Vietnam ... but Ireland ... but the class war on the globe OK?

In the back bedroom couples embrace ... Colin on the bed with Cathy together looking around, spinning head in passion throes, car lights dancing over the ceiling... Margaret on the floor, her skirt round her waist, shadows falling from walls, like drips from a tap, a bare backside in a maddening rhythm and dragging and forcing, a head pouring a soul into breasts... subverted and 'everybody was talking aboot revolution, revolution, revolution'.

Samadhi Samadhi one to the other an empathy of multi-centres with one soul between wi ... as the music made the glass panes rattle we were all as one.

Talking about my generation.

The hippies are just the fancy dress version of wi ... trying the pacifist road ... but THE HIPPIES ARE RIGHT. You want the war to end ... you've got to stop fighting it! Don't fight the fucking wars for the rich and the ruling class. You don't like the system ... you hate the system? Stop living the system. Mek all roads to reject the system. To not fight their wars. That's right. That's right ... we should find room for wasells in the universe ... we are communists ... universalists.

I'm talking about my generation...
my Degeneration, baby ... why don't you all f-f-f-fade away?
Don't try and dig what we all say.

The black struggle in the United States, the sickening men under the hoods, after a century of unabated beating of the black man, were now confronting the Panther Party. The Panther Party was wor party, we empathised deeply with it. Few shed tears when Martin Luther King was killed. 'Right, now let's stop the pacifism and get stuck into the gets' was a widespread reaction, my own in particular, at first. King's worth was understood later.

The last vestiges of British imperialism in Aden and Ireland were meeting a thunderous challenge.

On the streets of Harlem thug police would billy-club neymer Negroes without meeting instant retaliation from units of the black people's own forces.

While Labour sat in office at Number Ten, Denis Healey's wife launched nuclear submarines, as the wives of 'Labour leaders' still dey, while demonstrators breached police lines at Birkenhead.

Wilson was well and truly into his special relationship with America's dirty war in Vietnam, and the SAS trained Viet puppet forces to kill their own people, while revolutionary groups and solidarity campaigns loaded their mental rifles for what was promising to be demonstrations which would take the kids off their backsides and onto their feet.

Kelly came in the Bridge and mopped his brow. 'What fettle, marra, yee look like yi'v had a shock.' 'We've nearly all had a shock, ainly ye divinar it. Ye knaa David O'Connel?' Laughter.

The lone star rider, whey aye.'

'Ah was just on the bus with him, comin' doon alang Shields Road ye knaa?' 'Aye, gaan on.'

'Whey, ye knaa roond there the bus is all ower the road, and bumping alang and what not?' 'Aye!'

'O'Connel pulls a bottle oot of es pocket and ses "Ah hope this stuff l'll be alreet gettin bumped aroond." Whey, it's clear liquid ye knaa, like water. Ah says, "Gi's it here, Ah'll taste if foryi." Whey Ah thowt it wes potcheen. "Oh, it's not potcheen", he says. "It's nitro." '"Buggerrahell", says I. "Ye'll bla' aal Newcastle up from this end ti the ither." "Ah'd best get off and walk", he says. Bugger me if he dissent gaan an fall doon the stairs. Ah didn't put me fingers in me ears, Ah cudn't see much point.' 'Bliddy hell, where's he nuw?' 'Ah divinna but if wi sit ower there wi'l likely hear the bang.'

A T' Party with a difference.

We were back yem as usual, at one of those boozy, singing, political discussion parties, where other people still get up and jive and dance aboot, and are totally impervious to the words of profound wisdom and divine political philosophising gaanin' on. It was the hoose of Sid Ogalvy, who I thought as a southerner of sorts, but actually was a Newcastle tiler, and a member of the Revolutionary Workers' Party (Trotskyist), the RWP(T) for short, not a team I knew about much. I had taken much for granted about what would be common ground, the struggle against the bomb, etc., when he hit me with a concept which seemed at the time to be as reactionary as any I had ever heard.

He told me the struggle against the bomb was futile, because the nuclear war was inevitable. When I chided him for reactionary cynicism, he corrected:

'I'm not cynical in the slightest, comrade, because the world working class will win that nuclear war and world imperialism will be defeated!' I think it blew my mind and was torn between attacking him and crying with frustration,

'You're fucking mad', I responded.

'Am I mad? Is he mad?' he asked, pointing at Tom.

Tom', I enquired, as if he'd just broken a strike, raped my wife and shot my cat, 'Do you think the nuclear war is inevitable then?'

'I believe it might well be', he responded. 'And, that being the case, the workers' states have to take what action is necessary to limit the degree of damage which imperialism can inflict upon humanity.'

'Limit the damage? There'll be ney bliddy humanity if a nuclear war starts', I screamed.

'Nonsense', responded Sid

'Ah'll fuck ye, in a minute', I yelled, losing me cool and making to punch him.

This is not the time, not the place, for this discussion. You're too drunk, and it's too emotive to discuss in this atmosphere', offered Judy, Tom's girl-friend.

'Ah'll never be sober enough to advocate blowing up the whole world and everyone in it, inheriting an irradiated cinder, and in me dying breath turn to me kids and say,

"Nevor mind, kiddhas, we won."'

We left in disgust, raging all the way to Maureen's mother's place, about kamikaze communists. This workers' bomb thing was something the old Stalinists of the CP and the Trotskyists has in common. Both the Young Communist League and, for a time, the Young Socialists believed that the workers' states' bombs, or the degenerated workers' states' bombs, were different in quality from imperialism's and capitalism's bombs. They were 'defensive bombs'; imperialism's bombs were 'aggressors' bombs'. Which if you happened to believe that the so-called workers' states, degenerated or otherwise, were political and social gains for the working class which had to be defended you were forced to agree with. The anarchists used to sing to the tune of *The Red Flag*:

So raise the workers' bomb on high
Beneath its shade we'll live and die
And though our critics all shout 'Balls!'
We'll run to greet it when it falls!

Next day we'd been invited up to Tom's, where 'the comrades' from The Party' (the party was now the Revolutionary Workers' Party, full title Revolutionary Workers' Party (Trotskyist) British Section of the IVth International-Posadist).

It seemed quite a few of my comrades had been courted by The Party and were on the brink of joining.

The room of Tom's flat had been decorated with the IVth International flag, the red flag with the hammer and sickle interlaced with a figure 4. It was brilliantly imposing, the men from the party were very strict, very formal, gave the impression that there was much to be done and that it was they who had their finger on the pulse, around the whole world, that their views were based upon scientific formulations, not whim, that their road was The Road, that they were the Revolutionary Leadership of the Worldwide Working Class. When they spoke, they spoke as if for the class as a whole; how could they be challenged? The analyses of The Party' always began from a general description of the revolutionary process around the world and how it was interacting with each specific national centre. 'Right, now we shall fit Britain into the world' was the phrase with which they began what otherwise would have seemed like purely British developments in the class war but were soon sitting in the context of a world-wide perspective. Optimism and certainty: the world revolutionary process was moving forward, day by day, country by country.

Imperialism and capitalism had destroyed, were destroying, more men, women, and children daily and weekly, month in month out, year in year out, from starvation, disease, poverty and conventional war, than a nuclear war with capitalism could ever do. So even on a straightforward moralistic basis, finishing with capitalism through the war would be just, and better than giving humanity a slow, tortuous and numerically bloodier death. In any case there was no option. It was not a matter of choice. There was a global class conflict going on, war was the continuation of politics by other means, the class war was being fought out across the world with arms, the degenerated workers' states, the USSR and China primarily representing in a bureaucratic fashion the world working class, faced US imperialism primarily as a representative of all imperialisms and the capitalist system. In the final analysis imperialism would never throw up its hands and say OK, we surrender, you've won, without using everything in its armoury, including nuclear bombs. So what should we do, call off the class war? Say we were only kidding, we didn't mean we wanted it all? Bourgeois pacifists might make such concessions, but the working class could not.

Vietnam had experienced already the equivalent of a nuclear war. Did we call upon the Vietnamese masses to desist their struggle because of the horror unleashed by US imperialism upon it? Of course not. We called for victory to the struggle of the NLF, and yet Vietnam had already endured more bombs and bullets and high explosives than fired by all sides in two world wars, including the two atom-bombs dropped upon Japan! Was it just that the thought had struck home the class war was OK in Third World countries but when the bombs start to fall here and in the USA it's time to change the slogans? These were good questions. But they went further:

'In order to minimise the loss of life, by bringing imperialism down speedily, at certain moments of decisive conflict we have called upon the USSR to launch the nuclear war, to launch a pre-emptive strike against imperialism and NATO, hitting the government and military targets, avoiding civilian centres with no political or military significance, although of course western capitalist countries will be the hardest hit and suffer the most causalities, the masses will know at root it is the crime of imperialism not the workers' states.'

'But won't the world be destroyed? What about radiation?' I would venture.

'When the bourgeoisie talks of "the world" it doesn't mean us, the workers, or the masses of the Third World, it is talking about itself. When it says "the world will be destroyed", it is inconceivable to them that the world can live without them, and therefore they conclude the world will end. We've got news for them: humanity will survive and, sooner than many have predicted, will have restored itself and constructed a world socialist system.'

It was a gradual, process first towards Trotskyism and then

by 1972 actually into the party which had started that night, an adventure which I think took us to the edge of insanity at times, before we broke bitterly free, but we were only in the foothills of what was to become a long and winding road, in search of a plan to put the vision into reality, perhaps an never ending journey. But for now, we had neither time nor longevity, in the words of the Panthers, 'we wanted it NOW !".

Hope I die before I get old...
Talking about my generation
Not trying to cause a big sensation
I'm just talking about my generation
My generation, baby...

But this was still the 60s and the upstairs room of the Bridge was mobbed. The Tyneside Women's Socialist Action Group. Oh yis, the student folk already in boiler suits, with thin gold-rimmed glasses and an air of the Koran... The mod lasses with the bob hair and cut hair and eye make-up... The beat lasses with flowing hair and raggy jeans... The twinned-up motorbike lasses, who had become beats on wheels... The lasses from the coalfield: girlfriends and older wives... The lasses from the shops and factories, some of them poets and orators...

'COMRADES, SISTERS, FELLOW WORKERS but certainly not chicks, nor tarts.' (Cheers.) 'Lasses, aye, we'll accept .... Ney mer what will we put up with. Ney mer what we shall have given but what we shall dictate for wasells!'

'We will start from this proposition: wa bodies are wa an! The body belangs ti us! Or ti wasells mer particular! We are the socialist women and not the feminist women because, we believe, the situation of women is determined by the class system, by the existence of the ruling class and the subservient working class, and we the women are what James

Connolly yes, a man, but a fairly man called the slaves of the slaves. We do not hate men. Men are not the enemy but some men are the enemy. Whites are not the enemy of the blacks but some whites are the enemy of the blacks:

We will not be sexual niggers, and we won't be slaves to sexual rednecks!'

The massive cheering upstairs and stamping of feet brought wry glances from the men belaw, awaiting the female companions.

That's the garden shears out for wa bollocks.' (Laughter.)

'That's precisely the mistaken lumpen attitude which leads such women to separate themselves from the working-class movement as a whole.' Thus spake the Afghan-coated, denim-shirted lad who had previously been selling the *Militant*. And big Harry, the now heavily involved engineer, the archetypal informed proletarian communist, eyed him!

'What's ye mean, like, such women? Such women, bonny lad, are the working-class women of this city! Such women are the spokeswomen of their class, this class and their sex. Whey are yee, like?'

That's possibly correct', he attempted in English. 'Women ought not he separated from their male comrades. It is a class question.'

'Whey, that's a typically middle-class male reaction, if yee dinnit mind is seyin sey', says H.

The young class-hardened militant (he thought), an apprentice in the shipyard, never having had his class credentials challenged, in shocked reply shouts: 'Whey, where ye think Ah's from, like?'

Harry coolly eyed the ragged fringed coat, the 'I AM FOUR' badge in the lapel, which was a fashion among toon mods, and replied: 'Whey, judging by ya apparel, either Afghanistan or Disneyland.' The lad's gob smacked open and the pub fell apart... Afghanistan, yi bugger!

Up the stairs, the room filled with smoke, the women in deadly serious discussion.

'But what', asked the miner's grandmother, 'if these men won't give us what we want?'

A shoot: 'Then they dinnit get what they want!' And raucous laughter filled the rafters.

'It's not what they Will give us', said Cathy, now a person in total charge of her body, 'It's what we choose to take! They'll give us nowt. We'll have what we demand! Oh whey aye, ye'l laugh coz Ah've had a canny few of them.' (They laughed.) 'Ah might yet have a canny few mer. But Ah'll decide IF or NOT or if never. That's my right. This mightn't look much ti yee' (she wiggled her tits) 'but it's mine neybody else's. Ah will say, and Ah'm not a lezzie sorry, lasses, for them that are if that soonds insulting; Ah dinnit mean it ti be. But if Ah choose ti share my body wi the bonny lasses here, that's for me to choose' or not ti dee it at all and sit on me bonny arse that's for me, neybody else.

'Wor bodies alan. Else leave wi alan!'

A decision was made to immediately commission a banner carrying a pithead, the Tyne Bridge, and that slogan. Ye'll knaa Dave he's doonstairs in the bar, wondering who's gaana carry him yem. He's the leader of the revolution. Yes, aye, Ah love him. He's shown me this city Ah've always lived in and nivor seen. He's shown me art in the working people Ah was always afraid of. He's introduced me to a generation of miners in my family I thought of as family and not in a class sense. But he cannot show me *me!* And will not tell me *me!* Because I no longer will let him.

'I became a political person in big letters when Dave paid me ten bob to read *The Communist Manifesto*. I wouldn't read anything like that. I was a pacifist that was my soul. My feelings for fellow human beings had developed already, were devolving already like yours. Like a lot of young lasses like me. After all, this is wor world, is it not? Wor grannies must have told us all, of the waste of life the life from their loins, their nurturing, all that waste of women's efforts and squandered love. Not squandered love, real love lost! My reading snowballed from there, but the bloody ten bobs stopped! "What does a socialist woman expect to get out of socialism?" they ask. Ah'll tell yi. We'd expect to get less, because that is the lesson taught by socialist men.

'But socialist women have no intention whatever of allowing socialist men to dictate the terms. We too shall determine the route of that march of humanity. We working-class women ARE in fact the march of humanity. Aye, we want the men there. True, to wor feminist sisters, we divind need them: all kinds of substitutes are available, some of them perhaps better than some of the men on offer. But with them, without them, is an individual choice in bed. Personally I prefer as large a variety as possible.' (Cheers) 'But that's my choice, not theirs. And the path to a future world is unconditionally determined by us, the socialist womenfolk. We ask for nowt.

The family is a trap. It is the enslavement of the whole world, men, women and children. It is the encapsulation of capitalism into everybody's home and soul. No, that doesn't mean we walk out of the family. That doesn't mean the love we had and have in a family is a false or mistaken love. But it is a microcosm of the potential of humankind, freed from the family system. Humanity needs itself all of itself needs a consciousness of every living person and a responsibility and love for each other regardless of family and patriarchy and name and size of house or district or county or country or race. Yes, we must learn to see each other world-wide.

'Children do not BELONG to parents. Will we learn? Many of us are youth in revolt at wor parents. At the restraints and restrictions and we ignore the lot. We dey just what we want ti dee. But time is a slip of jig, and will o' the wisp. We soon shall be parents.

'Kath, comrades, is already a parent at fifteen. What shall we say ti wor kids?

'If you hate the slave system because you are a slave, that's not enough, that's not the point. And no matter how oppressed you are and how difficult your circumstances, you still dey not understand. This kills the myth that oppression breeds consciousness. It breeds resistance but not consciousness, which is why so many of wor militant and revolutionary men still do not REALLY understand. Neither does it mean that children and young uns belong to the community. They are instead part of the community. Nor is it a question of replacing individual monopoly and control with collective monopoly and control. But we are here better for the women. Our traditional role as women, in terms of children, is rather like that of the men to us. They, doon in the bar will not dictate wor road; and we shall not dictate the road of the children. They will, by what they do, by what they say, because they can and do speak if you listen, and anyway, just dey what they want. We must be aware that we shall not obstruct. The guy's doonstairs must also not obstruct. In this sense we will be together, different and together.'

'But for the neet', the miners' grandma shoots. 'There's mony will waak oota here nuw, and tha man'll tek them aside, and that's it. The gam's up. Back ti the canny wee hoosewifie. Ah'm reet, girls?'

'Whey huw there's a disco for us.'

The men are comin'?'

'Aye, lets mek a demonstration the' neet. We'll aal dance t'gether and with ney men ti show wi can if wi want.' (Wild cheers.)

It was a confused Geordie Cong male entry which went into the disco to show support for the womenfolk, ti find the answer at every turn was: 'Why should Ah want ti dance wi a man?'

'Are we the enemy?' we asked, like kids with a smacked arse.

'Na.' The rest was left dangling in impotence.

The Heaton window frames rattle.

TALKING ABOUT MY GENERATION

Things they do look mighty cold...' The gang: Talking about my generation.' My degeneration, baby.... 'Why don't you all f-f-f-fuck off!!'

Don't try and dig what we all say
Talking about my generation
Not trying to cause a big sensation
Just talking about my generation.

'WHY DON'T YOU ALL FUCK OFF!!'

We yelled once more, together and united, a generation in defiance.

The struggle continues...

Coaldust

When I was young and in me prime
Ee aye ah cud hew
Whey Ah wes hewin all the time
Nuw me hewin days are through-through
Nuw me hewin days are through
At the face the dust did flee
Ee aye ah cud hew
Nuw that dust is killing me
Nuw me hewin days are through-through
Nuw me hewin days are through
Av laid doon flat and shoveled coal
Ee aye ah cud hew
Me eyes did smart in the dust filled hole
Nuw me hewin days are through-through
Nuw me hewin days are through
Whey av had marra's and they were men
Ee aye ah cud hew
Whey they were men! and sons of men
Nuw me hewin days are through-through
Nuw me hewin days are through.
They say that work is made by men
Ee aye ah cud hew
But whey med dust ah dinnit ken
Nuw me hewin days are through-through
Nuw me hewin days are through
Its yon. That pit ney mer Ah'll see
Ee aye ah cud hew
Ah'll carry it roond-inside of me
Nuw me hewin days are through-through
Nuw me hewin days are through.[17]

Notes

1. In 1154 King Henry 11 seized Northumbria from Scotland when Malcolm the King of Scotland was a lad of 11 and annexed it to England. Following his death his brother 'The Lion' William never let this insult and theft pass. He concluded a formal alliance with France, known ever afterwards as 'the aud alliance' and in 1174 launched a rebellion to retake Northumbria for Scotland. An untimely mist among other things led to a massive defeat at Alnwick for The Lion. Now he was forced to sign The Treaty Of Falaise, subjecting Scotland to the feudal rule of England and Northumberland designated 'English' all Northumbrian and Scottish castles were then staffed by occupying Norman forces. It was these occupying forces that William Wallace pledged to oust and retake Northumberland and remove the insult of Falaise. So it was that Wallace freed Newcastle as part of his campaign. The Hollywood fiction of his life has him attacking York instead, probably for no other reason that Americans had heard of that city but not Newcastle, it mattered not that this made no historical sense. The Scot Nat's don't know it, but the 'flooa of Scotland' is Northumberland.

2. See Remembering George Stephenson, Robert Colls, chapter 12 in Newcastle Upon Tyne a modern history. Pg 284/5 Pub: Phillimore and Co Ltd. West Sussex. 2001.

3. A number of my quotes were used in the drafting of Wor Diary and by return I have quoted a number of theirs. See Wor Diary *www.wordiary.org*

4. See 'Print and Preach', Joan Hugman, chap 6 of *Newcastle Upon Tyne a Modern History* ed Robert Colls and Bill Lancaster pg 122 etal.

5. Ibid pg 130/131

6. Eeh knickers, by God they caught the attention. I almost developed a shoe fetish by the time I was eight. I loved going shopping for me shoes .Me Ma would on point of principle take me to Clarks where in addition to knickers you got to see your feet down the X-ray unit and where ya feet fitted in the shoes. Knickers? Girls of all ages and sizes were invariably trying on shoes, leg up, tying the shoe strap or laces, everywhere you looked, legs and knickers. Mind it can't just have been me, the later inventor of the space hopper was surely likewise effected. There are a lot more knickers in this story though I was finally purged of the obsession near its end, with the invention of the thong. The thong at once transformed the female bottom from a thing of dressed up sexiness to a thing of ugly flesh torn in two. The accompanying low-slung pants, which allow the damn article to be displayed along with a builders bum every time they bend over was a sure fire, cure for the wicked knicker voyeurism of my childhood.

7. The Leam Lane Estate, which they called Wardley but was actually between Wardley and High Heworth. The name came from the Viking lane which passed through The White Mare Pool and up towards Springwell and Kibblesworth. At one time a great scenic walk through blackberry bushes and wild flowers, birds and animals, now a slip road intersecting the back of the Leam Lane Estate.

8. After a life time in mining with an associated interest in fossils and geology, I have now come to the amazing though well considered opinion that this shiny blue rock was Opal

9. Modern howls of outrage about eating distorters and illness really didn't seem to apply to Bridgette this wasn't a Twiggy or a Shrimp. This wasn't a thin skinny little girl child, this was a busty well covered healthy female women. To us then thirteen she was of course a grown up, I didn't get to see her Nudey bit film until I was about twenty-five when she 'hands up' was forced to lift her hands from her breasts to reveal those magnificent tits. But for now the black and white photos of her naked with just a bit of her bum on display and the merest suggestion of her naked breasts sent us to body tingling showers of electric shocks we drooled; couldn't get that face and body out of our minds.

10. Lindisfarne is a surprisingly disappointing island from about the middle of the fifteen hundreds when the Southern ruling class decide to make it a principle defence against Scottish reclamation or northern autonomy. One of the Erringtons did succeed in seizing the castle in the rising of 1715 and ran up the Jacobite flag as a symbol for the locals to rise, but it seems they stayed abed. Little of its brief industrial history seems to be logged, but it has in my mind continued along a path of conservatism ever since. This might be due to its strict 'no camping' policy which as teenagers we deeply resented, or the tradition of being a source of anti social middle class residence and hostility which we encountered ever since. Still, not the islands' fault, the most exciting folk in their history were either the Celtic Brits or the raiding Vikings. The number of rules both official and unofficial on the island are not the most welcoming of features taken together with the sour face and warnings not to eat your chips on the public seats or lean your bike on the windows. A shag in the sand dunes is right out of the question.

11. We never knew Barney's full name, knew nothing of his past other than the bits which he revealed in the process of discussing politics. He had known Peter Kropotkin, more than that, had been a close political associate of the great Russian anarchist during his residency in The Toon. He embarrassed we young Geordie anarchists by both his formality and informality "Nuw A kenned weel ya Prince Peter Kropotkin". We didn't normally mention the 'Prince' bit. Barney always did, not in a mocking manner, but almost as a mark of the man's rank, and the fact he had come over to us. It was a point of pride to him and radical workers on that generation. It was not until Barney had passed on some twenty years after this scene in the Bigg Market, and twenty years further down the line from that I discovered firstly his full name and secondly a picture of that aud Northumbrian fighter's life. I am greatly indebted to the Tyneside Labour History Society for the facts following which I took from their journal and the well research article by Dave Neville. I have, though, corrected a slight mistake about Barney staying with the ILP until he died, the last time I met Barney he had just left in disgust at the party re-applying for affiliation to the Labour Party again.

Barney Markson. Had been born, incredibly, in 1893. He joined first the British Socialist Party at the age of 18 in 1911 the year of its inception. Its offices were on the corner of Leazes Park Road and Percy Street. The outbreak of world war one caused a split in the BSP with the majority supporting the war and actively campaigning for recruits. Barney and the others took this as utter betrayal and left. He faced a terrific battle against engagement in the war effort something which was a deeply unpopular among the majority of working class people. He took some serious abuse for his stand. He ended up back in Newcastle with the Peace Through Negotiation Movement. One of their first public meetings was attacked by 'Patriots' and Barney who took the blame for a Union Jack being ripped was lucky to survive.

In 1920 he moved to Toronto, becoming Secretary of The Toronto Branch of The IWW. He also joined the Workers Party. From there he moved to Peterborough, Ontario where he got behind efforts to raise practical support for the Russian revolutionaries, raising funds to send machinery and technicians. He became the centre for police and press attention, identified as 'a Bolshevik' in their midst's. The upshot was Barney was sentenced to six months jail, for an article he penned in *The Worker* condemning working conditions in the Peterborough factories. The action was brought by the Chamber of Commerce for 'publication of false news'

After coming back to England he briefly joined the Labour Party but was expelled for opposing coal reparations. By 1926 he had joined the Communist Party Of Great Britain. During the General Strike was influential with the *Workers Chronicle* which became the workers' paper throughout Tyneside, all other papers having been shut down. Two editions per day were produced to keep pace with demand and the army of newspaper sellers which had been recruited to circulate the paper. I learned, incidentally, that Barney was also present in the Big Market when police cleared the streets with batons and much ferocity, my Dad as a young striking miner had been there that day too and he often talked of it.

The defeat of the strike, and the crisis of political organisation caused Barney whilst still a member of the CPGB to criticise its timidity. He was expelled from them not long after the last of the miners returned to work in defeat. During the King George V visit to Newcastle in 1928 Barney was interned along with other prominent socialists in case he launched some sort of outrage upon his royal personage. Sometime after this he joined the ILP and in the 1950s became its National Organiser. He held this position for three years before coming back to Newcastle and opening a small fruit and vegetable shop. Jointly with this he was a keen member of the Tyneside Humanist Society. He stuck with the party until, it decided to re-affilate to the Labour Party, during which time Barney true to his principles left. I was actually in the Bridge the night the big battle took place. By now most of the members were extremely old and several had great difficulty getting up the long winding staircase. It wasn't long before the doors flung open and Aud Barney led the exodus of old guard, back out into the cold of a hostile political climate, but determined not to compromise their principles. That was the last time I seen him, flushed and panting with anger, with no sign that any of the fire in his aud belly had cooled any.

Barney died 7th January 1981. (Two years short of a hundred.)

12. Joni Mitchell, *Woodstock.*

13. It ought perhaps to be explained that petrol bombs were a novel weapon in Britain at this time; indeed, we may have been unique. Stone throwing had not been revived in any protests really since the general strike of 1926. The uprising in Ulster, which was to make the petrol bomb its symbol and weapon of choice, hadn't broken out yet. Even by 1981, the hard-core anarchist movement hadn't mastered this basic incendiary device. Class War founder Ian Bone says, "There had been an earlier legendary petrol bomb attack-before my arrival in Cardiff-where a target had gone up with a mighty whoof sending burning petrol back under the door and setting fire to the bomber's trousers! It was described to me as 'another Cardiff comedy classic's the perpetrator cycled-yes cycled!-off home with his inconspicuous corduroys glowing like fag ends as cop sirens and fire engines wailed past in the opposite direction. Cardiff anarchists were angrier than The Angry Brigade. They were the extremely fucking Angry Brigade and this one was angrier than most." *Bash The Rich*, Ian Bone, Tangent Books, Bath. Pg 101.

14. See Ian Bone's autobiography *Bash The Rich*, Tangent Books, Bath 2006. Ian's political trajectory and my own crossed paths on a number of occasions and doubtless, we were frequently in the same place at the same time, but didn't formally meet until the founding of Class War and the foothills of what was to be the miners' most determined stand in 1984. Ian was a founder member of Class War and one of its most visionary tacticians.

15. Stables in Yorkshire, these were the 'nueks' or corners of the coal face. An indent in the parallel line of the coal face at each end of the 'jud' or piece of coal being worked. The purpose to provide the 'bite' for the cutter drum. In the days of 'conventional' Lang wall it was to provide an inseam extension to the tunnels through which men and materials might access and egress the coal face particularly useful in the thin seam pits where working height was often less than two feet and on occasion little more than one.

16. It will be seen here that Maureen's words are directed against the bourgeois idea of 'the family' in those days the British state and its law had a high respect for 'the family' as an institution and granted it large areas of autonomy and discretion. A generation down the line from this speech and it is clear particularly with the advent of the Blair/Brown government that the nature of states relationship with the family has dramatically changed and this is reflected in large areas of legal imposition and control, particularly with the care and 'ownership' of children. Current arrangements suggest that all children belong to the state and they merely lease them to parents, this lease can be easily revoked as we have seen in numerous cases through multiple agencies. Parents and the sanctity of their relationship with their children are no longer recognised as the state deems to intervene and take away children without notice, often without evidence, often on whim, acting on panic or rumour. The distress of the children and their parents during these brutal enforced periods of state kidnap and detention, and the virtual law unto themselves that governs Social Service and Child Protection make the old days of the bourgeois family seem positively idyllic. New laws being worked on in the June of 2008 will refuse to register children births unless the mother reveals the name of the father. The degree of emotional bullying being applied here has the ring of the Third Reich about it. There are a million and one reasons why a mother might not wish to reveal who the father is, she might be underage and not wish to see the father jailed. The father could be married already and not ready to break-up the existing family. He might be a prat or worse a violent anti-social prat who she wants no part in her life of that of her child. As if this wasn't bad enough the legislation will allow 'authorities' to investigate who the potential father might be, from rumour, gossip and door to door enquiry if necessary. Alleged fathers will be legally forced to give DNA samples to disprove their fatherhood or otherwise. The heartlessness of this proposed legislation and the pressure placed upon a women, often a young women already under hard emotional pressure and social hardships is devoid of human consideration. The pressure not to reveal the father, will without doubt push many toward otherwise unwanted abortions. Our notion of communalised children and children held in common were regarded as slightly cold and heartless, at this time, little did we know what steely eyed cold indifference to parental relationships with kids the modern state would have up its sleeve.

17. *Ee Aye Ah Cud Hew*, Eddie Pickford.

Endnote — Picts

Jonties' history was as he learned it, through the oral tradition rather than extensive book histories, though he had done masses of that too. He never, as far as I knew, checked with accepted wisdoms and histories as to whether the world as he saw it was documented and authenticated. The history of the Picts is one much argued over. The word

Pict was given by the Romans, they were a confederation of tribes largely north of the Forth and Clyde. The word means 'to paint' and was probably because they painted themselves in war paint, or perhaps forms of tattoo, it could equally have been because of their great artistry and amazing ability to accurately draw animals. Nobody knows what language they spoke. They were matriarchal and traced their blood lines through their mothers, not their fathers. Bede suggested they came from Scandinavia, first to the northern part of Ireland, looking for new lands in which to settle. It is said that the inhabitants of that region, about whom we also know next to nowt about, advised them to try what is now Scotland. Some described them as dark skinned, very small statured folk. Their stone carvings of themselves have a distinctly Persian look about them in terms of beards and weapons and armour (but that's just to my eye). They converted to Gaelic Christianity quite early, along with most Scots. In the 700s they were defeated in war by the Northumbrians, and became absorbed into that nation. I have no idea if they survive as a distinct people. I had earlier been led to believe, probably by Jonty that they had settled in other remote areas of Britain, particularly Cornwall and Wales. although I have never found any academic support for this view.

Glossary

A

Aalreet, all right
Aan, own
Aboot, about
Ah, I
Ah'm, I am
Aheed, ahead
Ahint, behind
Ain, Own
Alang, along
Alain, alone
Alreet, all right
Amang, among
Anarl, and all
Ard Fheis, (Gaelic-'grand meeting' / National Conference)
Arthur (Scargill) For most this story President of the NUM, although initially Yorkshire Area president, and ultimately Honorary President of the NUM

B

Bairn (e) child
Banksman, the man at the top of the pit shaft in charge of the loading and lowering and raising of the cage with men or materials.
Bare-back (riding) unprotected sexual intercourse
Bla, blae, blow
Boards, wooden planks used underground for lagging
Boody, a precious child object of currency, normally recognised throughout Northumbria, Tyne, Tees Weir and Tweed, though probably not by adults. The true form was broken real bone china items, though with the expansion of northern populations and the diminution of real bone china

tea sets, any china pieces became currency too. In every child community expert children could decipher the ever smaller items of real bone china 'bonny bits' from the lesser varieties.
Bords, birds/girls
Boxhole, a sort of rudimentary underground 'office' much more in common with a cave, in which the overman deploys his deputies and gets reports from off going officials. It is a source of kists, and desks, picks and tools, and when no-one is around flaked out diesel drivers and fitters grabbing a quiet kip.
Bowk, to be sick (also used to describe the sound of the earth crashing down in higher seams, or falling in overhead cavities, whilst underground-the sound was thought to resemble someone being persistently sick)
Brek, break

C

Cannit, can not
Cannie, can not
Canny, cute, quite,
Caunch, Canch, the stone face of a tunnel or working coal face. (likewise Rip, Yorkshire)
Caunchmen, the 'stoneworkers' who work the caunch
Cla's (Santie) Father Xmas
Claes, clothes
Clarts, mud
Clarty, muddy
Clout, cloth
Clout, smack
Cowp, to hit in a sweeping motion by an object or circular blow
Cuddie, horse (also nick name for folk from Durham)

D

Dee, do
De'e, die
Dee, die
De'el ,the devil
Deent Daint, (Yorkshire) don't.
Dey, do
Der, (Netherlands,) The
Dinnet, divind, don't
Divind, Dinnet, Deen'd, Do not, don't.
Divinknaawhat, (ahdivinknaawhat) Don't know what/ I don't know what.
Dit (Netherlands) this
Doobt, doubt
Doon, down
Dook, duck (lower your head)
Duds, the pit clothes
Dunch, collide

E

Eerste (Netherlands) First
Eiyt, eight

F

Feller, fellow
Fernant/fernance, directly opposite
Flee, Fly
Fleein, Flying
Follies, Follows
Foond/Fund, found
Foya, for you
Forbye, that aside
Frau, (Netherlands) women

G

Gaan, go

Gaanan/gaanin, going

Gaanins, alleyways

Gaaninboard, track underground which links the bord and wall headings gaanins and the main roadway (gate)

Gadgies, usually an aud bloke, and generally a miserable bastard in charge of looking after something or stopping you doing something. They were cheap watchmen protecting holes in the ground or building sites at night.

Gallis/gallus (Glaswegian) cocky, boastful.

Galvie, Galvinated

Gate, road

Geet/Greet /Gret , Great

Geordie. Originally the inhabitants of Newcastle Upon Tyne, then by extension all Tynesiders. It was a term for those who supported King George against the Jacobites, in fact the 'geordies' were not 'Geordies' at all and there was a powerful movement throughout Northumberland and Durham which supported the Jacobites, this was particularly true of the Tyneside coal communities of both sides of the river. Newcastle was though the major garrison city of the north and the British army loyal to King George was stationed there. It was this which earned Newcastle the name of The Geordies, though the folks who lived there overwhelmingly were not. Others have thought the name came from the Tyneside pitmen's preference for the Geordie lamp as against the Davie lamp, they did, but the name predates that. Likewise the areas propensity to call each other 'Geordie' in the absence of a workmates real name, is a correct observation and almost everyone is 'Huw Geordie' at work, but this is not the source of the name.

Gud, good

Gud'un, good one

H

Had, hold
Had on, hold on
Hadawaycumback, (Kevin Gartland's (a boyhood neighbour who joined Wardley Colliery band with me) description of the slide trombone which has become a part of my language ever since, and I've noticed found its way into formal Tyneside dialect glossaries, without any reference to him or me, amazing.)
Hadaway, go away.
Hade, rather a complicated mining concept which is difficult to explain if you haven't seen it. Basically it is an unplanned hole which occurs in the strata above the area in which you are mining, and is usually composed of crushed minerals which continues to run out in small or large sizes. The hole can run forward in advance of the area you are working and to unlimited heights above your supports. It often accompanies geological faults and intrusions, and is a very volatile environment in which to work, with the risk of being buried alive or struck by falling boulders very high.
Hadin, holding
Hail (Netherlands) very
Ha'way, haweh, Come on
Het, have
Hev, have
Hoss, horse
Hoose, house
Hooses, Houses
Hoor, hour
Horseheed/head, A metal box attached to the last girder set, through which forepoling or girders are run in line with the tunnel and upon which the middle section of the arch girder will rest. Or a square metal box which attached to the adjacent girder on the coalface, which the adjacent girder

will sit in and be supported by when the props are withdrawn from beneath it and it is advanced.
Hinger, name for various clinging metal supports attached to last girder set which support the running girders as above.
Heed, head
Hingin, hanging
Hing, hang
Hyme (La'lands Northumbria the 'h' is silent, in La'lands Scots, it is pronounced), Yem/ Home

I

Inbye, in toward the face and away from the shafts

J

Ja, (Netherlands) yes

K

Knaa, know
Knaas, knows
Kiddha, kid, children. Used to address an adult it can be threatening, seriously or as mock rebuke.
Keek, to look
Keek (Netherlands)to look
Keeker, colliery 'viewer' on the surface who supervised the tubs coming to bank for quality and quantity of coal in each tub or corf.
Kijker (Netherlands) a look
Kist, box, usually deputies kist, at the corner of a mine district in which the reports of off going and oncoming shifts are made out and stored and men are deployed or assembled before and at the end of shifts.
Ken'd, understood, known,
Kleiner, (Netherlands) a little

L

La'r, the pitman's self gained knowledge
Lang, long
Lavie, lavatory
Lang'uns, Long ones (The trousers pitmen wear when not on the coal face, in outbye regions which tend to be cold or even freezing)
Langsyne, long time since.
Leds, lads
Leets, lights
Leng (Northumbrian) long
Les (Netherlands) lesson
Lig'ht (Netherlands) lie/lay
Loco, locomotive, either electric or diesel.
Lockers (Yorkshire) Drags (Northern) wooden or steel shafts about a foot long, used to slow the passage of tubs, by being thrown into the spokes of the tubs or minecars.
Lol, rest
Lope, bound
Loppin, bounding
Lowse, knock off time at the pit, meaning literally to 'lowse' or loose the coal bearing corfs and gear from the pit winding rope to accommodate loops or baskets or skips to carry the workers out of the mine.
Luek, look
Luekin, looking
Lurn, learn

M

Ma, mother
Ma, in the context of underground speech, a northern term for workmate, short for 'marra'
Manrider, means of conveying men underground, either on a manriding belt, or manriding set of vehicles pulled by a

loco (a Paddy in Yorkshire) or by rope

Mak, (usually Wearside varient of the Tyneside 'mek' as with their tak as against wor 'Tek' it is the origin of the much misunderstood and argued about term 'makums' for the folk of Wearside. It is simply the way they pronounce the dialect, which opens up new arguements about whether it is more or less Scottish than the Tynside version.)

Meedmen/man.Madmen/man (name we gave our adolescent gang)

Meg, make fun of

Mek (The Scots/Tyneside variant alang wi Tek which differenuates from wa Wearside comrades) Mak

Mel, Big hammer

Mer, more

Mickle (La'lands: Scots /Northumbrian) few

Mit (Netherlands) with

Mo (Netherlands) tired

Muckle (La'lands: scots/northumbrian) many

Mullergate (mothergate) Maingate, the main tunnel into the coal face, usually it is the intake road for fresh air, and has the conveyor belts running from the face

Mun, must

N

Na, no

Nae (Netherlands) no

Ney, no/nothing

Netty, toilet

Nay, no, nothing (modern infusion of La'lands)

Nowt, nothing

Nouce ,pitmans self gained knowledge (Yorkshire)

Nivor, never

O

Onsetter, the man at the bottom of the pit shaft who is in charge of riding of materials and men up and down the shaft.
On't (Yorkshire) On top of
Oot, out
Ootbye, away from the coalface toward the shaft
Oss (Yorkshire) horse
Ouseburn, one time self contained industrial community on the way to Byker from Newcastle, its surviving meandering river and abandoned condition ensured it would be 're-developed' largely by Yuppies, but also cheek by jowl by the Star and Shadow, and the Nuevo hippies along with a number of artists and academics. Features of the old community survive and the folkies too have adopted its four pubs for ceidhles and impromptu sessions. The overall effect, despite the upper class accents, and the presence of students and woolly middle class folk is a pleasant one.
Overmans, the Overman, a colliery official under the undermanager
Oversman, (scottish pronunciation of above)
Ower, over

P

Padmasana (Indian) lotus sitting position
Pinners, wooden wedges used in tightening supports
Pricker, the wire 'thread' which fits in the centre of the oil lamp base and makes connection with the wick to adjust its height for testing for gas levels.

R

Rammle, bits of abandoned tackle, ropes and wires etc
Retelt, re-told

R&B, a music genre intercepting basic blues with jazz, it was originally associated with the poor rural black southern states but spread to the urban black population, it was the root of Rock and Roll and then experienced a resurgence among the hip generation of '60s Britain and in particular Liverpool and Tyneside. It became the adopted motive force of the Rolling Stones, the Beatles, and the Animals among many others. The term in the '90s covers a far wider and non-specific field and to '60s' ears is now unrecognisable as 'true' R&B
Roon/Roond, Roonds, Round/rounds

S

Sand dancer, a resident of South Shields. A mix of the sandy shores and long time presence of Arabs has given the seafaring coalmining town's residents the name. Legend has it that the Arabs were the first real inhabitants of the town while modern research says they came with the invention of the steam ship as stokers from mainly Aden and Yemen. Seafarers and coalminers were often the same blokes, switching from one trade to the other seasonally or in accordance with their age and marital status. Early Durham Miners' certificates and membership diplomas clearly show Arab coal hewers in their cameos, so at least from the time of the Durham Miners' Association in the 1860s, Arab coalminers worked Shields coal seams along with their more Nordic Tynesiders. Who knows but the Romans called the local fort Arbeia, my Latin isn't too good since leaving the Catholic church but that sounds like 'Fort of the Arabs' to me.
Sark, shirt
Schlafsacken, (Netherlands) sleeping bag
Scrat, poke about in the dirt, sand or soil
Shelt, shalt, shall have

Shooted, shouted
Shoot, shout
Slooter, (probably Tyneside-Irish) to walk with the souls of ones footwear scraping or sliding along the ground
Snadgies, turnips 'snadged' or nicked from a farmers field
Soond, sound
Sook, (short for sook-up) groveller, toady
Spragged, propped up
Sprag (Yorkshire) tell tales on someone
Sprag, small props wedged under nicked jud prior to blasting at the coal face (A space is dug out from below the coal seam, the width and depth of the jud or portion of coal to be felled, it is supported by sprags prior to firing. The shot for maximum impact must have a space in which to absorb the blast through the coal seam, otherwise it would tend to fire back out of the shot hole and do little damage to the coal seam)
Sprake (Netherlands) speak
Spraken (Netherlands) speaking
Stot, bounce (On the stot) erection
Strags, strays
Swallie (Northumbria) a dip in an underground roadway
Swillie (Yorkshire) ditto

T

Tailgate, the smaller and — usually — the supply gate and return airway tunnel from the face. In the days of 'conventional' hand filled faces there would be two tailgates, one at either end of the coalface, with a main or mother(muller) gate running through the middle
Taitie/s, potato/potatoes
Tatty, a bit threadbare
Teds, Teddy Boys (Teens and Twenties working class lads, who dressed in Edwardian style clothes, or so it was said,

and took the name Teddy Boys; they were the post-war rock and roll generation, given to lots of violence, the head butt, the flickknife, gang fights some murders and a snog and a touch of breast before they were married, if they were lucky. The music was much cooler than they were, unless you were a middle class American in a red TB with white wall tyres making out overlooking the ocean. Newcastle teds were not like that.)

Tart, at one time a fairly common expression in the north for a young female companion or potential companion, a girl friend, sort of, but less serious, potentially sexual, potentially casually regular — but ney strings. Someone decided then to class 'tarts' as easy, and from that prostitutes, or loose women, 'tarty' like you, were dressed up for it and cheap. It became number one on the middle class feminists hit list of working class blokes' expressions for girls, though it is doubtful we ever meant the things they thought the word meant — so there's a surprise.

Te, too

Telt, told

Tellitale, child informer, sneak

Tey, to

Tha, their

Thiv, they have

Thorty, thirty

Thou,Tha,Thee, you

Thowt, thought

Thy,Thee, yours

Timmer, Timber, originally the wooden supports but then applied to all sorts of mobile and temporary roof support.

Ti'vis, to me

Twe, two

U

Up't'tash, (Yorkshire) Yorkshire sexual allegory for the drill being right at the end of its length up to the face of the stone or coal, as with a penis being fully inserted 'up to the tash' or pubic hair of the vagina. 'Tash' being shortened version of moustache. That's really ower much information I agree.
Us (Yorkshire) our

V

Vloer (Netherlands) floor
Vornie, very nearly

W

Wa/wa We/we are
Walla (probably a British army derivation of an Indian word) sort of hapless Joe Soap, dogsbody.
Wa'llers, wallers, big rocks used in construction of 'dry stone walls' underground.
Wasells, ourselves
(Yorkshire) Wasens, ourselves
Wee, small
Whey, who
While (Yorkshire) until
Wi, with
Wi, us
Wes, Was
Weel. well
Whey, who
Whee's, whose
Woorm, snakes, sea-serpents, and worms
Wo'ord. word
Workie-ticket, someone who pushes their luck in testing peoples patience

Workin ya ticket, trying others patience with provocative behaviour
Wor, our
Wors, ours

Y

Ya mooth, your mouth
Yasell, yourself
Ye, Ye's / You, You's
(Yorkshire) Yensen, yourself
Yersell, Yourself
Yi, Yi's / You, You's